L'ÉMIGRATION

et ses Effets dans le Midi de l'Italie

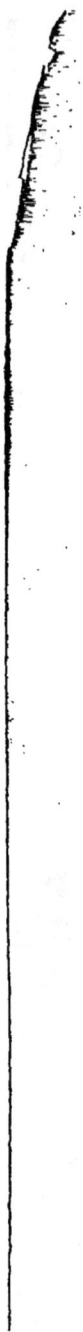

GIACOMO BARONE RUSSO

Docteur en Droit

Diplômé de l'Ecole des Sciences Politiques

L'EMIGRATION
et ses effets dans le Midi de l'Italie

Préface de Paul BEAUREGARD

MEMBRE DE L'INSTITUT

Professeur d'Economie politique à la Faculté de Droit de Paris
Député de la Seine

PARIS

Librairie des Sciences Politiques et Sociales
Marcel RIVIÈRE
31, rue Jacob et 1, rue Saint-Benoît
1912

A ceux qui me sont les plus chers
mes oncles
VINCENZO ET FRANCESCO BARONE D'URSO
mes initiateurs

Préface

Je me fais un plaisir de présenter au lecteur l'étude
de M. Giacomo Barone Russo : « l'*Emigration et ses
effets dans le midi de l'Italie* », qui constitue un sujet
d'un haut intérêt, pour l'Italie elle-même sans doute,
et d'abord, mais aussi pour d'autres pays, tels que l'Autriche-Hongrie où les phénomènes sont analogues, et
pour la science appelée à ouvrir un nouveau et important chapitre au livre de la colonisation. Le temps
n'est pas loin où l'on contestait encore l'avantage de
l'effort colonial pour le peuple qui l'accomplissait.
L'égoïsme naturel aux hommes dérobait à leur vue
tout profit qui ne se traduisait pas en un gain immédiat. Et nous avions fort à faire, mettant en face,
d'une part, les dépenses en argent, et de l'autre, les bénéfices moraux ou commerciaux, pour démontrer que
les derniers, dissimulés ou à long terme, l'emporteraient

quand même, et sensiblement sur les premiers. Aujour-
d'hui, un nouvel argument, saisissable à première vue
celui-là, apparaît. L'Emigration ne permet pas seulement à une nation de rester féconde sans encombrer
à l'excès son sol ; les émigrés, fidèles au pays d'origine, lui envoient leurs économies, lui fournissent les
capitaux nécessaires à la mise en exploitation des
champs. Au besoin ils lui procurent l'or qui lui manquait et, du coup, y redressent le change intérieur.

Ces phénomènes — non pas nouveaux, mais jusqu'ici
peu étudiés — M. Giacomo Barone Russo les met bien
en lumière, avec les statistiques nécessaires à l'appui
de ses argumentations.

Je recommande au public son livre, auquel je sou-
haite tout le succès que mérite une œuvre conscien-
cieuse et distinguée.

Paul BEAUREGARD,
de l'*Institut*.

CARACTÈRE ET PLAN DE L'ÉTUDE

———•———

« Les grands déplacements d'hommes
ont pour résultat définitif de mieux
répartir les forces productives des
sociétés, en désobstruant les parties
de l'arène industrielle où le travail
surabonde pour approvisionner
celles où les bras et les intelligences
sont rares ».

DE MOLINARI.

La question de l'émigration n'est pas nouvelle
et en présenter encore une fois une étude peut
sembler tout à fait inutile. En effet les publications sur cette matière sont très nombreuses soit
à l'étranger soit spécialement en Italie, qui dans
ce genre d'étude occupe à présent la première
place. Mais le problème est si vaste et si variable
que le dernier mot n'en a pas encore été dit.

Les manifestations de la vie sociale sont si
complexes qu'il est souvent difficile de pouvoir
bien en saisir la nature et la connexion. Les phénomènes s'influencent les uns les autres et il est
si difficile de distinguer les principaux des secondaires, que les conclusions qu'on peut tirer de
leur examen sont souvent inexactes, quoique

étant le fruit de patientes études. L'étude de l'émigration, comme toutes celles qui s'intéressent aux collectivités humaines, présente des problèmes sociaux infiniment difficiles à résoudre.

Les recherches sur cette question sont très abondantes, il est vrai, mais elles sont ou trop générales, plus des essais littéraires que des études scientifiques, ou trop minutieuses et spéciales, et telles, qu'à force de considérer l'émigration de trop près, on oublie son essence vraie ou on la confond avec ses causes mêmes. Ainsi une connaissance parfaite de ce phénomène, de ses qualités et de son rôle, fait défaut et presque toujours il y a une confusion d'idées et de théories, qui ne peut qu'augmenter l'incertitude qui domine dans ce problème si intéressant. Il est admissible que la complexité de ce phénomène empêche d'arriver à des conclusions exactes, mais, en général, les variations se produisent dans les manifestations extérieures du phénomène, qui reste toujours invariable dans son essence. Nous tâcherons dans cette étude de fixer d'abord les caractéristiques de l'émigration, et ensuite ses manifestations particulières dans l'Italie du Sud.

Dans les sciences sociales la méthode est un élément essentiel et nous croyons qu'avant d'examiner les manifestations d'un phénomène social, dans un lieu déterminé, il est très utile de connaître le phénomène indépendamment de son cas spécial, afin d'être en mesure de mieux en juger et d'éviter les inexactitudes produites par l'influence momentanée de facteurs passagers.

Cependant nous nous proposons d'étudier dans une partie générale les manifestations de l'émigration à ses différentes époques et chez les principaux peuples d'Europe; d'en déterminer rapidement les proportions atteintes, les causes et les effets; d'examiner les jugements des principaux économistes et publicistes; d'en fixer les traits essentiels, le rôle dans la société et de déterminer la tâche réservée aux gouvernements à son égard.

Dans une partie spéciale, nous étudierons l'émigration et ses effets dans l'Italie du Sud où elle se manifeste surtout à présent. En effet celle-ci fournit à l'émigration totale de l'Italie un contingent de 46,6 pour cent par an.

Ce phénomène est riche de nouveautés économiques et sociales, soit par son étonnant accroissement qui n'a point de précédents dans l'histoire, soit pour les effets en partie inattendus, auxquels il a donné lieu. Il a été un sujet d'études et de recherches de la part du gouvernement et des publicistes de tous genres et la cause des discussions les plus vives et les plus discordantes surtout dans l'appréciation de son utilité.

Cette question est aussi très intéressante pour la science étrangère, qui doit contribuer à l'étude des phénomènes qui, quoique ne se produisant pas dans leurs pays, peuvent indirectement les influencer, à cause de leur répercussion générale.

Nous exposerons d'abord l'ancienne question du Midi, à laquelle le phénomène de l'émigration est connexe et dont il représente la solution. Nous ferons ensuite un examen de l'ambiance des conditions économiques et sociales du pays, pour pouvoir mieux trouver les causes de l'émigration. Etant donnée la relation qui existe entre l'émigration et le mouvement de la population, nous croyons opportun d'étudier celui-ci dans ses différentes manifestations, déterminant par là même, la composition, les caractéristiques et le mouvement de celle-là. Après cette étude statistique nous examinerons les différentes causes et effets de l'émigration, soit démographiques, soit économiques et sociaux. Nous exposerons enfin l'œuvre du gouvernement et de la société pour la protection de l'émigration et nous tâcherons d'indiquer le chemin à parcourir encore.

La connaissance de la plupart des régions en question où nous sommes né, l'étude des diverses publications officielles du Ministère d'Agriculture, du Commissariat de l'Emigration, et de plusieurs autres ouvrages, Revues et Journaux, les informations que nous avons obtenues de personnes qui vivant dans le Midi de l'Italie sont directement intéressées à la question, nous font espérer que nous ne nous éloignerons pas trop de la réalité des faits.

Paris, Mai 1911.   Giacomo Barone Russo.

PARTIE GÉNÉRALE

« *Le monde est un tout dont chaque
partie est liée à toutes les autres
par des liens nécessaires et malheureusement méconnus;* »

GASPARIN.

CHAPITRE PREMIER

Esquisse Historique de l'Emigration

L'émigration dans l'antiquité. — L'homme primitif. — Les peuples agriculteurs. — Origine de la navigation. — Les Phéniciens. — Les Grecs. — Les Romains. — Les Invasions barbares. — (Les Croisades) Causes et effets de l'émigration.

Les hommes comme les animaux ont toujours été sujets à des déplacements. L'émigration n'est donc pas un phénomène récent, mais elle remonte aux époques les plus lointaines du développement économique de l'homme.

L'homme primitif est chasseur et a besoin d'une grande étendue de terres. Quand le gibier vient à manquer ou que les membres d'une tribu se multiplient, s'impose la recherche d'une nouvelle demeure.

M. Schmoller (1) dit, en parlant des Indo-Germains, qu'ils avaient l'habitude, quand ils étaient devenus trop nombreux, de mettre à part de la tribu une élite de jeunes hommes et de jeunes femmes, de leur donner des chefs, des armes, du bétail et de les envoyer au loin chercher de nouveaux moyens d'existence.

Quand les peuples commencent à s'occuper d'agriculture et à bâtir des maisons, ils deviennent plus sédentaires. Mais les besoins de chacun augmentant avec la civilisation, il leur devient impossible de se suffire et ils sont obligés de se mettre en rapport les uns avec les autres et de passer dans d'autres pays. Ainsi commencent la navigation, le commerce, se forment les grandes factories et les colonies commerciales.

Les Phéniciens furent un de ces peuples migrateurs, et ils ont laissé les traces de leur civilisation un peu partout; fondant des villes de grande importance telles que Carthage, Gades, Panormus, etc. Les Grecs aussi, poussés soit par la discorde civile, soit par des nécessités économiques, s'établirent dans l'Asie Mineure, dans l'Italie Méridionale, etc. Ils y exercèrent une grande influence, et encore à présent nous trouvons en Sicile des pays qui gardent les coutumes des Grecs et dont la langue est plus grecque qu'italienne.

_____

(1) *Principes d'Economie Politique*, Trad. Platon 1905, page 434.

Les Romains aussi émigrèrent : sous la République. il n'y eut pas de vraie émigration, mais sous l'Empire elle joua un grand rôle, et eut un caractère tout à fait militaire. Les provinces conquises étaient partagées entre les vétérans de l'armée et vers elles se dirigeaient des courants d'émigrés; ils étaient favorisés par le gouvernement pour se débarrasser des gens sans occupation qui étaient très nombreux.

Les *invasions barbares* nous offrent un exemple très large de peuples émigrants tels que les Huns, les Goths, les Visigoths, les Francs et les Normands, qui, poussés par les exigences économiques plus que par l'esprit de conquête, abandonnèrent leur patrie pour chercher ailleurs leur subsistance. Et même les *Croisades* ne sont qu'une grande émigration d'Italiens, de Français, d'Allemands en Palestine et en Syrie, où les premiers croisés avaient fondé des colonies européennes.

Causes et effets de l'émigration dans l'antiquité

La caractéristique principale de cette émigration est celle d'être collective, d'être une espèce d'invasion armée et conquérante. Ce sont des peuples entiers qui se déplacent d'un pays à l'autre; quelquefois imposant leur langue, leurs lois, leurs coutumes, à la population indigène, quelquefois les leur empruntant.

Souvent aussi, l'émigration avait comme conséquence de faire émigrer à leur tour, les peuples chez qui elle se portait.

L'infécondité du sol, la rigueur du climat, les nécessités économiques, politiques et religieuses étaient en général les causes qui poussaient ces gens à laisser leur patrie.

Les effets étaient soit économiques, soit politiques. Ce n'était pas seulement la langue ou la religion qui se répandait, mais aussi les mœurs, les plus importantes conquêtes de la civilisation, l'écriture, la monnaie, le commerce; et même les formes de gouvernement trouvaient dans ces migrations un moyen de diffusion car les peuples envahisseurs imposaient leur constitution politique aux vaincus, qui souvent aussi imposaient la leur aux vainqueurs.

L'Emigration dans le Moyen-Age

Le Moyen-Age n'est pas favorable à l'émigration. — Les Seigneurs et les Vassaux. — Les villes maritimes d'Italie. — Les Allemands en Hongrie

Le Moyen-Age ne présente pas beaucoup d'émigration. M. De Molinari, dit avec raison, « qu'il offre l'image d'une véritable pétrification sociale : l'homme meurt sur le coin de terre qui l'a vu naître comme l'huître sur son rocher, et avec la circulation des hommes on voit s'arrêter celle des richesses. »

En effet le seigneur, d'après le principe que la puissance croissait avec le nombre des vassaux ne pouvait pas voir de bon gré sortir des personnes de son territoire. Les colons étaient presque des esclaves, car non seulement ils ne pouvaient pas émigrer librement, mais ils ne pouvaient même se marier sans l'autorisation de leur prince. Les différents états étaient jaloux les (1) uns des autres et défendaient en général l'émigration.

---

(1) Schmoller, *Principes d'Econ. Polit.* page 434.

L'institution des couvents par le Christianisme fut également un empêchement à l'émigration : une quantité d'hommes qui autrement aurait cherché des ressources dans l'émigration, y trouvait asile.

Cependant c'est entre le ix⁰ et le x⁰ siècle que les émigrants d'Amalfi et ensuite ceux de Venise, de Gênes, de Pise, fondèrent en Orient des établissements commerciaux très florissants, qui leur valurent le monopole du commerce dans ces pays jusqu'à la découverte de l'Amérique.

M. Duval (1) parle aussi de paysans et d'ouvriers allemands qui, dès le xii⁰ siècle allèrent en Hongrie et en Transylvanie pour y chercher du travail.

(1) *Histoire de l'Émigration Européenne et Africaine.* Paris, 1862.

L'Emigration Moderne

La découverte de l'Amérique. — L'Auri sacra fames. — L'émigration pacifique.

Avec la découverte de l'Amérique, l'émigration commence à se réveiller pour prendre graduellement des proportions remarquables dans les xviii° et xix° siècles.

Naturellement la découverte de nouvelles terres très fertiles, et riches de minéraux très importants, ne pouvait se passer sans produire une révolution dans la vie économique et démocratique des peuples. Tout d'abord l'émigration fut une espèce d'invasion d'aventuriers, qui poussés par « l'auri sacra fames » employaient toutes sortes de moyens pour arriver à leur but. L'Espagne et le Portugal travaillèrent ainsi à l'épuisement de leurs colonies, persuadés que l'or constitue la seule richesse d'une nation. Ce fut après plusieurs années, quand on vit les mauvais effets de ce système qu'on changea d'avis; et à l'émigration rapace se substitua une émigration pacifique de personnes actives et intelligentes, émigration qui dure encore et qui contribue à la richesse et à la puissance des états modernes.

L'EMIGRATION DANS LE ROYAUME UNI

Walter Raleigh. — William Penn. — La reine Anne favorise l'émigration. — Les actes parlementaires de 1719, 1750, 1782. — L'émigration libre. — L'introduction des machines. — Différentes périodes de hausse et baisse dans l'émigration. — Pays de destination des émigrants. — Périodes de prédominance des Anglais, des Ecossais ou des Irlandais. — Causes et effets de l'émigration.

C'est du Royaume Uni que sort le premier puissant courant d'émigration.

Dès 1584 et 1587, Walter Raleigh avait appelé des anglais dans la Virginie. En 1620, les Puritains poussés par l'intolérance religieuse avaient émigré en New-England et en 1600, William Penn faisait avec des émigrants une tentative de colonisation dans la Pensylvanie.

Poussée par la grande misère, que la famine de 1709 avait produite, la reine Anne offrit le passage gratuit en Amérique à tous les émigrants qui se présentaient. Mais bientôt, craignant que les colonies formées par ces émigrés ne devinssent des rivales à la mère patrie, les actes parlementaires de 1719, 1750, 1782 prohibèrent l'émigration des ouvriers et l'exportation des métiers et des machines.

Cependant le malaise causa l'émigration d'agriculteurs, et les paroisses établirent un fond spécial pour payer le passage aux pauvres qui devenaient de plus en plus nombreux.

Ensuite le gouvernement n'aimant pas appliquer des lois contraires à la liberté, supprima toute entrave à l'émigration, qui, surtout après la révolution française, prit un grand essor.

Avec l'introduction des machines, un grand nombre d'ouvriers se trouvaient sans travail, le Parlement en 1827 s'avisa de favoriser l'émigration et près de 95.000 âmes furent envoyées dans les colonies. Mais le développement de la production dû au progrès de la mécanique fit bientôt sentir le besoin d'ouvriers nouveaux et alors on chercha à les retenir.

Nous avons jusqu'ici parlé de l'émigration britannique déterminée par des nécessités économiques, mais il ne faut pas croire, que celles-ci en aient été la seule cause. De nombreux groupes d'émigrants furent poussés à abandonner la patrie pour des motifs religieux, comme par exemple les Puritains et les Quakers ; d'autres étaient constitués par les criminels et les condamnés politiques déportés ailleurs, pour débarrasser la patrie.

Les proportions de l'émigration britannique présentent de fortes variations.

Les mauvaises récoltes de 1846 et 1847 qui avaient aggravé la situation économique des Irlandais, causèrent un nouvel élan d'émigration.

De 93.000, en 1845, le chiffre monta en 1852 à 368.000. Pendant et après la guerre de Crimée le courant d'émigration diminua tant, que dans l'année 1859 on compte seulement 120.000 émigrants. En 1861 l'émigration monta de nouveau. Dans la période de 1871 à 1875, le chiffre des émigrants est de 969.000 tandis que dans la période 1856 à 1860, il était de 617.000.

Le mouvement de baisse recommence avec l'année 1876 (109.000 h.), mais dans l'année 1883 l'émigration atteint le point culminant au xixe siècle, soit 320.000 individus.

L'émigration britannique au xixe siècle ne présente pas de grandes différences, elle oscille entre 100.000 et 270.000. De 1815 à 1906 cette émigration a été un total de 16.940.000 individus dont 11.182.000 se sont rendus aux Etats-Unis, 2.668.000 dans les colonies anglaises du Nord, 1.887.000 en Australie et Nouvelle Zélande, 1.196.000 dans les autres pays, y compris l'Afrique du Sud (1).

Cependant l'émigration des anglais aussi bien que celle des Irlandais (qui ont fourni le contin-

(1) Gonnard. *L'Émigration Européenne au XIXe siècle.* Paris, 1906.

gent principal avec un maximum de 103.000 en 1883) tend à baisser.

En 1894 le chiffre des émigrants anglais est de 99.000, en 1899, de 87.000, tandis qu'en 1883 il était de 183.000.

Le chiffre des émigrants Irlandais diminue aussi depuis 1888 (73.000 émigrants) jusqu'en 1899 (42.000).

Avec le XXe siècle l'émigration britannique semble avoir de nouveau une tendance à s'élever. On y distingue encore des éléments écossais, anglais et irlandais, mais alors qu'au XIXe siècle les éléments principaux en étaient anglais et principalement irlandais, et que l'émigration écossaise était peu remarquable, (11.000 en 1878 et 16.000 en 1899), au contraire au XXe siècle, il y a une notable augmentation de l'émigration écossaise et anglaise, tandis que celle de l'Irlande décline depuis 1889.

En effet en 1901, les anglais sont 111.000, les écossais 20.000 et les irlandais 39.000. Il est vrai que dans les années suivantes l'élément écossais augmente de nouveau, mais il ne dépasse plus le chiffre de 1888, alors que le chiffre des écossais et des anglais s'élève comme jamais depuis 1878, et atteint chez les écossais 53.000 émigrants en 1906, 66.000 en 1907 et chez les anglais 219.000 en 1906, 285.000 en 1909, chiffres jamais atteints auparavant.

EMIGRATION BRITANNIQUE

Années	Anglais	Irlandais	Ecossais	Total
1878	72.323	29.432	11.087	112.842
1879	104.275	41.296	18.703	164.274
1880	111.845	63.641	22.506	197.992
1881	139.976	76.200	26.826	243.002
1882	162.992	84.132	32.242	279.366
1883	183.236	105.743	31.139	320.118
1884	147.660	72.566	21.953	222.179
1885	126.260	60.017	21.367	207.644
1886	146.301	61.276	25.323	232.900
1887	168.221	78.901	34.365	281.487
1888	170.822	73.233	35.873	279.928
1889	163.518	64.923	25.354	253.795
1890	139.979	57.434	20.653	218.146
1891	137.881	58.430	22.196	218.507
1892	133.815	52.902	23.325	210.042
1893	134.045	51.132	22.637	208.814
1894	99.590	42.008	14.432	156.030
1895	112.338	54.349	18.294	185.181
1896	102.837	42.222	16.866	161.925
1897	94.658	35.688	16.124	146.470
1898	90.679	34.395	15.570	140.644
1899	87.400	42.890	16.072	146.362

1900	102.448	45.905	20.472	168.825
1901	111.585	39.210	20.920	171.715
1902	137.121	42.256	26.285	205.662
1903	177.581	45.568	36.801	259.950
1904	175.533	58.257	37.445	271.435
1905	170.408	50.159	41.510	262.077
1906	219.765	52.210	53.167	325.137
1907	265.229	64.096	66.355	395.680
1908	276.986	38.352	42.273	263.199
1909	285.623	44.076	52.916	288.865

Causes et Effets de l'Emigration Britannique

Les causes qui ont déterminé l'émigration en Grande Bretagne, sont de deux sortes, morales et économiques.

Dans la première période, ce sont les causes morales, persécutions religieuses et politiques, qui prévalent ; les causes économiques quoique prédominantes pendant quelques années, n'ont qu'une influence secondaire.

Mais bientôt les déterminants économiques prennent le premier rang et se maintiennent jusqu'à nos jours. C'est la misère et la révolution apportée par le machinisme, (qui a été en même temps cause de chômage et de surtravail), ce sont *les mauvaises conditions de l'agriculture* qui ont été surtout cause du grand courant d'émigration britannique. La transformation des systèmes de

culture et précisément la substitution du pâturage
à la culture de la terre fût cause de fortes crises.
Le *landlordisme* a été aussi une plaie inguérissa-
ble. Les propriétaires, dit M. Gustave de Beau-
mont dans son livre « L'Irlande sociale, politique
et religieuse », qu'une odieuse confiscation a constitué les maîtres du sol, prélèvent sous forme de
rente une part excessive des produits, et n'en
restituent rien au pays, car ils consomment leurs
revenus loin des terres, que la plupart n'ont jamais vues et qu'ils administrent par le double intermédiaire d'un fermier général et d'un agent local, le *middleman*, dont la servilité et la cupidité,
ne recule devant aucune oppression. La propriété territoriale, grevée d'hypothèques aux
mains d'un maître plus obéré encore, indivisible
et insaisissable, tente en vain l'ambition des Irlandais qui voudraient en faire l'instrument de
leur prospérité... Pendant des siècles, les lois ja-
louses de l'Angleterre ont empêché l'industrie,
la navigation, le commerce de l'Irlande de s'établir ou de se développer.

Il faut encore y ajouter un taux des salaires très
bas et de nombreuses famines qui produisirent
tant de misère.

Les conditions agricoles de l'Angleterre quoique meilleures que celles de l'Irlande n'étaient
pas excellentes.

Si la libre importation des produits agricoles
du dehors, assurait bien aux ouvriers une vie à

bon marché, et permettait d'obtenir des concessions douanières pour les produits industriels anglais, elle fût aussi la cause de la ruine de l'agriculture nationale qui ne put pas résister à la concurrence étrangère.

Les effets de la grande émigration britannique ont été des plus satisfaisants. C'est grâce à elle que le Royaume Uni a créé un Empire « large comme le monde » selon le mot de Monsieur Chamberlain. Elle a donné un grand développement à son commerce et à son industrie et à ses finances. Et pour l'Irlande aussi, l'horizon s'est éclairci, les conditions économiques sont meilleures et l'émigration est de beaucoup diminuée.

Un des facteurs essentiels du bon succès de l'émigration britannique a été la nature même des anglais, qui loin de leur patrie ne perdent pas leurs habitudes, leur langue, leurs sentiments d'amour et d'attachement au sol natal.

L'action de l'émigration a été aussi secondée par différentes lois, celle de Ashbourne en 1885, celle de 1891 de 1896 et de 1903, qui visent à la constitution de la petite propriété et à l'abolition du landlordisme, qui, au dire de M. Paul Dubois (1), avait tous les inconvénients de la très grande propriété, joints à ceux de la très petite culture, sans avoir l'avantage ni de l'un ni de l'autre de ces régimes.

---

(1) Réforme Sociale, Mars, 1904. *La question Agraire en Irlande.*

L'ÉMIGRATION ALLEMANDE

L'Allemagne, à juste raison surnommée le réservoir des peuples, a toujours eu des tendances à l'émigration. La plupart des invasions barbares étaient constituées par des peuples qui demeuraient en Germanie. Au XVIe siècle, l'Allemagne ne prend pas une part active à l'occupation de l'Amérique car elle était encore morcelée en plusieurs petits états en lutte pour la suprématie, et de plus, engagés dans les querelles religieuses suscitées par la Réforme.

C'est aux XVIIe et XVIIIe siècles que se forme un courant d'émigration d'allemands vers l'Amérique du Nord, où ils furent attirés d'abord par Penn et les Hollandais ; mais c'est seulement au XIXe siècle que l'émigration prit des proportions plus considérables et que des milliers d'allemands envahissent l'Amérique, et aussi une partie du vieux continent, presque pendant tout le siècle. Cette émigration est, au commencement, tout-à-fait agricole, et opère par masses, car il y a des villages entiers qui émigrent. La proportion des émigrants diffère de province à province, ils sont par exemple plus nombreux dans la Bavière que dans le Wurtemberg ou la Bade. En général on peut penser que là où l'agriculture ne suffit pas à satisfaire les besoins de la population, l'émigration est plus fréquente.

Les gouvernements allemands ne furent pas toujours favorables à cette émigration ; d'abord sous l'influence des idées de Jean-Baptiste Say, qui considérait l'émigration comme une perte, on prit des mesures pour entraver et supprimer l'émigration ; tandis qu'ensuite, sous l'influence des idées de Malthus sur l'accroissement de la population, non seulement on la laissa libre, mais même on travailla à l'augmenter par différents moyens. On peut dire que cette émigration, née avec le xixᵉ siècle, meurt avec la fin de ce siècle au milieu duquel elle touche à son apogée. On n'a des statistiques que depuis 1815. D'après Gäber [1], l'émigration allemande jusqu'à 1844 n'a pas dépassé le chiffre de 33.000 individus par an. — En 1844 il monte à 43.000 pour arriver à 250.000 en 1854.

De 1855 à 1870, il y a une période de baisse pendant laquelle elle se maintient au-dessous de 100.000 personnes. De 1871 à 1873 elle remonte à plus de 100.000, mais ne dépasse pas 132.000 âmes. Entre 1874 et 1879 il y a encore une baisse dont le chiffre se maintient entre 21.000 et 56.000 émigrants par an.

La période de 1880-1884 présente de nouveau

---

[1] Hübner. *Jahrb. der Volkswirthschaft und Statistik.*

une notable augmentation ; le chiffre des émigrants atteignant 106.000 en 1880, 220.000 en 1881 ; ce qui est le maximum (116.000) de l'émigration allemande. Depuis 1885 commence la période de décroissance définitive qui dure jusqu'à 1896.

Il est vrai que dans cette période on rencontre quelques chiffres élevés comme 120.000 en 1891, mais en 1894 on a un total de 41.000, en 1895, 37.000, et en 1896, 33.000 ; c'est-à-dire le même nombre à peu près qu'on signalait avant 1844.

Avec l'année 1897 (pendant laquelle les émigrants sont seulement 24.000) commence la lente agonie de la grande émigration allemande.

Au XXe siècle on pourrait dire qu'elle est finie en effet, elle oscille entre 20.000 et 27.000.

L'émigration allemande s'est principalement portée aux Etats-Unis, parce que le taux des salaires y est plus élevé qu'ailleurs, et parce que les lois y sont plus libérales.

Elle a ainsi beaucoup contribué au progrès de ce pays. Les autres états de l'Amérique, le Canada, le Mexique, l'Argentine et le Brésil ont toujours essayé d'attirer chez eux les émigrants allemands, mais ils n'ont réussi qu'à en faire venir un faible courant. L'arrêt de cette émigration n'est sûrement pas dû à la diminution de la population allemande; en effet de 41.000.000 de personnes en 1871, elle est arrivée en 1905 à 60.641.278. Cependant le coefficient de natalité est baissé de 40,7 de la période 1874, — 79 à 37,5 dans la période 1891-95 (1).

Mais puisque le taux de mortalité est diminué de 27,2 pour 1.000 en 1871-80 à 20 pour 1.000 en 1903, on observe que la population augmente toujours et l'excédent annuel de 550.000 âmes en 1881-1890 s'est élevé à 730.000 en 1891-1900.

C'est le grand développement industriel et économique qu'on doit considérer comme cause de l'arrêt de l'émigration, car l'Allemagne à présent peut nourrir et occuper un nombre de gens bien supérieur qu'auparavant. Et il est bien évident que la population reste dans un pays où elle trouve les moyens nécessaires à la satisfaction de ses besoins jusquà ce que ceux-ci viennent à manquer pour une raison ou pour une autre.

(1) P. Leroy Beaulieu. *La question de la dépopulation. Revue des Deux-Mondes*, 15 Octobre 1897.

EMIGRATION ALLEMANDE

Années	Emigrants	Années	Emigrants
1844	43.000	1877	41.000
1845	67.000	1878	46.000
1846	94.000	1879	33.000
1847	109.000	1880	106.000
1848	81.000	1881	220.000
1849	89.000	1882	203.000
1850	82.000	1883	173.000
1851	112.000	1884	149.000
1852	162.000	1885	116.000
1853	156.000	1886	83.000
1854	250.000	1887	104.000
1855	81.000	1888	103.000
1856	98.000	1889	96.000
1857	116.000	1890	97.000
1858	53.000	1891	120.000
1859	45.000	1892	116.000
1860		1893	87.000
1861	Moyenne 41.000	1894	41.000
1862		1895	37.000
1863		1896	33.000
1864		1897	24.000

1865		1898	22.000
1866		1899	24.000
1867	Moyenne 107.000	1900	22.000
1868		1901	22.000
1869		1902	32.000
1870	79.000	1903	36.000
1871	102.000	1904	27.000
1872	154.000	1905	28.000
1873	132.000	1906	31.000
1874	74.000	1907	31.000
1875	56.000	1908	20.000
1876	50.000	1909	25.000

Causes et effets de l'Emigration Allemande

En considérant les conditions sociales de l'Allemagne, on peut trouver deux espèces de causes à l'émigration : l'injustice des lois et la mauvaise distribution et culture des terres.

Nombreuses étaient les entraves au mariage, qui dépendait de la possession de quelques biens ou de l'accomplissement du service militaire. Les droits de succession étaient contraire à toute répartition équitable des biens ; les impôts étaient excessifs, le service militaire très lourd.

Dans quelques provinces, comme dans le duché de Bade ; le morcellement de la propriété était extrême, tandis que dans d'autres états, comme

dans la Bavière et le Wurtemberg, c'est le mal
contraire qui cause l'émigration, car des lois
s'opposaient à la division du sol.

A celà il faut adjoindre les mauvaises récoltes,
les conditions déprimantes de l'industrie, le chômage produit par l'introduction des machines,
les persécutions religieuses, qui poussaient fortement les malheureux à chercher ailleurs le
bien-être qui leur manquait dans leur patrie. Le
paupérisme était très enraciné : « On trouve,
écrit M. Duval (1), des familles parquées en une
seule chambre avec une ligne de craie pour
toute séparation. Celles-là se croient privilégiées, qui possèdent une chaise, une
table, un lit pour tous ; un pot de grès pour tout
ustensile. Il en est qui vont, vêtues de lambeaux
en défroque, dont les enfants vont à peu près nus
et sans chaussure même en hiver. »

Cependant en Allemagne aussi les conditions
économiques ont favorisé une forte émigration.

Certains économistes et publicistes allemands
comme Roscher ont soutenu que l'émigration a
été cause de dommages à l'Allemagne ; considérant qu'elle n'a pas donné lieu à des résultats
importants comme des colonies sociales, qu'elle
enlève des bras, des capitaux et des consommateurs à la patrie. Les allemands, disent-ils, s'a-

---

(1) *Histoire de l'Émigration dans le XIX· siècle*
pag. 65.

daptent très facilement dans le pays d'immigration et sont tout-à-fait perdus pour la patrie.

Quoique l'allemand perde facilement son caractère germanique, on doit convenir que ces craintes sont trop exagérées. L'allemand en général réussit dans l'émigration ; il est patient, persévérant, travailleur et il sait supporter tous les ennuis d'une nouvelle demeure.

L'émigration a profité autant aux émigrants qu'aux Etats d'où ils sont partis. Elle s'est en plus grande partie produite parmi les classes pauvres, a déchargé l'assistance publique, et diminué le paupérisme.

On a pu constater une diminution de la criminalité, des faillites, des ventes forcées et une grande extension des débouchés de l'industrie. La marine marchande a pris un grand développement. Des compagnies très puissantes de navigation comme la Norddeutscher Lloyd, Bremen, et la Hamburg Amerika Linie qui possèdent des centaines de vaisseaux se sont constituées. Et la production allemande aussi, concomittamment au développement du commerce s'est fortement accrue. En 1872, l'Allemagne exportait 141.000.000 kilogrammes de coton écru, en 1904, elle en exportait 451.500.000 kilogrammes.

L'exportation des articles en fer et en acier est montée de 57.000 tonnes en 1872, à près de

1.200.000 tonnes dès 1898 (1). La production de la houille est passée de 29 millions de tonnes en 1871, à 120 millions en 1904.

Quoique enfin les Allemands n'aient pas de grandes colonies comme les Anglais, ils ont cependant de nombreuses colonies sociales un peu partout et dans des conditions très florissantes qui font toujours honneur à la patrie.

———

(1) Gonnard. *L'Émigration Européenne etc.*, pag. 129.

L'Emigration Italienne

Quoique les Italiens aient dans l'antiquité et le moyen âge donné des preuves de facile expatriation, et qu'ils aient une étendue considérable de relations commerciales, surtout Gênes et Venise, ils n'émigrent pas beaucoup avant le XIXe siècle.

Avant l'unification de l'Italie. Il y avait des déplacements de personnes qui d'un petit état passaient dans un autre voisin, mais ne dépassaient pas la frontière.

Au XIV siècle, l'émigration commence à devenir un phénomène remarquable surtout dans la seconde moitié du siècle.

Avant 1869, nous ne possédons que des documents fragmentaires sur l'émigration.

A Montevideo en 1842, sur 33.000 émigrants, 7.894 étaient piémontais et sardes, et en 1852, sur 2.116 Européens, 674 étaient Italiens.

A Buenos-Ayres, sur 5790 Européens arrivés en 1850, il y en avait 2.788 Italiens, en 1859, les Italiens montaient à 15.000 et en 1860 à 41.957.

En Algérie, on compte en 1860, 12.755 Italiens.

Aux Etats-Unis, la statistique constate 7.185 immigrants Italiens, entre 1819 et 1855, et 1240 en 1858.

Le chiffre baisse en 1860, à 1.019, à 811 en 1861, et à 566 en 1862 ; au contraire, avec 1866, recommence la période de hausse et le chiffre atteint 1.382 ; dans l'année 1867, on compte 1624 Italiens et 1.408 en 1868.

Depuis 1869, les documents statistiques sont plus exacts, car les Préfets des Provinces étaient obligés de donner des informations sur les mouvements de population.

Cependant cette statistique présentait des défauts, car elle n'était soumise à aucun contrôle ; à partir de 1876, elle est digne de foi, car elle résulte des rapports des Maires, de ceux des autorités des ports italiens et étrangers. d'embarcation, et des autorités des pays d'immigration.

Depuis 1904, les statistiques sont faites avec les nouvelles fournies par les registres de la Police, où sont annotés tous les passeports qu'on a accordés.

Voilà les chiffres de l'émigration depuis 1869 jusqu'à 1909.

Année	Emigration permanente	Emigration temporaire	Emigration clandestine	Total
1869	22.201	83.565	14.040	119.806
1870	16.427	83.588	11.444	111.459
1871	15.027	96.384	11.068	122.479
1872	140.680		5.585	146.265
1873	139.860		11.921	151.781
1874	91.239		17.362	108.601
1875	76.095		27.253	103.348
1876	19.756	84.015		108.771
1877	21.087	78.126		99.213
1878	18.535	77.733		96.268
1879	40.824	79.007		119.831
1880	37.934	81.967		119.901
1881	41.607	94.225		135.832
1882	65.748	95.814		161.562
1883	68.416	100.685		169.101
1884	58.049	88.968		147.017
1885	77.029	80.164		157.193
1886	85.355	82.474		167.829
1887	127.748	87.917		215.665
1888	195.993	94.743		290.736
1889	113.093	105.319		218.412
1890	104.733	112.511		217.244
1891	175.520	118.111		293.631
1892	107.369	166.298		223.667
1893	124.312	122.439		246.751
1894	105.445	119.808		225.323
1895	169.513	123.668		293.181
1896	183.620	123.862		307.482
1897	165.420	134.426		299.855
1898	126.787	156.928		283.711
1899	131.308	177.031		308.339
1900	153.209	199.573		352.782
1901	251.577	281.668		533.245
1902	245.217	286.292		531.509
1903				507.976
1904				471.191
1905				726.331
1906				787.977
1907				704.775
1908				486.674
1909				625.637

Ces chiffres révèlent la puissance migrative
de l'Italie qui prend ainsi la première place parmi les grandes nations émigrantes. On se trouve
vis-à-vis d'un rapide mouvement toujours ascen-
dant.

En 1885, l'émigration italienne dépasse celle
de l'Allemagne, qui était encore très forte (émi-
grat. ital. 157.000 émigr. allem. 116.000). En réalité, tenant compte du rapport de l'émigration à
la totalité de la population et à sa densité, l'Italie
a dépassé l'émigration de l'Allemagne dans une
époque antérieure à celle que nous indiquons.

En 1891, l'Angleterre est aussi dépassée
(émigr. ital. 293.000 émigr. angl. 218.000) et dé-
sormais l'Italie prend la première place en la
maintenant jusqu'à présent. Ainsi en 1896, le
chiffre de 300.000 est dépassé, et à partir de 1900
jusqu'à 1909, plus d'un demi-million d'émigrants sort chaque année de l'Italie.

La baisse de l'émigration est très frappante
dans les années 1904 et 1908, au-dessous du demi-million à cause des crises économiques en
Amérique. En effet, une fois la crise finie, l'émigration remonte de 471.000 en 1904, à 726.000 en
1905, et de 486.000 en 1908, à 625.000 en 1909.

Cette émigration n'est pas dirigée toute vers
les pays transocéaniens, il y en a une grande

partie qui reste en Europe (répartie en France, Suisse, Autriche-Hongrie, Allemagne, Angleterre) et dans les pays de la Méditerranée. Ainsi on fait la distinction suivante :

Année	Pays transocéaniens	Europe et pays de la Méditerranée	Total
1900.....	166.000	186.000	352.000
1901.....	279.000	253.000	533.000
1902.....	284.000	246.000	531.000
1903.....	282.000	225.000	507.000
1904.....	252.000	218.000	471.000
1905.....	447.000	279.000	726.000
1906.....	511.000	276.000	787.000
1907.....	415.901	288.774	704.000
1908.....	238.000	248.000	486.909
1909.....	357.850	267.787	625.637

Les pays d'Europe vers lesquels se dirige de préférence l'émigration italienne sont la France, l'Allemagne, la Suisse, l'Autriche, la Hongrie, et en Afrique l'Algérie, l'Egypte, la Tunisie et Tripolitaine.

En Amérique, ils immigrent de préférence dans les Etats-Unis et la République Argentine; cependant, il y en a de répandus aussi dans les autres états. Dans les pays d'Amérique, la population italienne est ainsi répandue.

	Population italienne
Etats-Unis, Mexique, Canada	1.782.487
Amérique centrale	4.481
Amérique méridionale	2.638.952

Dans le Brésil seulement, il y en a 1.500.000. Dans la République Argentine les Italiens jouent un rôle essentiel. Ils sont un million, dit M. G. Bevione (1) à peu près la sixième partie de la population. Ils forment le 65 % de la population agricole qui est la plus prolifique et nécessaire, la vraie source de la prospérité nationale. Sans les Italiens, l'Argentine ne pourrait pas vivre. Si les Italiens ne travaillaient pas pendant une semaine, la République souffrirait la faim et serait paralysée. Si notre gouvernement prohibait pendant une seule saison l'émigration temporaire, les récoltes pouriraient pour les trois quarts sur les champs.

Les différentes régions de l'Italie ne participent pas également à l'émigration. Les régions agricoles, l'Italie du sud surtout, et aussi la Vénétie, le Piémont, l'Emilie, sont les régions dont sort le plus grand nombre d'émigrants, mais de cela nous traiterons avec plus de détails dans la partie spéciale.

De ces chiffres extraordinaires, il faut sous-

(1) *Gli Italiani nella Repubblica Argentina*. Conférence tenue dans le Théâtre Argentina à Rome, le 7 février 1911.

traire les émigrants qui chaque année font retour en Italie ; car *l'émigration se compose de deux catégories de gens*, les uns qui s'éloignent, non sans idée de retour, mais sans savoir exactement quand ils reviendront (émigration permanente) et les autres qui reviennent à leur patrie après être demeurés quelques mois à l'étranger, pendant la saison où le travail est très abondant (émigration temporaire), et cela a lieu aussi bien pour les pays d'Europe que pour l'Amérique. Ainsi en 1908, les immigrés étaient 224.000 et seulement ceux de provenance des Etats-Unis, Argentine, Uruguay, tandis que l'émigration pour les pays transocéaniques était de 238.000, le total étant de 486.000. Dans les huit années de 1902 à 1909 sur 2.366.391 émigrants pour les pays transocéaniques, 1.382.863 rentrèrent dans leur patrie, c'est-à-dire 58 0/0 avec une augmentation plus remarquable pendant la période de crise dans le Nord d'Amérique en 1904 et 1908 (1).

Cependant on parle d'émigration permanente seulement de façon relative ; en réalité, il s'agit d'une émigration à temps indéterminé, car, quand l'émigrant est parvenu à épargner une certaine somme d'argent, qu'on calcule de 5.000 à 10.000 francs, dans une période normale de 2 à 5 ans, il retourne dans sa patrie.

L'émigration est surtout celle de la *classe agri-*

(1) *Relazione sui servizi dell'emigrazione*. Roma, 1909-10.

cole. M. Bosco (1) donne à l'Italie la deuxième place parmi les autres nations pour l'émigration agricole.

_____

(1) *Le correnti emigratorie e agricole fra vari Stati
e il collocamento degli emigranti*. 1906.

EMIGRATION AGRICOLE DES DIFFÉRENTS PAYS D'EUROPE

	Chiffres absolus	Proportion o/o
Italie (1899-1903)	284.000	56.7
Autriche (1899-1903)	41.000	64.3
Belgique (1898-1902)	1.500	27.9
Suisse (1898-1902)	1.300	37.4
Allemagne (1899-1903)	9.000	37.5
Angleterre (1899-1903)		10.4
Ecosse (1899-1903)	30.000	14.0 } 15
Irlande (1899-1903)		44.0

Cependant il y a parmi les émigrants un nombre élevé d'ouvriers, de maçons, de terrassiers. Ceux-ci forment principalement l'émigration temporaire, et se dirigent surtout vers les pays européens. Depuis quelque temps, il se produit aussi vers l'Amérique une émigration intellectuelle, qui en général n'est pas bien vue, surtout en Argentine.

Cause et effets de l'émigration Italienne

Des causes et des effets de l'émigration italienne, nous en parlerons ensuite, mais dès à présent, nous pouvons dire que pour l'Italie, ils sont d'ordre économique, social et politique, démographique.

Le malaise économique, le manque d'équilibre entre le capital et le travail, la crise agraire, spécialement la crise des vins et des « agrumi », l'arrêt du développement de l'industrie, la misère des classes agricoles vis-à-vis de la puissance progressive des grands propriétaires (latifondisti) les mauvais effets d'une législation uniforme pour des populations de différents sentiments et besoins, la faiblesse d'un gouvernement jeune, incapable de résoudre à la fois et toujours avec exactitude les questions les plus différentes et les plus vitales pour une nation qui compte à peine cinquante ans d'existence, ont été et sont les causes principales de l'émigration. Mais il ne faut pas oublier l'augmentation de la population qui n'a pas toujours la possibilité de se procurer les moyens de subsistance.

L'Italie comparativement aux autres pays qui ont une prédominante économie rurale, présente la plus grande densité de population. qui, de 26.800.000 habitants en 1871, s'est élevée à 28 millions 400.000 en 1882, et à 34.200.000 en 1909. Ainsi pour un territoire de 286.682 kilom. 2, il y a une densité de 119 habitants par kilom. 2, tandis que pour l'Allemagne, elle est à peu près de 111 habitants et beaucoup moins pour la France.

Voyez quelle différence il y a entre ces deux

nations et l'Italie ? Combien sont plus florissantes les conditions économiques de la France et de
l'Allemagne, qui, à une économie agraire très
active, peuvent ajouter une industrie et un commerce très développés !

L'Italie au contraire a un commerce et une industrie d'un développement tout à fait récent, et
ses ressources principales viennent d'une agriculture presque encore extensive. Il faut ajouter
que de 28.664.843 d'hectares (total de la superficie de l'Italie), seulement 15.419.000 hectares sont
cultivés : et vous voyez combien il est difficile à
l'Italie de fournir les moyens de subsistance à
ses habitants. Cependant les effets de l'émigration sont tout à fait bienfaisants.

Elle a amélioré les conditions économiques et
morales des émigrants qui, restés en Italie, n'auraient pas pu acquérir les moyens de se créer une
position, n'auraient pas suscité le mouvement ac-
tuel de réaction contre les vieilles idées et les
vieux systèmes, et n'auraient pas fait sentir le
pressant besoin d'une réforme sociale.

Elle fait affluer de grands capitaux en Italie;
les sommes envoyées des Etats-Unis sont de 400
millions de francs en 1907 et 320 millions en
1908; le Commissariat de l'émigration calcule
que normalement les rentrées d'argent des émigrés italiens sont de 500.000.000 par an, sans
compter l'argent qu'ils apportent directement
en rentrant chez eux. C'est l'émigration qui a

augmenté le sentiment de la liberté individuelle
qui a développé celui de l'épargne et a diminué
les crimes et le nombre des illettrés.

Le commerce, la marine ont subi des avantages remarquables et l'Italie a aidé à former ces
colonies sans drapeau, de grande importance,
comme on en rencontre aux Etats-Unis, au Brésil et surtout en Argentine, colonies qui pourraient devenir une source de richesse et de force
pour l'Italie, si elle savait protéger et y répandre la culture nationale.

Cependant plusieurs crient contre l'émigration
et l'envisagent comme un fléau qui cause la dépopulation et laisse des terres incultivées.

Ces craintes et d'autres encore sont sans aucune importance et d'un intérêt bien inférieur
aux avantages apportés par l'émigration. Dès à
présent, nous faisons observer qu'il n'y a aucun
péril de dépopulation pour l'Italie, quoique l'é-
migration ait surpassé le chiffre d'un demi-million par an.

En effet, l'excédent de naissances est toujours
si élevé, qu'il dépasse 350.000 personnes par an
(taux de natalité en 1901 : 32.5 p. 1000 et de la
mortalité 22.5 p. 1000) et de plus, 58 0/0 des
émigrants reviennent chaque année en Italie.

Ainsi, la population augmente partout à l'exception de la Basilicate qui se trouve sous l'influence de causes morbides spéciales que nous
examinerons en son temps.

L'Emigration en Autriche-Hongrie

L'Autriche-Hongrie est un centre d'émigration tout à fait moderne. Quoiqué les notices statistiques commencent en 1850, l'émigration prend une certaine imporatnce à partir de 1880. Aujourd'hui l'Autriche-Hongrie occupe la quatrième place parmi les Etats Européens par rapport à l'émigration. Pour abréger, nous donnons un résumé de la statistique de cinq en cinq années.

Années	Total émigrés	Hongrie	Autriche
1850	—508	—	—
1855	4.005	—	—
1860	2.032	—	—
1865	2.954	—	—
1870	5.920	—	—
1875	7.659	1.065	6.594
1880	29.759	8.766	20.993
1885	28.720	12.348	16.372
1890	67.451	28.745	38.706
1895	65.773	19.757	46.016
1900	116.685	54.080	62.605
1901	136.432	71.349	65.083
1905	372.929	249.200	123.729

1906	449.521	313.167	136.354
1907	563.882	386.528	177.354
1908	157.489	101.275	56.214
1909	415.792	272.260	143.532

Ces émigrants se sont dirigés presque tous vers l'Amérique où en 1900 on comptait 1.000.000 d'Austro-Hongrois, dont 430.000 Autrichiens, 350.000 Bohémiens et 216.000 Hongrois.

Le plus grand contingent d'émigrants a été fourni jusqu'à 1900, par l'Autriche, mais dès 1901, l'élément Hongrois dépasse l'Autrichien et dans les années suivantes on peut bien dire qu'il a été deux fois plus nombreux. En 1900 les Hongrois étaient 54.000 et les Autrichiens 62.000, en 1907 les Hongrois sont 386.000 et les Autrichiens seulement 177.000

Causes et effets de l'émigration en Autriche-Hongrie.

Cependant la densité de la population n'est pas très forte. Le pays en grande partie montagneux et agricole n'est pas bien peuplé. Si la densité de l'Autriche atteint le chiffre de 94 (en 1908), celle de la Hongrie n'arrive qu'à 63, tandis que la densité totale du pays est de 76.

Ce fait a beaucoup alarmé les Hongrois au point qu'un économiste a dit que « l'émigration jette une ombre noire sur la situation économique et sociale de la Hongrie... elle constitue une perle sèche... La perte en hommes causée en Hongrie par l'émigration est aujourd'hui déjà supérieure à l'accroissement naturel de la population » (1).

Nous ne pouvons pas examiner en détail la question mais nous pouvons dire qu'il y a de l'exagération dans ces affirmations.

La densité de la population Hongroise qui, en 1900 était 59 s'est élevée en 1908 à 63 : il n'y a pas une grande augmentation, mais il y en a cependant une. Dans ce rapport l'Autriche a fait plus de progrès car sa densité, de 87 en 1900, s'est élevée à 94 en 1908.

La cause de cette émigration est surtout le malaise agraire. La principale occupation des habitants est l'agriculture, mais elle ne donne pas de bonnes productions à cause des mauvais moyens de culture employés, des capitaux insuffisants et manque d'instruction. Mais le mal le plus aigu, c'est le grand nombre de vastes propriétés; ainsi la famille Esterhazy possède en Hongrie des étendues de terres grandes comme un département français et en Bohême le prince de Schwarrenberg possède 1/30e de la superficie du pays.

En outre l'industrie n'y est pas beaucoup développée à l'exception de la Bohême, de l'Autriche inférieure et de quelques autres provinces.

Quoiqu'on ait voulu envisager comme un mal

---

(1) M. Mailath. *Revue économique internationale*, Juin 1905.

l'émigration dans ce pays, nous pouvons constater qu'elle fait rentrer chaque année plus de 120 millions de francs dans le pays, montant des épargnes des émigrants (1).

En outre l'émigration a déterminé un grand réveil de ces peuples qui se sont mis sur la rive du progrès. Des importantes améliorations ont été apportées aux terres ; et l'industrie, surtout en Hongrie, avec l'aide du gouvernement. se répand de plus en plus.

(1) Pasanis'. *Geografia*, Roma, 1909.

L'ÉMIGRATION EN RUSSIE

L'émigration en Russie n'est pas tout à fait moderne, mais existe en réalité depuis longtemps, seulement elle n'a pas frappé l'attention, car elle se produisait dans des conditions spéciales, dues surtout à sa position géographique.

La Russie se trouve en contact direct avec ses colonies, qui semblaient constituer un état homogène avec elle, par conséquent, on ne remarque pas facilement les mouvements de population d'un pays à l'autre. Ainsi on calcule que l'émigration en Sibérie en 1889 était de 50.000 âmes, en 1895 de plus de 100.000, et de 200.000 en 1896. Les émigrés dans le bassin de l'Amour et dans l'Asie sont aussi très nombreux. Cependant cette émigration doit être considérée comme tout à fait spéciale, car, quoique les causes et les manifestations extérieures du phénomène puissent se rapprocher en général de celles des émigrations chez les autres nations, les effets à l'égard de l'état et de l'émigrant sont en grande partie modifiés. En effet, les émigrants, restant sous le même régime politique pourront améliorer leurs conditions économiques, mais non leur état moral.

L'émigration extérieure a eu dans une première période un caractère religieux (émigration des juifs) et politique (émigration des Polonais). L'émigration à causes économiques a commencé à se développer au XIXᵉ siècle.

Le gouvernement russe a été par principe toujours contraire à l'émigration, il avait même interdit l'émigration des juifs sous peine d'amende et d'emprisonnement. Malgré cela, l'émigration avait continué à se produire et à présent elle atteint un chiffre élevé.

Naturellement ces émigrants ne sont pas tous de race russe, car il y a aussi des Polonais, des juifs, des Allemands.

Depuis 1901 jusqu'à 1906, le nombre de tous les émigrants russes est de plus de 874.611, tandis que l'Annuaire des finances russes évaluait à 499.514 l'émigration de 1857 à 1879 : on voit évidemment quelle forte augmentation elle a subi au XXᵉ siècle.

Emigration Russe

Années	Emigrants	Années	Emigrants
1871.......	2.480	1901........	120.000
1875	6.752	1902	111.323
1880.......	5.162	1903........	157.656
1885.......	18.550	1904.........	128.211
1890.......	85.548	1905........	218.371
1895.......	36.725	1906........	139.050
1900.......	51.626		

De l'émigration russe, une partie se déverse en
Amérique (Etats-Unis, Argentine, Canada, Brésil, mais surtout dans les Etats-Unis où de 1901 à
1903 sont allés plus de 328.000 hommes).

Mais une grande partie des émigrants se dirigent en Sibérie où de 1896 à 1907 sont allés
1.560.905 hommes.

EMIGRATION EN SIBERIE

Années	Emigrants
1903	84.556
1904	30.704
1905	29.126
1906	125.800
1907	415.287

Considérant la grande superficie de la Russie
et la faible densité de sa population (24 habitants
par kilomètre carré) il ne semblerait pas possible
qu'elle pût donner lieu à une si vaste émigration.
Au contraire, elle semblerait un pays d'immigration.

Causes et effets de l'émigration Russe

La cause de l'émigration russe est principalement économique, et en seconde ligne politique.

Les conditions de l'agriculture ne sont pas très

heureuses, quoique celle-ci constitue la source principale de la richesse russe. Les forêts recouvrent 39 0/0 du territoire russe : au Nord, le climat froid et la qualité de la terre ne permettent pas la culture ; dans le Midi, se trouvent des steppes qui comprennent toute la Russie, à l'Est du Volga jusqu'à la Kama, et des plaines sablonneuses privées en général d'eau, car si les grands fleuves ne manquent pas, les canaux irrigatoires y font défaut. Les 2/5 seulement du territoire sont capables de culture, et pourraient nourrir la population agricole russe, si des conditions spéciales ne l'en empêchaient.

Ainsi par exemple la distribution de ces terres est très irrégulière ; il y a des lieux où les terres fertiles abondent, mais la main-d'œuvre manque, il y a au contraire, des endroits très populeux où les terres cultivables font défaut. Les moyens et les systèmes de culture employés ne sont pas perfectionnés, mais anciens et mauvais ; l'engraissement des terres n'est pas employé, l'irrigation est très rare. Quoique le servage de la glèbe soit aboli depuis 1863, il existe encore des rapports de soumission entre les paysans et leurs maîtres dans les immenses étendues de terres (latifondi) qui sont une caractéristique de la Russie.

L'industrie aussi n'est pas très développée, quoique depuis 1890, l'adoption d'un tarif protectionniste ait causé un réveil industriel.

Les conditions politiques et sociales sont très mauvaises. M. Lauwikc (1) nous dit que le gouvernement russe présente des vices profonds. Il étouffe toute autonomie des administrations provinciales et locales et fait une situation intolérable aux libertés politiques et civiles des sujets. La liberté de conscience n'est en Russie qu'un leurre, il y a absence complète de liberté de la presse et de liberté de réunion ou d'association. Si on considère encore les vexations pécuniaires infligées aux paysans, le régime d'exception qu'on fait aux Polonais, aux Finlandais et aux juifs, on comprendra facilement que dans des conditions pareilles, l'émigration doit se présenter souvent comme le seul moyen qui puisse rendre la vie moins misérable à tant de malheureux. L'émigration russe n'a pas réussi à créer des colonies sociales, mais elle a produit des effets plutôt heureux, car elle a amélioré les conditions misérables de tant d'émigrants et a fait diminuer leur ignorance.

L'émigration, en déterminant un mouvement de va-et-vient des gens, est un grand facteur de progrès, surtout pour ce pays, où les idées de civilisation, ne pouvant pas se répandre par les livres et les journaux, se diffusent par les hommes qui, revenant de pays plus libres et plus

_____

(1) *La crise politique et sociale en Russie.* — Paris-Pedone 1905.

avancés, peuvent rapporter dans la patrie ces germes bienfaisants pour l'amélioration de ses mauvaises conditions.

L'ÉMIGRATION EN ESPAGNE

Dans l'émigration espagnole, on peut distinguer trois périodes. Dans la première, qui va de la découverte de l'Amérique jusqu'à l'indépendance des républiques hispano-américaines, s'était établi un courant d'émigration constant de l'Espagne vers l'Amérique du Sud et l'Amérique Centrale, qui, en peuplant ces pays, ouvrit aux autres nations la voie de l'émigration transocéanique.

Après l'indépendance des républiques hispano-américaines, l'émigration espagnole s'est arrêtée pendant plusieurs années et recommence vers la deuxième moitié du XIXᵉ siècle. L'Espagne n'ayant une statistique que depuis 1882, (1) on ne peut pas bien se rendre compte du nombre des émigrants, mais cependant on calcule à 172.000 le nombre des émigrants dans la période 1871-1880, à 367.000 dans la période 1881-1890 et à 756.300 dans la période 1894-1900.

(1) C'est l'année de la création de l'Institut Géographique et de Statistique.

C'est surtout pendant le xxᵉ siècle que cette
émigration prend progressivement un développement tel que l'Espagne vient se placer au premier rang des grandes puissances migratives, où
elle se classe après l'Italie, l'Angleterre, l'Autriche-Hongrie et la Russie.

Emigration Espagnole

Années	Emigrants	Années	Emigrants
1882	25.000	1903	57.012
1885	23.315	1904	87.067
1890	37.023	1905	126.067
1895	36.220	1906	126.771
1900	59.266	1907	130.640
1901	56.323	1908	159.137
1902	51.266	1909	142.717

Cette augmentation de l'émigration, a soulevé
en Espagne, de telles inquiétudes qu'on l'a souvent appelée un fléau terrible (1) auquel l'Etat a
toujours, inutilement, essayé de remédier. (2) Des
lois et ordonnances se sont succédées depuis

(1) Angel Marvaux. *Le problème de l'Émigration en
Espagne.* Questions diplomatique, 16 août 1908. Lepel-
letier F. *Les mesures contre l'Émigration en Espagne.*
Réforme Sociale 1ᵉʳ mars 1906.

(2) La emigracion informacion legislativa y biblio-
grafica de la seccion primera tecnica administrativa
(Madrid 1909).

1848 « qui ont essayé de résoudre le problème
sous ses différents aspects, sans parvenir d'ailleurs à donner satisfaction à tous les intérêts en
jeu ». En général, l'Espagne a, presque toujours,
cherché à enrayer l'émigration, croyant ainsi résoudre le problème de son malaise économique et
social.

La loi du 21 décembre 1907 reconnaissant « le
droit d'émigrer à tout citoyen espagnol » bien
qu'ayant de bonnes dispositions, pour éviter la
mauvaise exploitation de l'émigrant, contient en
réalité des entraves à la liberté des émigrants.

Cependant, il y a un décret du 18 juillet 1881,
qui aurait dû servir d'enseignement et de guide à
l'Espagne mais qui, au contraire, a été oublié
pendant plusieurs années. Ce décret admettait
« qu'il serait vain de prétendre y remédier, (à
l'émigration) au moyen d'une seule disposition lé-
gislative et de ne se servir de la loi que pour entraver la liberté économique, ce principe fécond
des peuples modernes... Il faut au contraire élar-
gir les sphères de l'agriculture et de l'industrie. »

Causes et effets de l'émigration espagnole

Sûrement, on ne peut pas considérer la surpopulation comme cause de l'émigration en Espagne. Dans ce pays, au contraire, il y a presque
une dépopulation. — En effet, la densité de la
population est très faible. Elle est de 36,88 par

kilomètre carré (18.607.674 hommes pour une superficie de 504.516 kilomètres carrés) selon la statistique de 1900, et présente relativement à la statistique de 1870 (34 habitants par kilomètre carré), une minime augmentation, tandis que dans d'autres pays il y a des augmentations bien supérieures.

	Habitants par kil. car. 1870	Idem 1900	Augmentation
Angleterre.........	110	133	23
Italie.............	93	113	18
Allemagne.........	75	104	29
Hollande..........	110	157	47

Les vraies causes ont été et sont politiques, sociales et économiques.

Le soudain enrichissement par l'exploitation des colonies américaines détourna les espagnols du travail de la terre et de l'industrie, et les capitaux au lieu d'être bien placés servirent au faste et à l'oisiveté. Les couvents, avec leur abondante charité, augmentèrent le nombre des mendiants ; le manque de sécurité a détourné les gens de la campagne ; et si on considère encore les salaires très misérables, les impôts et les droits de douane très lourds, les crises industrielles, la mauvaise répartition de la terre, très morcelée (comme en Galice) ou très concentrée entre les mêmes mains on comprendra comment la vraie cause de l'émigration repose dans cette triste situation du pays. L'émigration a donné des avantages à l'Espagne. Elle lui a ouvert des débouchés pour ses légumes, fruits et vins, lui a diminué le nombre des mendiants, lui a fait maintenir des rapports avec les républiques de langue espagnole, et lui sert maintenant de stimulant pour remédier au malaise économique qui persiste.

L'emigration en France

La France à présent n'est pas un pays d'émigration. Les émigrants arrivent seulement à quelques milliers par an, qui se dirigent préférablement vers l'Amérique et l'Algérie. Cependant autrefois, les conditions n'étaient pas les mêmes, et si aujourd'hui quelques auteurs craignent le manque de l'émigration française (1), vers la fin du xviii° siècle, nous en trouvons d'autres qui craignent le contraire. Ainsi, Moreau (2) disait que : « Quoique la France par la beauté de son climat, la fécondité de son sol, les plaisirs qu'on y trouve, l'élégance de son luxe, les charmes de la société, les agréments de celui des deux sexes qui attire l'autre, semble devoir fixer dans son sein ceux qui ont le bonheur d'y être nés, il n'est peut-être pas d'Etat dans lequel l'émigration cause des maux plus sensibles... il semble qu'en France, l'expatriation soit une maladie nationale. »

En 1778, Moreau évaluait de 20 à 23.000 le nombre des Français qui émigraient chaque année : en 1803, il n'y en avait que 5.300. Dans l'inter-

---

(1) Gonnard. Pages 290-291
(2) *Recherches et considérations sur la population.* Paris 1778.

valle d'un siècle, les choses sont changées du tout au tout. Il est évident que la cause de cela est dûe à l'état économique très florissant de la France, et à la liberté dont jouissent ses habitants. Il est possible que l'aliénation des biens nationaux, et le Code Civil, en attribuant à tout héritier un droit à la propriété du sol, aient augmenté l'amour des Français pour la terre dont ils acquéraient une partie et que l'excessive centralisation embrassant les entreprises dérivant de l'effort personnel, laissent peu d'initiative aux individus (1), mais la vérité est, qu'étant bien chez eux, les Français n'ont pas la nécessité d'émigrer et ils n'ont pas l'esprit d'envoyer leurs enfants au dehors (Colson). Du reste, l'augmentation de la population est devenue très lente : le taux de natalité en 1903 était de 21.2 et celui de mortalité de 19,3, c'est-à-dire un excédent de naissance de 2, tandis que cet excédent était bien plus élevé chez les autres nations :

	Taux de natalité 1903	Taux de mortalité 1903
France	21.2	19.3
Grande-Bretagne	28.5	15.6
Italie	32.1	22.7
Allemagne	33.9	20 »
Autriche	37.6	24.1
Hongrie	37.7	26.8
Russie	49.0	31.0

(1) Duval. Page 109.

En outre, le grand développement de l'industrie de la France donne de l'occupation à un grand nombre de personnes, qui, au contraire, auraient été contingent de l'émigration dans une période où l'économie industrielle ne se serait pas encore substituée à l'économie agraire.

Du reste, il ne faut pas oublier l'influence de la Révolution française qui, d'un côté, a été la cause de l'expatriation d'un grand nombre de personnes privilégiées et de l'autre, a arrêté l'émigration naturelle, si nombreuse avant, spécialement vers le Canada.

Voici la statistique de l'émigration française depuis 1853.

Elle n'arrive pas jusqu'à présent, car on ne fait plus de statistiques en France (1).

1853	9.694
1854	18.074
1855	19.957
1856	17.997
1857	18.809
1858	13.813
1859	9.164
1860	6.786
1861	6.334
1862	5.036
1863	4.285
1864	4.057

(1) Voir à tel propos: *Questions diplomatiques et coloniales*, 1 août 1907, *Émigration en France*.

1865............................	4.489
1866............................	4.531
1867............................	4.938
1868............................	5.274
1869............................	4.837
1870............................	4.845
1871............................	7.109
1872:...........................	9.581
1873............................	7.161
1874............................	7.080
1875............................	4.400
1876............................	2.867
1877............................	3.600
1878............................	2.316
1879............................	3.634
1880............................	4.612
1881............................	4.456
1882............................	4.848
1883............................	4.011
1884............................	3.768
1885............................	6.063
1886............................	7.314
1887............................	11.170
1888·...........................	23.339
1889............................	31.354
1890.......... :................	20.560
1891............................	6.217
1892............................	5.200
1893............................	5.300

L'EMIGRATION CHEZ LES PUISSANCES
SECONDAIRES D'EUROPE

Nous avons jusqu'à présent exprimé rapidement le rôle que l'émigration a joué chez les principales puissances européennes. Nous n'avons pas parlé des puissances secondaires, non parce que chez elles, on ne rencontre pas de traces d'émigration, mais parce que ce phénomène joue dans ces pays un rôle moins important.

Cependant pour compléter cette esquisse, nous rapporterons les données statistiques des petites puissances européennes et pour abréger seulement par chaque quinquennat.

PORTUGAL

Le Portugal par rapport à sa population de 5.423.132, et avec une densité de 61, a une forte émigration. Les notices statistiques commencent en 1872.

Années	Emigrants
1872	17.284
1875	15.440
1880	12.597
1885	13.153
1890	28.945
1895	44.419
1900	20.861
1905	33.610
1906	38.094

L'émigration portugaise se dirige de préférence vers le Brésil.

La Belgique a une émigration inférieure à celle du Portugal, quoique sa population (en 1900 de
6.693.548, et en 1909 de 7,451.903) et surtout sa
densité (253 habitants par kilomètre carré, soient
de beaucoup supérieures.

Années	Emigrants	Années	Emigrants
1841-50....	45.470	1890........	2.976
1851-60....	88.607	1895........	1.318
1865......	12.015	1900........	2.215
1870......	7.326	1905........	27.963
1875......	10.157	1906........	32.858
1880......	766	1907........	32.350
1885......	1.286	1908........	32.294

Bien que l'émigration ait augmenté dans les
dernières années, la Belgique qui est un pays
fortement industriel présente peu de tendance à
l'émigration, et si l'on considère le chiffre de l'immigration, qui est chaque année supérieur à celui
des émigrants, on pourrait dire qu'en Belgique,
il n'y a pas d'émigration.

Années	Emigrants	Immigrants
1905...............	27.000	36.000
1906...............	32.000	37.000
1907...............	32.000	38.000
1908...............	32.000	38.000

Les Pays Scandinaves

La Suède et la Norvège sont des pays qui ont donné une abondante émigration, quoiqu'ils aient une densité de population très faible, correspondant à leurs caractéristiques économiques qui sont la sylviculture, l'agriculture, et pour la Norvège, la pêche.

Ainsi la Norvège avec une population de 2.240.032 (en 1909), a une densité de 7 habitants par kilomètre carré, et la Suède, avec une population de 5.476.441, a une densité de 12 habitants par kilomètre carré.

Ci-dessous la statistique des émigrants qui se dirigent en général vers les Etats-Unis.

Suède

Années	Emigrants	Immigrants
1851...............	1.102	
1855...............	1.087	
1860...............	348	

1865	0.691	
1870	20.003	
1875	9.727	
1880	36.398	
1885	18.466	
1890	30.126	
1895	15.104	
1900	20.669	
1905	24.046	8.609
1906	24.704	9.581
1907	22.978	8.913
1908	12.496	9.818

Norvège

Années	Emigrants
1866	15.955
1870	15.552
1875	4.845
1880	20.212
1885	13.281
1890	10.991
1895	0.207
1900	12.931
1905	21.059
1906	21.967
1907	22.135
1908	8.497
1909	10.281

SUISSE

Depuis longtemps, les Suisses ont la coutume d'aller à l'étranger pour y travailler ; mais tandis qu'avant cette émigration était temporaire, depuis quelque temps, elle est devenue permanente, en se dirigeant avec préférence vers les Etats-Unis.

Le courant a été presque toujours stationnaire, car il n'a pas subi de variations très fortes. Relativement à la population de 3.525.256, et à sa densité de 85 habitants par kilomètre carré (en 1907), l'émigration est abondante, cependant elle reste proportionnellement inférieure à celle de la Norvège. La raison est dans ce que la Suisse, quoique pauvre par nature, a su donner un grand développement aux industries. et a su tirer profit des grands pâturages.

Emigration Suisse

Années	Emigrants	Années	Emigrants
1870	3.494	1900	2.650
1875	1.772	1905	5.049
1880	3.517	1906	5.296
1885	6.928	1907	5.710
1890	6.693	1908	3.656
1895	3.107	1909	4.915

La Suisse présente en compensation un bon excédent de naissances sur les morts.

Années	Excéd. de Naissances
1905	34.010
1906	32.853
1907	36.400
1908	38.544
1909	34.700

PAYS-BAS

Quoique la Hollande ait une très forte densité, de 176 habitants par kilomètre carré, avec une population de 5.853.037 (en 1909), et soit un pays agricole. l'émigration n'y est pas nombreuse et présente une tendance à baisser.

La cause évidente est la florissante condition économique de ce peuple, principalement dûe au grand développement du commerce, qui est deux fois et demie plus grand que celui d'Italie, malgré que celle-ci ait une population sept fois plus nombreuse.

Emigration Hollandaise

Années	Emigrants	Années	Emigrants
1870........	8.528	1900..........1.899	
1875........	9.035	1905........	2.277
1880........	9.454	1906........	2.548
1885........	2.146	1907........	4.393
1890........	3.526	1908........	3.030
1895........	1.314	1909........	2.939

Par suite d'un fort excédent de naissance qui
a une tendance marquée à la hausse, la population hollandaise a subi une grande augmentation
qui de 1899 à 1907 a été de 177 0/0, et le phénomène de l'émigration est presque négligeable.

Excédent de naissance

1905	. . . .	85.737
1906	. . . .	87.695
1907	. . . .	88.156
1908	. . . .	84.927
1909	. . . .	90.483

DANEMARK

L'émigration ne joue pas un rôle principal en
Danemark. Elle a touché son apogée vers 1882,
avec un chiffre de 11.614 âmes, et après a eu une
constante tendance à diminuer. Seulement dans
les premières années du XXᵉ siècle, elle s'est élevée jusqu'à 9.000 en 1904, mais pour décroître de
nouveau dans les années suivantes.

Le plus fort contingent est donné par les cam-
pagnes, et les paysans constituent ainsi 80 0/0
des émigrants. Ceux-ci se dirigent de préférence vers les Etats-Unis, le Canada et l'Australie.
Les Danois, étant doués de très bonnes qualités, sont bien acceptés dans les pays d'immigra-

tion, où ils trouvent toujours moyen d'améliorer
leurs conditions économiques.

Emigration Danoise

Années	Emigrants	Années	Emigrants
1870	3.525	1900	3.570
1875	2.088	1905	8.051
1880	5.658	1906	8.516
1885	4.346	1907	7.850
1890	10.298	1908	4.558
1895	3.607	1909	6.782
1908	10.298	1908	4.558

Pour mieux observer les oscillations que l'émigration a subies dans les principaux pays d'Europe pendant les dernières années, nous réuni-
rons les différents chiffres dans le tableau suivant à partir de 1905 jusqu'à 1909. La méthode
suivi dans la formation des statistiques étant
différente de pays à pays, nous ne pouvons pas
faire de comparaisons entre les différentes nations. Seulement, puisque l'émigration est un
phénomène démographique qui est connexe à la
densité de la population et à l'excédent des naissances sur les décès d'un pays, nous allons es-
sayer de donner les chiffres de ces phénomènes.
On pourra ainsi mieux juger l'action de l'émigration dans chaque pays.

L'émigration chez les principaux pays d'Europe de 1905 à 1909

États	Population	Densité	1905			1906			1907			1908			1909		
			Emigr.	Excéd. de nais- sance	Immigr.	Emigr.	Excéd. de nais- sance	Immigr.	Emigr.	Excéd. de nais- sance	Immigr.	Emigr.	Excéd. de nais- sance	Immigr.	Emigr.	Excéd. de nais- sance	Immigr.
Italie............	34.269.701 en 1909	119	426.331	354.478	316.592	787.977	374.403	444.603	704.675	302.000	378.896	486.674	358.607	298.890	625.037	377.206	548.678
Angleterre........	45.006.421 en 1909	142	262.077	492.078	205.493	325.137	489.244	230.105	395.680	488.000	203.638	363.440	492.743	342.922	288.865	478.042	284.325
Russie	140.503.868 en 1909	21	218.371	»	446.904	139.080	»	302.798	315.387	»	207.836	»	»	»	»	»	»
Autriche-Hongrie...	51.450.026 en 1908	70	123.729	421.002	»	136.354	509.683	»	177.334	554.470	»	56.244	377.242	»	443.552	»	»
Allemagne........	60.641.489 en 1905	112	28.075	782.839	»	31.074	910.273	»	31.696	862.084	»	19.883	879.564	»	24.921	»	»
Espagne............	20.068.891 en 1909	40	120.067	479.282	68.037	196.771	451.367	73.208	130.640	174.332	79.352	139.437	196.740	87.773	142.717	484.054	92.042
Portugal	5.493.132 en 1909	61	33.010	»	»	38.094	»	»	44.980	»	»	40.036	»	»	»	»	»
Suède............	5.470.411 en 1909	17	24.016	52.986	8.609	24.701	60.954	9.581	22.978	58.644	8.913	12.499	68.306	9.812	21.002	64.800	8.074
Norvège............	2.240.032 en 1900	7	21.059	28.905	»	21.967	30.122	»	22.435	27.923	»	8.497	27.537	»	16.924	29.393	»
Pays-Bas..........	5.858.717 en 1909	176	2.727	85.737	»	2.348	87.000	»	4.392	88.155	»	3.030	84.027	»	2.039	89.463	»
Belgique........ ...	7.451.903 en 1909	243	27.963	69.094	36.040	32.858	67.387	37.282	32.350	69.794	38.924	32.294	61.850	38.155	»	»	»
Suisse............	3.525.236 en 1907	85	5.049	31.010	»	6.296	32.658	»	5.740	36.409	»	3.636	38.544	»	4.945	31.700	»
Danemark..........	2.605.268 en 1906	66	8.051	34.484	»	8.546	38.986	»	7.850	37.062	»	4.558	37.454	»	6.782	40.404	»

CONCLUSIONS ET DEDUCTIONS

L'humanité n'est pas le bœuf à courte haleine,
Qui creuse à pas égaux sou sillon dans la plaine
Et revient ruminer sur un sillon pareil ;
C'est l'aigle rajeuni qui change son plumage ;
Et qui monte affronter de nuage en nuage
De plus hauts rayons de soleil !

LAMARTINE (*Harmonies poétiques*)
Les Révolutions.

De tout ce que nous avons examiné jusqu'à présent, on relève que l'émigration est un fait qui se produit chez tous les peuples ayant un peu de civilisation.

L'esprit humain change avec l'évolution progressive et revêt des formes différentes.

Autrefois quand les communications étaient difficiles, et que tout étranger était considéré comme un ennemi, l'émigration n'avait lieu qu'à main armée. L'individu n'en pouvant affronter

tout seul les périls, c'était par grandes masses
se déversant sur des nations affaiblies et tom-
bées en décadence qu'elle avait lieu. Ainsi pri-
rent place les invasions barbares. D'autres fois
le désir de faire fortune et d'augmenter le bien-
être se transformait en un enthousiasme religieux ou social qui, s'accroissant avec le temps
poussait à des expéditions lointaines : telles les
Croisades.

Et la colonisation n'est elle-même qu'une phase de l'émigration. Aussi y rencontrons-nous la
caractéristique d'individus, qui sortent de leur
patrie en masse ou isolément. C'est le but qui
varie, car les hommes, sous le régime de la colonisation, fondent des établissements qu'ils considèrent comme un prolongement de leur patrie,
ou des marchés pour y employer leurs capitaux.
Une fois les terres libres occupées et capables
d'être soumises à la culture et d'être exploitées.
une fois que le progrès de la civilisation fait res-
pecter tout état constitué et que l'homme civilisé
cesse d'être hostile à l'homme civilisé, et que
les étrangers sont ainsi sauvegardés et presque
considérés comme des nationaux, une fois que
les moyens modernes de communication ont
supprimé toute barrière existant entre nation et nation et que le travail peut circuler comme les marchandises, l'émigration a changé encore une fois
d'aspect.

Elle est devenue pacifique et se produit tous

les jours presque sans qu'on s'en aperçoive, prenant des proportions toujours plus grandes. Les
émigrants modernes vont chez des Etats constitués et vivent pacifiquement avec la population
indigène à laquelle parfois ils se fondent. Et
même le plus grand peuple colonisateur moderne, qui dans le passé était porté à la colonisation, préfère maintenant émigrer aux Etats-Unis,
où il constitue l'élément prédominant.

« En réalité, le mouvement obéit aux mêmes
lois naturelles que dans l'antiquité et le moyen-
âge ; il coule de la même source : le désir du
mieux; il tend au même but : le bien-être. C'est
dire que l'émigration loin d'être un caprice ou
un accident, fruit d'une fantaisie ou d'une fata-
lité passagère, a ses profondes racines dans les
besoins et les instincts innés de l'homme, sa jus-
tification dans les conditions essentielles des
sociétés, qu'elle est une phase légitime de l'évolution de notre espèce en ce monde, compensant
les douleurs qui l'accompagnent par d'immenses
bienfaits ». (Duval)

On pourrait dire que l'émigration est le phénomène social par lequel doivent passer tous les
peuples qui marchent vers la civilisation et vers
leur développement économique.

Ainsi elle a été très importante en France vers
la fin du xviii⁰ siècle (1) et en Allemagne jusqu'en

_____

(1) Voir page 50 l'Émigration en France.

1882, et maintenant que ces nations avec leur grand développement industriel et économique ont atteint un très fort degré de bien-être, elle diminue graduellement.

L'émigration n'est donc pas un phénomène permanent, ni spécial à une nation (1). Vers la moitié du XIX⁰ siècle, elle se manifeste généralement dans l'Europe occidentale, tandis que dans l'Europe orientale où la population est très faible et la civilisation n'est pas encore développée, elle ne joue presque aucun rôle.

Vers la fin du XIX⁰ siècle et surtout au commencement du XX⁰ siècle, le phénomène se propage aussi dans l'Europe orientale à un tel point que quelques-uns de ces pays (Russie-Hongrie) viennent à occuper une des premières places entre les nations à forte émigration. De même, tandis que jusqu'à la deuxième moitié du XIX⁰ siècle les Allemands et les Anglo-Saxons ont fourni une émigration plus grande que les peuples latins, à partir de la fin du XIX⁰ siècle et principalement dans le XX⁰, ceux-ci ont pris la première place et ont maintenant une émigration presque trois fois plus grande.

En 1885, les émigrants latins (Italie, Espagne, Portugal, France) étaient 200,000 tandis que les Allemands et les Anglo-Saxons étaient 323.000. Une vingtaine d'années après, en 1905, la proportion est tout à fait changée : les Latins attei-

_____

(1) Voir Preziosi. Il Problema d'Italia d'oggi p. 12.

gnent le chiffre de 886.000, sans compter les
Français, et les Allemands et les Anglo-Saxons
ne sont plus que 290.000.

Mais entre tous les pays européens, c'est l'Italie qui tient la tête dans le mouvement migrateur, qui constitue pour elle un des principaux
phénomènes sociaux. Le courant d'émigration
italien a dépassé depuis 1891 celui des autres
pays, et il est monté graduellement jusqu'à prendre chaque année des proportions sans précédent dans l'histoire.

Il y a quelques années, écrivait M. Dingley (1), la
race latine dans les Etats-Unis était représentée
principalement par un Italien de rencontre avec
son petit orgue et son singe, ou avec sa meule
à affuter, plus une curiosité pour la population
qu'un facteur de recensement ; aujourd'hui .es
Italiens aux Etats-Unis, Canada et Mexique sont
plus d'un million et demi.

*Les causes de l'émigration sont aussi très va-
riées.* Elles changent avec le progrès graduel de
l'humanité et sont en connexion avec les conditions des différents peuples (2), mais leur
fond commun est toujours le même : c'est-à-dire
le facteur économique et social. Il est vrai que
des causes politiques, la guerre, les dissensions
civiles, le désir de propager une religion, (sou-

(1) *European Emigration*, Washington 1891.
(2) Voir Wagner. *Grundlegung der politischen Œko-
nomie.* Leipzig 1892. page 550 et la suite.

vent pour en tirer des avantages politiques ou re
ligieux), la passion de la conquête, les persécu
tions religieuses ont été souvent cause de l'émi
gration ; mais même alors, on trouve que leur
vraie base économique et sociale.

Aujourd'hui ces causes ne jouent presque plus
aucun rôle, ce sont les difficultés économiques
de la vie, l'insuffisance de production, les diset
tes, les inondations, les tremblements de terre,
les difficultés de la vie industrielle, le taux trop
faible des salaires, la mauvaise répartition de la
propriété qui déterminent la grande émigra
tion moderne. Le désir du bien-être, les conquè
tes progressives de la civilisation (comme la fa
cilité et sûreté des communications, le grand
développement des lignes de navigation, la pro
tection des droits des hommes et la liberté per
sonnelle de se déplacer et de vivre où l'on pré
fère) ; les relations de parenté ou de nationalité
entre les émigrés et leurs compatriotes, les
mauvaises spéculations des agents d'émigration
sont des conditions et des phénomènes qui favo
risent aussi l'émigration et quelquefois exercent
sur elle une grande influence. Mais ce qui joue
le plus grand rôle, entre les causes secondaires,
c'est la facilité de la correspondance par le pro
grès des services postaux et télégraphiques, qui
font connaître aux émigrants la situation, sou
vent variable des pays d'immigration avec sûre
té et rapidité. Autrefois il fallait des mois pour

avoir des nouvelles des pays transocéaniques et souvent plus dangereuses qu'utiles, car, ne pouvant pas être facilement contrôlées, elles étaient tendancieuses. Au contraire à présent, en quelques heures, une nouvelle peut arriver d'Amérique et être propagée en Europe.

La *surpopulation* n'est pas une cause de l'émigration, comme quelques économistes l'admettent. (1) C'est une chose essentiellement relative (2) : certes dans un pays à population très dense, un certain malaise peut se produire, mais cela arrivera seulement si les habitants ne peuvent pas utiliser leur activité et se procurer un peu de bien-être. Si les conditions économiques sont, au contraire, telles qu'elles rendent possible à tout le monde le travail, ce malaise n'aura pas lieu.

La question de la surpopulation se réduit donc dans ce cas à celle de la *suffisance des moyens d'existence*. C'est quand les moyens de subsistance ne sont pas proportionnés au nombre des habitants qu'on a vraiment une surpopulation qui exercera une forte influence sur l'émigration : la plus grande densité de la population n'en présente en elle-même aucune. Ainsi souvent les pays à forte densité émigrent moins que d'autres d'une densité bien inférieure. La Rus-

---

(1) Voir Cauwès. *Econ. Polit*. page 68, Paris 1893.
(2) Voir Gonnard. *L'émigration européenne du XIX*e page 281

sie, la Hongrie, les Pays Scandinaves qui sont très peu peuplés ont en effet une émigration proportionnellement bien plus étendue que la Belgique et la Suisse qui ont une population très dense.

Nous avons vu comment l'émigration est plus forte dans les pays où la *population est agricole* (Irlande, Hongrie, Italie, Espagne, etc.) que dans les pays industriels (Belgique, Suisse), car ceuxci peuvent mieux régler leur production et leurs échanges et se procurer les moyens de subsistance, tandis que dans les premiers, la misère, souvent causée par une insuffisante production ou une mauvaise répartition de la propriété, pousse les paysans à chercher ailleurs la fortune qu'ils ne peuvent se procurer chez eux. Et dans un même pays, l'émigration se produit principalement dans les régions agricoles : en Italie, ce sont les populations agricoles du Midi qui émigrent le plus. De même l'émigration slave, est constituée en plus grande partie par des paysans, et on peut dire qu'il en est de même du Royaume Uni.

Un peuple agricole, en effet, qui, ayant occupé tout le terrain cultivable disponible, n'a pas de place suffisante pour sa population croissante, se trouve facilement dans de mauvaises conditions économiques, et par conséquent recourt beaucoup à l'émigration. Un peuple à économie industrielle au contraire, a la possibilité d'occuper dans un territoire peu étendu, une grande quantité d'hommes, qui pourront ainsi gagner de quoi vivre.

Il est vrai que dans un pays agricole aussi, les progrès techniques, la substitution de l'agriculture intensive à l'extensive, l'emploi des machines et de l'irrigation, le développement des communications, ou le passage à l'industrie manufacturière, pourraient faire augmenter la production des moyens de subsistance et employer un nombre plus grand d'hommes; mais ces passages sont très lents et très difficiles. « Quand on jette un coup d'œil, dit M. Schmoller (1) sur l'histoire de l'agriculture, on se rend compte que les progrès de l'économie rurale sont les faits de l'histoire les plus rares et les plus fameux : ils ont eu beaucoup de peine et ont mis beaucoup de temps à se répandre ».

L'émigration est en rapport *avec des crises :* elle s'accentue dans le moment de crise et diminue dans la période de la hausse des salaires.

Dans la Lombardie (2), l'émigration permanente, qui en 1876, était de 6.000 h., monta à plus de 18.000 en 1891, année de forte crise.

---

(1) *Principes d'Économie Pol* Trad. Platon 1905, page 454.

(2) Colajanni. *Statistica e Demografia*, Napoli 1909,

Mais avec l'introduction de nouveaux tarifs, le développement industriel une fois favorisé, elle diminua tant qu'en 1901, elle était seulement de 6.461 âmes, quoiqu'elle ait augmenté dans les autres provinces italiennes.

De même en Allemagne, avec le développement industriel produit par l'introduction du protectionnisme de Bismark, l'émigration qui, en 1881 avait atteint son maximum, commence graduellement à diminuer; ainsi en 1901, elle est de 22.000 individus. Ensuite à cause de la crise de 1900-1901, l'émigration monte à 32.000 en 1902, et à 36.000 en 1903.

M. Wagner (1), avec une grande richesse d'exemples, prouve l'influence des crises économiques sur le mouvement émigrateur dont l'oscillation se produirait en fonction du mouvement total économique et admet l'existence d'un parallélisme des masses transocéaniques des émigrants européens dans toutes les principales nations participantes. *Les conditions économiques favorables ou défavorables* de l'Amérique du Nord, dit-il, se réfléchissent dans une augmentation ou diminution du mouvement migratoire, dans un maximum et dans un minimum de l'émigration par chaque période.

Mais ce n'est pas seulement la crise du pays d'où sortent les émigrants, qui a une grande influence sur le cours du phénomène que nous étu-

(1) *Grundlegung*. Leipzig 1892. page 557.

dions; *si la crise se produit dans le pays d'immigration*, il en est aussi influence. Dans ce cas,
au contraire, on relève une baisse dans le nombre des émigrants. Les crises économiques de
l'Amérique en 1904 et en 1908 ont déterminé une
forte baisse dans l'émigration européenne. En
effet, une fois la crise terminée, nous constatons
que :

L'émigration italienne monte de 471.000 en 1904,
à 726.000, en 1905, et de 486.000, en 1908, à
625.000, en 1909.

De même en Autriche-Hongrie, l'émigration
qui, en 1906 était de 157.000 personnes, monte à
415.000 en 1909.

On pourrait cependant, par les conditions de
l'émigration , juger de l'état économique des
pays et Bismarck avait bien raison de dire que :
« *die periodische Vermehrung der Auswanderung grade auf Verbesserung der Wirthschaft-
lichen Lage hinweise.* » Ainsi le gouvernement
en connaissant les qualités du phénomène migrateur, pourrait souvent connaître en même
temps les besoins de la population et être mis
au courant des conditions économiques et sociales de la nation, afin de prendre les dispositions
nécessaires pour en découvrir les tares et les soigner, au lieu de chercher inutilement, du reste,
à empêcher l'émigration (1).

(1) M. De Luca est du même avis. Voir *Dell'emigrazione europea 1910* Parte III, page 5.

CHAPITRE II

Différentes manières de considérer l'émigration

Quoique l'émigration soit un phénomène très ancien, jusqu'à présent on ne s'est pas mis d'accord pour déterminer son essence et son rôle dans la société.

Cette discordance d'idées, de principes, entre les hommes d'état, les économistes et en général entre les auteurs qui ont étudié cette question, a déterminé une action politique souvent contradictoire et par suite des effets contraires aux prévisions.

Par exemple : l'*Espagne* a pendant longtemps empêché l'émigration en Amérique, considérant ses colonies comme un objet d'exploitation commerciale et non pas comme un débouché pour ses produits et sa population. En *Allemagne* elle fut tout d'abord libre ; (en 1784, presque 17.000 âmes émigrèrent aux Etats-Unis) mais ensuite, sous l'influence des idées mercantilistes, qui considèrent l'émigration comme une perte sèche d'hommes et de capitaux pour le pays, on la prohiba avec amendes, prison et confiscations. En *Italie* vers la fin du XIXe siècle il y avait une forte tendance à limiter l'émigration.

En 1887, Crispi proposa d'accorder au gouvernement le pouvoir d'arrêter l'émigration et de frapper de sanction ceux qui l'encourageraient. En 1888 on fit une loi pour empêcher tout individu, sujet au service militaire au-dessous de trente-deux ans, d'émigrer sans la permission du ministre de la guerre [1].

Au contraire, la loi de 1901 et celle de 1910 est inspirée par des sentiments plus libéraux.

En *Angleterre*, si en 1709, après un très mauvais hiver, on favorise l'émigration en Amérique, elle fut ensuite limitée à plusieurs reprises (1719, 1750, etc.) et la sortie des machines et des ouvriers prohibée. Au XIXe siècle, à nouveau, on la considère comme utile, on la rend libre, et même on la stimule.

L'étude scientifique proprement dite de ce problème commence avec *Malthus*. Frappé par la forte augmentation de la population en Angleterre, et par le paupérisme qui en résultait, celui-ci avait publié en 1798 son fameux « Essai sur la population » où il étudiait à fond ce phénomène, et envisageait aussi la question de l'émigration.

---

[1] King et Okey. *Italy To-day*. London 1909. page 319

Mais, quoique Malthus ait le mérite d'avoir appelé l'attention des savants sur l'émigration, il n'aperçoit pas toute l'importance qu'elle a dans la vie sociale. Impressionné par les mauvais résultats des tentatives d'émigrations collectives de Raleigh à la Virginie ; des Puritains, à la Nouvelle Angleterre ; des Français, à la Guyane ; etc., c'est-à-dire par les effets de l'émigration artificielle, et en trouvant les causes dans des passions (soif d'or, goût d'aventures), il la considère comme un « faible palliatif » pour un pays surpeuplé et appauvri (1).

Il a dit que ses avantages seraient de très courte durée, qu'elle est un mal pour les individus et qu'en Angleterre, à l'heure même de son grand développement, l'indigence ne fut pas diminuée, mais qu'au contraire, l'on eût toujours recours à l'assistance par les paroisses.

L'erreur de Malthus est évidente, car il a commis la faute de considérer l'émigration dans sa manifestation artificielle, d'émigration recrutée, subventionnée, et non pas sous son aspect naturel, d'émigration régulière et libre. Mais, si ses arguments n'ont pas de valeur au point de vue du phénomène naturel, il n'en est pas moins vrai qu'ils sont bien fondés contre l'émigration systématique et sont la meilleure preuve de ses défauts. Avant Malthus on considérait comme un devoir des États

_____

(1) Malthus. *Essai sur la population*. Paris 1852. Trad. Prévost page 346.

de favoriser l'accroissement de la population, et on avait pris des dispositions pour encourager les mariages et défendre l'émigration (1). Malthus posait le principe destiné à triompher partout, que « si d'un côté on ne peut démontrer que les gouvernements sont tenus d'encourager l'émigration d'une manière active, de l'autre, c'est, de leur part, non seulement une criante injustice, mais encore une mesure fort impolitique de la défendre » (2).

Si Malthus ne s'était pas trompé, n'avait pas confondu l'émigration naturelle avec l'émigration artificielle, il eût certainement conservé en cette matière une appréciation exacte. C'est ce qui apparaît des restrictions mêmes qu'il a apportées à ses principes en écrivant ; qu'elle fait le bien général ; que la facilité d'émigrer en Amérique « est incontestablement fort heureuse pour un pays, qui a ainsi un doux asile, ouvert à sa population excédente ; et qu'elle paraît utile et convenante à étendre la civilisation et la culture sur la face de la terre »

En général, on trouve dans l'histoire *deux ou trois courants d'opinions opposées.* Les uns ont considéré l'émigration comme un malheur à éviter ou bien à combattre, les autres comme un bien absolu ou un spécifique applicable à diverses ma-

---

(1) Costa. *Il principio di popolazione secondo Malthus.* Bologna 1895.
(2) *Essai* page 352.

ladies sociales : d'autres encore comme un phénomène naturel capable de produire de bons résultats chaque fois qu'il est dégagé de toute influence
artificielle.

Nous parlerons dans ce chapitre des deux premières théories, en nous réservant de relater la
troisième dans le chapitre suivant. Celle dernière
nous peut seule expliquer l'essence vraie et le rôle
exact de l'émigration.

Ceux qui ont cru que : *l'émigration est un fléau
qui ôte aux pays où elle se produit une grande
partie de leur vigueur et de leur vitalité*, ont été
principalement impressionnés par l'idée que l'émigration cause une diminution de population et
une sortie de capitaux du pays, et par conséquent
un affaiblissement. Cela n'est pas tout-à-fait vrai.
La place vide produite par ceux qui émigrent est
rapidement remplie par les nouveau-nés, à
moins qu'on emploie des moyens qui empêchent
la génération.

Si une population a le sentiment de l'émigration,
si elle ne craint pas de voir partir ses fils au-delà
de l'Océan ; elle n'est pas portée à empêcher d'une
façon quelconque la génération, et l'accroissement
de la population n'est pas arrêté (1).

Et en effet les nations qui ont la plus grande

---

(1) Leroy-Beaulieu. *La colonisation chez les peuples
modernes*. Vol. 2ᵉ page 44.

émigration ont aussi en général le plus grand coefficient de naissance (1).

En Italie, quoique dans la période de 1871 à 1909 émigrèrent 11.498.000.000 d'âmes la population s'est accrue de 7.400.000 personnes qui représentent un accroissement net de 134.737 âmes par an. Il est clair, que si une population est accoutumée à l'émigration, la certitude d'avoir ce débouché, lui assurera un accroissement de natalité. L'émigration enracinée représente ainsi une demande d'hommes, à laquelle l'offre tend à s'égaler. « La demande d'hommes règle nécessairement la production des hommes » disait Adam Smith.

J.-B. Say (2), dit que c'est une puérilité pour les chefs d'une nation de s'imaginer qu'elle s'affaiblit par l'émigration. Les provinces d'Espagne d'où sortirent les aventuriers, qui conquirent le Mexique, furent toujours plus populeuses. Il y a une île en Ecosse, l'île de Skye, qui comptait en 1755 plus de 11.000 habitants, dans les années suivantes elle en perdit 8.000, qui émigrèrent : après cette émigration la population augmenta à 14.000 âmes (3).

On pourrait objecter qu'en Irlande la population a diminué beaucoup par l'effet de l'émigration ; mais nous nous trouvons en ce cas dans des con-

---

(1) Mayo-Smith. *Emigration and Immigration.* New-York 1898. page 23.
(2) *Cours complet d'écon. pol.* Paris 1840, page 193
(3) *Statistique* de sir Jon Sinclair.

ditions spéciales et morbides qui ont donné lieu
à cette vaste expatriation :Malthus a aussi soutenu cette théorie (1). Rocher (2), donne une bril-
lante démonstration de ce phénomène: « l'augmentation de la population étant donnée la nature
humaine,a une tendance à s'étendre autant que le
permet la masse des subsistances (dans le sens le
plus large du mot) comparé avec les besoins
usuels dans le pays; cette loi de la nature est,dans
sa sphère,aussi incontestable que la loi de gravita-
tion. Toute extension relative à la masse des subsistances,qu'elle provienne d'une production plus
abondante, ou d'une restriction dans les besoins
des travailleurs,entraîne après elle un accroissement de la population. Or,il est incontestable que
*la croyance universelle,à une extension des subsis-
tances, doit avoir le même effet que cette extension
réalisée.* Si par exemple,pendant que l'Emigration
est en faveur, des millions d'Allemands s'imagi-
nent que non seulement les émigrants sont dans
une position plus satisfaisante qu'auparavant,
mais qu'encore ceux qui sont restés dans le pays,
vont se trouver également dans une position meilleure, ce simple espoir suffit pour conclure un
grand nombre de mariages et produire un grand
nombre de naissances. qui sans lui n'auraient pas
eu lieu ».

(1) Voir *Essai sur la population*. Pages 266, 209, 307.
(2) Roscher und Jannasch-*Kolonien, Kolonial Politik
und Auswanderung*. Leipzig 1885.

Plusieurs économistes, Say, Roscher, von Phi-
lippovich, Marshall, Leroy-Beaulieu, Cauwès,
etc., ont essayé de *déterminer la quantité de capital* (1) *que chaque émigrant porte avec soi,*
la valeur de l'émigrant, la somme des frais d'édu-
cation supportée par la nation, et plusieurs d'entre eux se sont laissé impressionner par les résultats de cette recherche, plus ou moins chimérique,
et sont parvenus à des conclusions qui sont en
général la réflexion de la célèbre phrase de Say:
« Le départ de 100.000 émigrants par an, équivaut
à la perte d'une armée de 100.000 hommes, qui tous
les ans serait engloutie avec armes et bagages en
passant la frontière ».

Or, cette crainte de perte de capitaux par la patrie des émigrants est également sans fondement.

---

(1) *Roscher* estimait que les émigrants emportent ordinairement avec eux un capital supérieur à la moyenne
individuelle du capital dans leur pays d'origine, et ap-
pauvrissent par suite celui-ci. *M. Leroy Beaulieu,* par-
tant du point de vue que l'émigration se recrute parmi
les classes les plus pauvres de la nation, affirme qu'elle
n'enlève qu'une masse de capitaux peu considérable.
M. Becker, directeur du bureau de statistique de Berlin,
évalue de 800 à 900 marks la perte de capital que subit
l'Allemagne par chaque émigrant. *M. Cauwès* estime
que de 1820 à 1890, l'Allemagne a donné aux Etats-
Unis, par ses émigrants, un capital de 4 milliards et
demi (cours d'écon. Polit. Vol. II, p. 71). (Gonnard.
Emigration Européenne, p. 101).

Il suffit de penser que, en général, ce sont les gens qui n'ont pas une bonne situation économique qui émigrent, et que, par conséquent, ils ne peuvent pas emporter avec eux beaucoup de capitaux. Une grande partie d'entre eux émigrent avec l'argent que quelque parent leur a envoyé d'Amérique, donc pas d'emploi de capitaux nationaux. Les émigrants sont généralement des hommes qui, ne pouvant pas travailler et gagner suffisamment à cause d'une forte offre de bras, représentent un capital très faible, et souvent inutilisé. Et, à ce propos, Ferrara, le grand économiste Italien (1) disait: « une richesse quelconque perd avant son caractère de capital, après, perd le même caractère de richesse, si elle est inerte, paralysée, impuissante à produire. Ce que l'émigrant emporte de son pays, c'est précisément cette portion de capital, qui pour une cause quelconque, restait improductive, et dont la production était tellement limitée, qu'elle ne méritait pas qu'il y consacre son temps et son travail. ».

Mais même en admettant une sortie de capitaux, d'hommes et d'argent, il faut voir, avant de parler de perte, si leur rendement aussi sort du pays d'émigration. Nous croyons qu'il n'est pas une exagération d'admettre que non seulement ce rendement va à la mère patrie; et qu'en général, quand l'émigration est naturelle et dégagée de toute influence artificielle, elle est capable en quel-

---

(1) Colojanni *Demografia*. 1909, page 409.

ques années, de restituer à la mère patrie, un capital bien plus grand que celui qui en est sorti.

En effet, dans les pays d'émigration, souvent l'industrie ou l'agriculture n'offre pas d'emploi utile à tous les habitants, qui, ainsi, sont poussés à émigrer. Il est évident que si les émigrés étaient restés dans leur patrie, leur production ou le rendement de leurs capitaux auraient été très bas, et sans doute bien inférieur à ce qu'aurait été dans un pays où les bras manquent et où l'agriculture et l'industrie offrent les moyens de gagner beaucoup. On pourrait objecter que ce plus grand rendement est un bénéfice seulement pour l'émigrant, et que la même patrie n'en reçoit aucun avantage. Mais il suffit de regarder les chiffres des envois en argent faits par les émigrants à leur patrie, pour se convaincre du contraire. Les émigrants Britanniques de 1848 à 1869, envoyèrent à leur patrie 274 millions de francs. A présent on estime que les émigrants d'Autriche-Hongrie envoient à leur patrie 325 millions par an, et ceux du Royaume-Uni 125 millions (1).

Pour l'Italie le « Commissariato dell'Emigrazione » (2) estime que les remises faites par les émigrants montent à un chiffre pas inférieur à 500 millions par an, auquel il faut adjoindre encore

---

(1) Colajanni- *Demografia*. Page 412.
(2) *Relazione sui servizi dell'emigrazione per l'anno 1909-1910.* Roma 1910. page 395.

l'argent importé par les émigrants eux-mêmes, qui leur est bien propre, ou qui leur a été confié par des parents ou des amis, afin de le remettre à leurs familles à la métropole.

Mais à part l'argent envoyé ou importé, il faut considérer l'accroissement du commerce entre la mère patrie et les pays d'émigration, il faut tenir compte des avantages moraux, diffusion de la langue, de la race, des idées, etc., et alors on ne pourra pas ne pas admettre, qu'en conditions normales, la mère patrie obtient des émigrants une utilité plus grande que celle qu'elle aurait eu s'ils étaient restés chez eux. Plusieurs ont voulu soutenir que la *restriction de la natalité apporte des avantages plus efficaces que l'émigration* des adultes. Cela n'est pas du tout conforme à la réalité. L'émigration, nous l'avons dit, favorise les échanges de produits divers avec les pays d'immigration où les émigrants diffusent les goûts et les mœurs de la mère patrie.

Ces avantages ne seraient pas possibles avec l'autre système. Ceux qui estiment que *l'émigration est un bon régulateur de la population et qu'en la favorisant, en l'autorisant, ou en la prohibant à propos, elle pourra maintenir l'équilibre entre capital et population*, ont été poussés à admettre cela par l'exagération des mérites de l'émigration, qu'ils ont considérée comme un spécifique mis à la disposition du gouvernement

pour guérir une grande partie des maux sociaux.
L'émigration serait ainsi un remède contre l'excès de la population, la misère et les crimes et
un moyen pour faire élever le taux des salaires.
Ainsi Lord Bacon conseillait en 1606 à Jacques Ier
de coloniser l'Irlande pour éviter la misère produite par l'accroissement de la population, qui
n'avait été arrêtée par aucune guerre. On voit
déjà ici un prélude à l'émigration systématique,
qui trouva ensuite son défenseur et son cham-
pion le plus ardent en Wakefield.

Mais cette école n'a abouti à rien, Malthus (1) nous raconte comment les trois
tentatives, faites par M. Raleigh à la Virginie, échouèrent, et les gens moururent par la
famine et la maladie, ou tués par les indigènes.
Des 12.000 Français, qui, en 1668 essayèrent de
faire un puissant établissement à la Guyane,
10.000 périrent dans l'inaction, dans le besoin,
dans le ravage de la contagion : 2.000 furent
ramenés en France, 26 millions de francs furent
perdus.

Des 75.000 chrétiens de l'empire Ottoman con-
traints par le gouvernement russe d'émigrer en
Crimée, seuls 7.000 survécurent, les autres, dépourvus d'abri, périrent dans la misère. D'un
autre côté, il ne faut pas croire que réellement
cette émigration systématique *soit le remède contre l'excès de la population.*

_____

(1) *Essai.* pages 347-318.

Il est vrai qu'une émigration régulière, spon-
tanée, et bien dirigée, peut remédier jusqu'à un
certain point à l'excès de la population, mais cela
arrive parce que les émigrants, avec leurs gains
et leurs économies faites à l'étranger peuvent,
en favorisant le développement de l'industrie,
de l'agriculture, et du commerce dans leur patrie,, ouvrir ainsi de nouvelles sources d'emplois
et de travail aux autres nationaux et réduire
un surplus de population peu utile.

L'émigration recrutée et suscitée, n'ayant, en
général, pas bon succès, elle ne créera pas des
débouchés réels à la population : au contraire,
celle-ci, par la croyance à une trompeuse extension des subsistances, qui ne se réalisera pas,
tendra encore plus à un accroissement qui sera
un malheur encore plus grand pour le pays (1).

On a même soutenu que l'émigration serait
un *bon moyen pour débarrasser une nation, des
malheureux* sans ressources et pour combattre le
paupérisme. Il est évident que ce n'est pas un
bon système de soigner une maladie par l'élimi-
nation du malade : il faut toujours combattre la
cause du mal qui, dans notre cas, n'est pas l'homme en lui-même, mais les mauvaises conditions
économiques, produits de différentes forces sociales.

Malheureusement il arrive souvent que les plus
besogneux ne sont pas capables d'activité in-

(1) Voir page 78

dividuelle ni de ressort. Les privations, les gênes, les contraintes fâcheuses, conduisent généralement à la passivité, à l'indifférence et au désespoir.

Ainsi ces malheureux, affaiblis par le vice ou la misère, pas habitués, ou incapables, pour la plupart, du travail, privés de toute initiative et d'esprit d'entreprise, périront certainement.

Nous croyons que cela représente le comble de l'inhumanité, à moins que la patrie, pour les aider, ne fasse des sacrifices qui seront sans doute bien plus grands que ceux qu'elle aurait pu faire chez elle (2).

Ainsi pas de bénéfices à la patrie et pas aux émigrants.

On obtient les mêmes effets quand on veut employer *l'expatriation des criminels* pour en décharger la patrie.

Les mauvais résultats de Botany-Bay pour les convicts d'Angleterre et de Nouvelle-Calédonie, pour ceux de la France, montrent l'inefficacité du système. Les criminels sont en général de mauvais travailleurs, leur placement chez les colons établis est difficile et ils empêchent l'affluence des émigrants libres, dans les lieux où ils se trouvent, qui deviennent ainsi de vrais centres criminels. L'emploi de l'émigration forcée pour combattre une religion quelconque n'a pas été plus heureux.

(1) Colson. *Cours d'écon pol*. Paris 1907.

Les idées ne sortent pas d'un pays avec les
hommes, tandis qu'une exportation de travail,
d'énergie, de capitaux, ne restant pas en relation avec leur pays d'origine, sera pour lui une
perte sèche. Ainsi, l'expulsion des Juifs et des
Maures, fut un désastre pour l'Espagne, et la
révocation de l'Edit de Nantes appauvrit plusieurs provinces de France, où les protestants
représentaient la richesse et le travail. On a soutenu : que l'on pourrait employer l'émigration
pour produire une hausse des salaires, en dimi-
nuant la concurrence. L'émigration, ôtant au
pays une grande quantité de bras, produit une
diminution de l'offre de travail, de sorte que la
demande sera supérieure à l'offre et les salaires
subiront une hausse. C'est-à-dire : quand la population augmente, l'offre de travail hausse et
la demande baisse; quand la population diminue,
l'offre de travail baisse et la demande augmente.

Le principe n'est pas faux, et nous l'admet-
tons aussi : mais il est évident que le taux des
salaires ne varie pas seulement avec l'augmentation ou la diminution de la population et que
l'émigration n'est pas un moyen de diminuer la
population. Nous avons précédemment démontré que l'émigration n'influe pas beaucoup sur
le dépeuplement, et qu'au contraire, elle donne
à une population une plus grande élasticité
d'augmentation.

Il est possible qu'à un moment donné, la sortie

rapide d'une grande quantité de bras, produise une augmentation du taux des salaires, mais cette augmentation sera momentanée, car à mesure que des hommes jeunes viendront à remplir les vides, le salaire tendra de nouveau à baisser. En outre, si, en général, ceux qui ne trouvent pas de travail dans leur pays émigraient, le rapport entre l'offre et la demande ne changerait pas; l'émigration des ouvriers qui travaillent, aurait le même effet, car ils seraient remplacés par ceux qui ne travaillent pas. Si la sortie de la force de travail devient systématique, cela peut même donner lieu à des crises désagréables. Justement M. Leroy-Beaulieu dit (1) que « toute hausse de salaire, qui n'est pas justifiée par une production plus grande du travail de l'ouvrier, toute hausse qui provient de moyens artificiels, des coalitions, d'une émigration sur vaste échelle, cette hausse-là n'est pas durable, elle n'est pas bienfaisante, elle peut, elle doit amener des crises industrielles ».

En 1827, le Parlement anglais, par suite de la crise produite par l'introduction des machines, décida d'envoyer aux colonies 95.000 ouvriers qui étaient sans travail. Quelques années après, l'Angleterre manqua de bras pour l'industrie qui avait pris un grand développement et elle en

(1) La colonisation chez les peuples modernes. Vol. II page 440.

arriva à regretter, inutilement d'ailleurs, les hommes qu'elle avait expatriés, et qui, eux-mêmes, étaient très malheureux aux colonies.

Mais si l'émigration n'a pas une influence directe sur la relation entre les variations de la population et l'offre de la demande de travail, si la hausse de salaire produite par une émigration artificielle est dangereuse, *faut-il nier à l'émigration toute influence sur le taux des salaires ?*

Nous croyons qu'elle exerce, en effet, une influence sur le taux des salaires, mais cela indépendamment d'une diminution d'offre de travail, que nous n'avons pas admise, et à condition qu'elle soit naturelle, sentie par le peuple et privée de toute influence artificielle.

Si nous considérons les causes qui peuvent amener une hausse du taux des salaires, nous trouverons entr'autres, les suivantes : Les conditions de la vie qui changent continuellement; les besoins qui augmentent sans cesse, l'enchérissement des aliments, des loyers, etc., correspondant à une augmentation relative des salaires, absolument nécessaire, sans quoi la vie deviendrait impossible.

Le passage de l'économie agricole à l'économie industrielle, cause chez celle-ci une augmentation dans la demande de travail. Pour avoir des travailleurs, il faut les retirer de l'agriculture en leur offrant des salaires supérieurs. Cela produira en même temps une hausse des salaires dans les autres branches où l'offre vient à diminuer, car ils tendent toujours à s'équilibrer.

Or, l'émigration augmentant les connaissances des peuples, favorisant le passage de l'économie agricole à l'économie industrielle, et à l'économie commerciale, exerce indirectement une influence bienfaisante sur les salaires.

Les capitaux que les émigrants envoient dans leur pays, les avantages tirés d'un commerce plus actif avec les contrées d'immigration, donnent lieu à la constitution de nouvelles industries, au développement des anciennes, et, par suite, à une augmentation de demandes de travail à laquelle correspond une hausse des salaires.

Et cette hausse qui découle de cette augmentation de travail, est tout-à-fait naturelle, et, au lieu d'être dangereuse comme celle produite par une émigration artificielle, elle est bienfaisante et produit un soulagement effectif chez les classes ouvrières.

CHAPITRE III.

CE QU'EST L'EMIGRATION ET QUELLE DOIT ETRE

L'ACTION DE L'ETAT.

Nous avons vu dans le chapitre précédent comment les deux courants d'idées, dont l'un considérait l'émigration comme un mal à combattre, et l'autre, comme un moyen de défense sociale à la disposition du gouvernement, sont privés de tout fondement; examinons maintenant la troisième manière de considérer l'émigration, qui, quoique née à côté des deux précédentes, s'est affirmée vers la moitié du XIX⁰ siècle, et à présent tend à prévaloir sur les autres tendances

Elle considère *l'émigration comme une phase naturelle de l'évolution humaine, qui, dégagée de toute influence artificielle et anormale, permet une meilleure utilisation des forces humaines et représente un avantage pour l'Etat et l'individu.*

Nous avons, en effet, vu comment elle se pro-

duit dans tous les pays qui sont parvenus à un
certain degré de civilisation, et nous avons ob-
servé les différents avantages qu'elle a apportés
aux nations dont nous nous sommes occupés précédemment.

Quand les richesses naturelles du sol sont insuffisantes pour faire vivre les hommes qui l'habitent, ou que les conditions des habitants leur
font sentir la nécessité d'une jouissance, plus
grande de la vie, l'émigration a lieu.

Les courants humains qui abandonnent la patrie, sont composés de ceux qui trouvent un
champ nouveau d'application de leurs forces,
de ceux qui désirent pouvoir vivre et souffrir
moins; et leur vie active à l'étranger même, devient plus utile à la patrie (1).

Cependant nous pouvons définir l'émigration
comme le *déplacement d'un pays à un autre,
d'hommes qui ont l'espoir d'améliorer leur situation.*

Elle est un phénomène tout-à-fait naturel, produit par le marasme et le malaise d'une société,
qui tend à rendre plus actives les forces de cette
société et à augmenter leur utilisation.

Si un Etat ne peut pas, ou ne sait pas soigner
un mal social, ou s'il ne sait pas seconder l'œuvre de la nature, celle-ci ne s'arrête pas à cause
de cela, mais parvient quand même toute seule
à établir l'équilibre de la société.

(1) Voir Mosso, L'émigrazione, Nouva Antologia 16
juillet 1905.

L'émigration n'est pas un mal à soigner, mais c'est un remède qui fonctionne contre un mal, et qui, libre de toute influence hétérogène, peut faire ressusciter à une vie nouvelle, des régions désolées.

Certes, le fait d'un déplacement dans l'ordre usuel des choses et la création d'un ordre nouveau, est cause d'un certain malaise; mais celui-ci, sous la bonne influence du nouvel état des choses, disparaît bientôt, et donne lieu à des bénéfices.

Si nous restons pendant quelques jours au lit, à peine nous remettons-nous en mouvement, nous nous sentons courbaturés, mais cette indisposition sera vite suivie par un bien-être général produit par la reprise de l'activité de notre organisme.

« De même des maux accidentels peuvent surgir d'un brusque mouvement de circulation imprimé à des populations, naguère vouées à l'immobilité, mais combien, en revanche, le rapprochement et l'agglomération des masse laborieuses ne sont-ils pas favorables à la diffusion des connaissances humaines et aux progrès de la sociabilité ! (1).

Il ne faut pas s'alarmer si les bons effets de l'émigration tardent à se faire sentir; comme tous les bons remèdes, elle n'a pas une action rapide,

_____

(1) Voir De Molinari, *Dictionnaire d'Econ. Pol.*

mais il faut attendre quelque temps pour constater les bénéfices qu'elle apporte.

L'émigration opère sans besoin de stimulants ou de palliatifs, qui n'ont aucune valeur vis-à-vis de la puissance des forces naturelles : elle se produit dans des conditions déterminées et cesse naturellement une fois que ces conditions viennent à manquer.

Il est donc inutile de vouloir l'arrêter ou l'empêcher avec l'imposition, ce qui ne ferait qu'aggraver la situation d'une société. Lorsqu'on empêche une population surabondante dit J.-B. Say, de sortir par la porte des frontières, elle sort par la porte des tombeaux. Chacun a le droit de respirer plus à l'aise, et c'est respirer plus à l'aise, que de subsister plus facilement.

C'est seulement en combattant les causes qui déterminent l'émigration qu'on pourrait réussir à l'arrêter. Mais dans ce cas encore, il faut être très prudent. Dans la vie sociale, il se produit des répercussions qu'on ne peut prévoir, et nous croyons avec M. Colson (1) qu'il vaut mieux laisser les hommes souffrir les maux qui sont la conséquence normale de leur disposition naturelle, que de leur en infliger d'autres, d'autant plus difficiles à supporter qu'ils seraient l'effet de mesures voulues.

Il est inutile, à notre avis, de discuter *jusqu'à quel point l'émigration, à moins qu'elle ne soit*

(1) Econ. Polit. page 50.

artificielle, devient un bien ou un mal. Aussi
quand elle est supérieure à l'excédent de naissance, elle ne peut pas être considérée comme
un mal, car si elle existe, c'est la conséquence
des mauvaises conditions économiques, sociales ou politiques; et il est évident, dans ce cas,
que l'émigration ne peut pas être considérée comme un mal, car il est toujours préférable que la
population aille chercher les moyens de subsistance dans d'autres pays, au lieu de rester cris-
talisée dans la contrée où persiste un état morbide, et où elle ne peut vivre et travailler com-
modément. On se préoccupe souvent du mal que
l'émigration fait à la patrie, mais pourquoi ne
pense-t-on pas au mal que les conditions, dans
lesquelles se trouve la patrie, font aux individus ? Il serait inhumain d'obliger des hommes
à vivre dans un pays où les conditions sociales
sont pire que celles faites aux habitants d'autres
pays. Et, comme l'a dit Monseigneur Scalabrini:
qui pourrait contenir un peuple qui se détend
sous les convulsions du ventre, si ce n'est l'espoir de trouver un moyen de gagner son pain
quotidien ?

Du reste, en Irlande aussi, où la population fût
de beaucoup réduite par l'émigration, celle-ci a
apporté des effets bienfaisants, comme dit M.
Duval, et a miné, selon Bolton King (1), la domination du *landlord* et du prêtre.

---

(1) Italy To day, page 312.

Mais une fois que l'émigration est en général un bien, *est-elle toujours désirable ?* Il est impossible de répondre à cette question complexe par l'affirmative ou la négative. Nous croyons qu'un léger courant d'émigration est toujours désirable afin de favoriser les échanges, la diffusion de la culture, des idées, de la langue d'un pays; car une forte émigration est toujours le signe d'une mauvaise condition économique ou sociale d'un pays. N'importe comment, elle est toujours préférable à l'immobilité morbide d'une population, qui ne pouvant pas se répandre, donnerait lieu à un plus grand malaise économique et social.

Par conséquent, *l'émigration ne doit pas être prohibée, ni favorisée, mais laissée libre.* Seulement puisque l'influence d'éléments artificiels pourrait la faire dégénérer, il faut la soumettre à une tutelle et à une protection.

C'est seulement depuis le XIX⁰ siècle que le principe de la liberté et de la protection de l'émigration est généralement admis.

En France, encore en 1791, le droit d'émigrer était soumis à la permission d'une commission, et en Allemagne on essaya de l'empêcher jusqu'à 1825. L'Angleterre s'est occupée de la question depuis 1803 en protégeant les émigrants de l'exploitation d'une foule d'agents malhonnêtes, en réglant le nombre des émigrants pour chaque vapeur, la quantité de nourriture et d'eau, la navigabilité des bateaux etc.; et les autres états ensuite l'ont imitée.

On n'est arrivé à admettre ces principes, comme nous l'avons dit, que graduellement et qu'une fois qu'ont échoué tous les efforts pour arrêter l'émigration, la recruter ou la favoriser.

Mais le progrès des sentiments de civilisation, le grand respect des droits des hommes, les proportions toujours plus grandes que le phénomène assumait, les abus commis par les agents qui, attirant par des promesses fallacieuses beaucoup de gens, les transportaient, dans des conditions déplorables, dans des pays où ils ne pouvaient pas travailler, eurent aussi beaucoup d'influence sur l'admission de ces principes.

Voilà ce que plusieurs écrivains ont dit à ce propos.

Burke : « Il est aussi naturel aux hommes d'affluer vers les contrées riches et propres à l'industrie, quand pour une cause quelconque la population y est faible, qu'il est naturel à l'air comprimé de se précipiter dans les couches d'air raréfié » (1).

---

(1) It is as natural for people to flock into a lensy and wealthy country, that by any accident may be thin of people, as it is for the dense air to rush into these parts which are rarefied.

Malthus s'exprime ainsi : «Si d'un côté on ne peut démontrer que les gouvernements sont tenus de l'encourager d'une manière active, de l'autre, c'est de leur part, non seulement une criante injustice, mais encore une mesure fort impolitique de la défendre » (1).

Say, quoiqu'il considère l'émigration comme une perte d'hommes, comme un mal, (2) il s'oppose énergiquement aux lois cœrcitives de l'émigration. « Il ne faut pas, dit-il, s'armer contre elle, parce que c'est une violation du droit naturel, toute société peut bien imposer les conditions qu'il lui plaît aux associés qui viennent se réunir à elle, ou qui consentent à vivre dans son sein; mais elle n'a aucun droit sur ceux qui veulent la quitter lorsqu'ils prétendent rien emporter qui appartienne à l'Etat ou aux particuliers. S'y opposer n'est pas seulement un passe droit, c'est une barbarie et une maladresse (3).

---

(1) Essai. Trad. Prévost, page 352.

(2) « Il ne faut pas conclure que je ne regarde pas comme un mal une émigration d'adultes, surtout si ce sont des hommes laborieux, savants et utiles... elle (l'émigration) est cause que des hommes faits sont remplacés par des enfants, des hommes forts et capables par des êtres débiles et qui seront pendant plusieurs années à charge à leurs familles et à leur pays au lieu de leur être utiles ». Say. *Traité d'écon. pol.* page 151. Guillaumin 1861.

(3) Voir Say. Traité d'écon. pol., page 233.

Bentham (1) à propos d'empêchement à l'émigration, dit que : « c'est changer l'Etat en prison, c'est publier au nom même du gouvernement, qu'il ne fait pas bon y vivre. Il semble qu'un tel édit doit toujours commencer ainsi: Nous, etc... ignorant l'art de rendre nos sujets heureux, bien assurés que si nous leur laissons la liberté de fuir, ils iraient chercher des contrées moins opprimées, etc. ».

On peut distinguer quatre périodes de temps dans lesquelles les Etats ont exercé une action différente sur l'émigration; mais ces périodes ne sont pas contemporaines dans les divers états, et ne se succèdent pas avec régularité dans un même état. Ainsi dans la première, quand le citoyen était considéré comme la propriété du Seigneur, les Etats, craignant que l'émigration ne devienne dangereuse, cherchaient à l'arrêter en la défendant. Dans la seconde, les Etats ne se préoccupent pas de ce phénomène et le rendent presque libre; dans la troisième ils favorisent beaucoup l'émigration, et dans la dernière enfin ils laissent l'émigration libre, intervenant seulement pour la protéger contre les influences hétérogènes.

Aujourd'hui on admet presque partout que l'Etat ne peut pas prohiber l'émigration, et que le

---

(1) Théorie des peines et des récompenses. Tome II, page 310.

citoyen a le droit d'émigrer. Mais de même que l'Etat, dans l'intérêt de l'ordre public, règle le mariage, la famille, la filiation, qui sont tous des droits naturels des hommes, de même il faut admettre son intervention dans l'émigration pour la protéger de toute mauvaise influence, afin d'éviter une dégénérescence du phénomène.

Le gouvernement doit exercer une surveillance sur les émigrants soit au moment du départ, soit à celui de l'arrivée dans le pays d'immigration.

Dans le premier cas, afin d'éviter que les émigrants soient exploités par des agents d'émigration, par des hôteliers, etc., il doit leur assurer de bons moyens de transport, et un voyage dans des conditions hygiéniques, afin d'empêcher qu'ils ne se trouvent en conflit avec les lois de l'Etat (service militaire, individus mineurs, etc.).

Dans le deuxième cas, afin de protéger les émigrants contre les vexations, les fraudes qu'ils subissent souvent dans les pays d'immigration, il doit prêter assistance aux ouvriers qui chôment ou qui sont victimes de malheurs et d'infortunes, et éviter qu'ils perdent la conscience de leur nationalité par la création d'écoles nationales.

PARTIE SPÉCIALE

« *In another century..... Italian
will be, after English and Rus-
sian, the most widely spoken of
Aryan tongues* ».
Bolton King *et* Thomas Okey.

CHAPITRE PREMIER

*L'émigration dans le Midi de l'Italie et la
question du Midi*

Si on suit le mouvement des publications italiennes on est frappé de la place énorme occupée
dans les revues et les journaux, par les questions
relatives à l'émigration dans le Midi de l'Italie,
questions qui sont généralement traitées en connexion avec les problèmes économiques et sociaux qui intéressent le pays. Précédemment
au contraire, c'était la vieille question du Midi,
dont nous allons parler, qui occupait beaucoup
les publicistes de tous genres.

On pourrait penser que cette question et celle
de l'émigration du Midi d'Italie sont deux problèmes distincts; mais selon nous ils n'en constituent qu'un seul, dont l'émigration peut être
la solution.

Le Sénateur Franchetti dans une conférence tenue à Milan s'exprime ainsi : pendant qu'on écrivait des livres, pendant qu'on prononçait des discours et que l'on compilait des lois pour résoudre le problème du Midi, les paysans méridionaux commençaient à la résoudre silencieusement par eux-mêmes. Ils allaient en Amérique créer les capitaux nécessaires à la fécondation de la terre de leur pays (1).

Nous avons eu l'occasion de montrer dans la première partie de cette étude, comment le phénomène de l'émigration est strictement connexe à la vie économique, sociale et politique d'un peuple, et comment elle est pour ainsi dire la valve de sûreté naturelle à laquelle les populations recourent lorsqu'elles sont dans des conditions de vie misérables et insupportables.

L'Italie du Sud nous offre la preuve la plus frappante de cela.

Les mauvaises conditions économiques du Sud de l'Italie ne sont pas récentes, mais existent déjà depuis si longtemps qu'elles sont devenues en quelque sorte traditionnelles.

A l'étude fragmentaire de l'un ou de l'autre aspect de la vie du Midi, succéda bientôt une étude systématique des conditions économiques et morales de ce pays où l'on essaya d'en déterminer les causes et les effets, d'en indiquer les remèdes; des enquêtes agraires et parlemen-

(1) Giornale di Siciliai 25-26 février 1911.

taires furent faites, et de tout cet ensemble
d'études et de faits naquit la question qui fût appelée « la question du Midi ».

Plusieurs politiciens et économistes (Villari,
Nitti, Ciccotti, Ferraris, di San Giuliano, di Son-
nino, Franchetti, Sacchi, Arcoleo, etc.) sociolo-
gues et anthropologues (Lombroso, Ferri, Ferria-
ni, Loria, Sergi, Colajanni, Squillace, Renda,
Marchesini, Niceforo, etc.) et publicistes de tous
genres se sont occupés de cette question, y ap-
portant une intéressante contribution d'observations et de propositions, mais cependant soit par
indolence, soit par apathie des gouvernants et
des gouvernés, on n'a abouti qu'à des résultats
très maigres.

Mais si le gouvernement et les hommes n'ont
sû ou n'ont pû remédier au malaise du Midi,
les forces sociales ont naturellement réagi, et la
question a trouvé dans l'émigration un moyen
de solution. Elle a en effet réveillé le peuple de
sa longue léthargie, lui a ôté des yeux le ban-
deau qui lui empêchait de voir les conditions misérables, dans lesquelles il se trouvait, et comme remède héroïque a détruit les petits propriétaires, qui vivaient dans l'oisiveté et opprimaient
les paysans.

C'est l'émigration qui pousse les paysans à s'é-
manciper, et qui secoue le gouvernement de son
apathie, en le stimulant à déployer une plus
grande activité pour le bien de ses sujets.

Etant donné que l'émigration est strictement liée aux conditions du pays, nous croyons utile de tracer rapidement les conditions de l'ambiance, où elle se produit afin de pouvoir ensuite retracer mieux ses causes et ses effets.

CHAPITRE II.

Les conditions économiques et sociales du Midi de l'Italie.

En regardant dans un Atlas géographique, l'Italie se trouvant coloriée d'une même teinte, on pourrait penser qu'elle est un état homogène. Malheureusement cette idée n'est jusqu'à présent qu'une illusion. Il y a une Italie, disait M. Lombroso, mais elle n'est pas unifiée « *L'Italia è una, ma non è unificata* ».

En réalité, l'Italie est politiquement une, mais sociologiquement elle est comme une palette de peintre, où sont délayées des couleurs discordantes : en un mot, elle est si différente d'un bout à l'autre, que l'on peut considérer chez elle des sociétés diverses pour la civilisation, la vie sociale et l'état économique. C'est-à-dire *l'Italie du Nord et l'Italie du Sud*.

Le Nord est un pays plat, ouvert, sillonné par

de grands fleuves et canaux; le Midi, (1) étroit et prolongé, est traversé par les Apennins, qui rendent la région semée de gorges et de vallées d'une communication difficile.

Qui voyage dans la Basilicate, dans la Calabre, dans la Sicile, ne rencontre souvent, pendant plusieurs heures de chemin de fer, que des grandes étendues de terre, désertes, sans habitations, qui sont soumises à une culture extensive. Les villes ne sont pas fréquentes, les bourgs sont la caractéristique du Midi, quoiqu'ils aient le nom de villes et ils se trouvent en général dans une position montagneuse et loin les uns des autres (2).

Dans ces villes, propriétaires, fermiers, paysans, ouvriers, vivent entassés dans de vieilles *maisons privées* d'air et de lumière, abritant à la fois la famille et ses animaux domestiques.

Les maisons n'ont généralement qu'un seul étage, ayant pour tout parquet la terre battue, avec une petite lucarne qui sert à faire entrer l'air et la lumière et à faire sortir la fumée; souvent elles sont souterraines, creusées dans les rochers, de vraies grottes troglodytiques.

Souvent, dit M. Lombroso, relativement à la Calabre, les cloisons y font défaut; on a un seul

(1) Qui comprend sept régions: la Campanie, la Calabre, l'Apulie, la Basilicate, les Abruzzes et Molise, la Sicile et la Sardaigne.

(2) Voir Cicotti-*Sulla questione Méridionale*, Milano 1904, page 2 et suiv.

lit pour toute la famille, enfants et vieillards, et
une partie de la famille dort sur la terre nue.

Dans les champs les maisons sont rares, et en
général on ne trouve que des « pagliai » (1) espèce d'abris formés de pierres sans ciment et re-
couverts de paille.

Si l'on fait un tour dans une de ces villes, l'on
est frappé par l'aspect des rues qui semblent plutôt des lieux de réunion et de travail. Presque
devant chaque porte des femmes s'occupent des
différents travaux de leur ménage, des enfants
souvent pieds nus, et demi-nus, jouent entre
eux; des bottiers, tailleurs, serruriers, etc., travaillent en plein air, plutôt que dans leur sombre
maison; et sur les places, surtout vers le soir,
se trouvent des cercles de paysans, d'ouvriers, de
journaliers de tous genres qui, en attendant d'ê-
tre engagés par quelqu'un, causent entre eux.

C'est ainsi que les affaires privées des différentes personnes viennent à la connaissance de tout
le monde, si par exemple un tel est parti pour
l'Amérique, si un autre a fait fortune; c'est là,
en plein air, qu'on lit les lettres qui arrivent d'A-
mérique, et qu'on en fait la critique; c'est là qu'on
s'occupe de ses propres intérêts et de ceux d'autrui; les bonnes et mauvaises nouvelles se pro-

(1- Voir Taruffi, De Nobili, Lori. *La questione agra-
ria a l'émigrazione in Calabria*-Firenze 1908, page 762,
et aussi Colajanni. *Statistica e demografia*. vol. II
Napoli 1909, page 46, 47.

pagent rapidement de bouche en bouche, et l'on remplace ainsi les journaux, généralement in-connus ou pas lus.

La caractéristique du Midi de l'Italie est cette *agglomération* de la population qui dans les Abbruzes, la Campanie, l'Apulie, la Sicile, la Calabre, la Basilicate et la Sardaigne atteint son maximum pour l'Italie : 82 à 93 0/0 (1).

L'agglomération est la cause d'inconvénients soit pour l'hygiène, soit pour l'exécution de la loi sur l'instruction obligatoire, soit pour la ré-partition des impôts.

Ce phénomène empêche une meilleure culture de la terre, la population n'ayant pas un contact direct avec elle; il rend les champs peu sûrs et fa-cilite de brigandage et « *l'abigeato* », c'est-à-dire le vol de bestiaux.

Au contraire, celui qui voyage en Toscane, en Piémont, en Lombardie, ne trouve pas un coin de terre non cultivé, mais partout remarque les beaux produits de la culture intensive. Les villes y sont plus nombreuses, et dans une condition très flo-rissante, favorisées par la facilité des communi-cations et par le déplacement du centre du monde civilisé de la Méditerranée à l'Atlantique.

Le Midi, dépourvu d'irrigation, avec un com-merce en déficit, une industrie peu développée.

---

(1) Colajanni *Statistica e Demografia,* vol. 2, pag. 39. Napoli 1909.

loin des nouveaux centres de civilisation, se trouve dans des mauvaises conditions économiques
et sociales et dans une civilisation rétrograde.

*La différence entre la civilisation de la ville et
celle de la campagne est très grande.*

Leurs habitants vivent et pensent diversement
et ne font aucun effort pour arriver à une entente.
Ce sont en général les citoyens des villes qui s'intéressent aux questions nationales et politiques,
tandis que les paysans ne s'occupent jamais de
telles matières, ne lisent pas les journaux, vivant
de leur travail et préoccupés presque seulement
de leurs intérêts personnels. Ce phénomène, dit
justement M. Pasquale Villari (1), a une origine sé-
culaire. Les Romains faisaient cultiver les champs
par les esclaves. Les communes du Moyen-Age,
riches et civilisées, étaient des oasis de liberté parmi des terres tout à fait retranchées de la vie politique. Les paysans n'ont pas pris part à l'indépendance italienne et une fois libres de l'oppression intérieure, ils n'hésitent pas à émigrer.

Dans ces régions, il y a *une grande foule de déclassés*, dont plusieurs sont les victimes des mauvaises conditions économiques, d'autres sont les
auteurs volontaires de leur mécontentement et de
celui d'autrui. Des classes entières flottent entre
des conditions incertaines et mobiles, dont on
peut se rendre compte si on fait la connaissance

(1) Nuova Antologia-*Sulle questione nell'Italia Meridionale*, 18 dicembre 1907, pag. 461.

avec quelques-uns des *types* de ces régions désolées.

Il y a un « *contadino urbano* » (1) c'est-à-dire
un *paysan urbain* (forme bâtarde d'agriculteur,
qui chaque soir rentre en ville, au lieu d'habiter
l'endroit de son travail, et préfère s'en aller à la
bourse du travail pour bavarder).

Le *paysan ouvrier*, attiré par un salaire plus
élevé dans les ouvrages industriels, ne retourne
pas aux champs.

Le *petit propriétaire* d'une maison ou d'un
fonds aime à vivre de ses rentes et pousse ses fils
dans des carrières qui donnent le plus grand nombre de déclassés, avocats, prêtres, militaires.

Le *petit capitaliste*, qui possède quelques milliers de francs, cherche à en tirer par l'usure un
profit suffisant pour vivre avec sa famille.

Le *grand propriétaire* vit de ses rentes dans les
grandes villes, ne s'intéressant ni à celles-ci puisqu'il y est étranger, ni à son pays natal, parce
qu'il n'y réside pas.

Les *femmes des classes inférieures* vivent en
général du travail de l'homme.

Celles des *classes moyennes* commencent à se
réveiller cherchant à obtenir quelque place dans
un bureau : mais en majorité sont aussi des para-
sites.

Les *dames* n'aiment pas à se mêler aux ques-

---

(1) Voir Arooléo: *Forme Vecchie e idee nuove* et
Taruffi: De Nobili, Lori, ouvrage cité page 780 et suiv.

tions économiques et politiques, préférant ne pas abandonner leur champ d'action « le salon ».

La personne de talent ne voyant pas chez elle le moyen de faire fortune va le chercher dans le Nord ou à l'Etranger.

Le cercle des civils c'est le lieu où toute la journée se rassemble une multitude vagabonde de gens qui ne savent quoi faire, parce qu'ils ont réussi à réaliser.une petite rente suffisante à satisfaire leurs besoins limités; et d'autres. qui attendent que la fortune vienne les aider, ou qu'un bon mariage vienne améliorer leurs conditions économiques et sociales.

Leurs discussions principales sont : la médisance, la satire, la critique injuste de tout ce qui est bon et de tout ce qui est mauvais. L'occupation principale c'est le jeu. Ce cercle est l'officine centrale des oisifs de tous genres qui fuient le travail mais qui demandent à avoir un emploi.

Si l'on se prend à considérer *les conditions hygiéniques* de l'Italie du Midi (1), faisant exception des quelques grandes villes principales qui n'ont rien à envier aux autres villes modernes, on se trouvera souvent obligé de se demander si ce sont des hommes ou des animaux qui habitent certains endroits.

Plusieurs pays sont dépourvus de service de propreté urbaine, les ordures sont jetées.dans la

(1) Voir Rossi- *Vantaggi e danni dell'emigrazione nel Mezzogiorno*-Bollettino dell'émigrazione 1908 n° 13.

rue et seulement la pluie, le vent et quelquefois les cochons sont les seuls balayeurs.

Les fontaines et les aqueducs sont rares, il y a des pays qui sont obligés de boire de l'eau de fleuve, l'eau de source coûtant très cher, quand il faut l'amener de loin, dans de petits chariots traînés par des ânes; ou dans des vases portés par les femmes, sur la tête. Les fontaines et les lavoirs publics font défaut, le linge est souvent lavé et séché dans l'unique chambre d'habitation, ou dans quelque petit cours d'eau.

Il y a beaucoup de maisons qui n'ont pas de latrines, les égouts n'existent souvent pas ou sont défectueux. L'éclairage public est un luxe quoique l'électricité commence à s'introduire partout. C'est l'éclairage à pétrole qui triomphe encore; il y a certains pays qui sont même éclairés à *l'acétylène*, mais par contre, il y en a qui n'ont que la lune pour tout éclairage. Les entrepreneurs d'éclairage public sont des adorateurs de la lune, car, lorsqu'elle apparaît, ils ne sont pas obligés d'allumer les lampes dans les rues.

Les hôpitaux sont peu nombreux. Le peuple du Midi n'aime pas beaucoup se faire soigner par le médecin, et a une aversion pour l'hôpital.

Les conditions de *l'alimentation* sont aussi très misérables.

L'importance de l'alimentation dans la marche de la vie sociale et de la civilisation même des peuples, écrit M. Niceforo, (1) est si influente, que, certains peuples sont supérieurs à d'autres par-ce qu'ils mangent mieux.

Voulez-vous savoir ce qu'un paysan sicilien mange généralement ?

Le matin — pain, oignons, poivres d'Espagne.

A midi — pain, oignons, ou salade d'oignons et tomates, ou pommes de terre.

Le soir — soupe de pâte et légumes (choux, choux-fleurs, fèves, haricots) cuits dans l'eau et avec du sel et de l'huile, (quand on l'a pour tout assaisonnement). Comme boisson — eau ou vin très léger coupé avec eau.

Quelquefois l'oignon est remplacé par un morceau de fromage, et dans les fêtes, la soupe cède la place à un plat de *macaroni* aux tomates.

Mais naturellement l'alimentation change quelque peu de pays à pays, et il y a des lieux dans le Midi (Calabre, Basilicate, etc.) où on ne mange pas de pain de blé, mais seulement du maïs, de l'orge, des fèves, des herbes cuites, ou des figues d'Inde (2).

La viande est un aliment de luxe; il y a des familles qui en mangent seulement une fois ou deux par an.

Voilà les chiffres qui représentent la consom-

---

(1) *Italiani del Nord e Italiani del Sud*. Torino 1901, page 163.

(2) Taruffi, De Nobili, Lori, ouvrage cité pag. 772 et suite.

mation moyenne de viande, en kilogrammes, par individu et par an dans le Midi de l'Italie :

Italiens de l'Italie Méridionale (1) 6,4

Italiens de la Sicile 5, 0

Italiens de la Sardaigne 12, 2

Comme on voit, la consommation est minime proportionnellement surtout à la Lombardie (21) et au Latium (26), Dans la Basilicate et dans l'Apulie la proportion est seulement de 3 kilogrammes par individu !

Le lait et les œufs sont aussi des aliments qui ne font pas partie du menu d'un ouvrier ou d'un paysan; se sont les classes plus riches qui en mangent.

En confrontant le Sud de l'Italie avec le Nord, M. Nicéforo (1) s'exprime ainsi : « Le Sud mange beaucoup moins de viande et beaucoup moins d'œufs que le Nord, à peine un peu plus de blé, beaucoup moins de céréales, une quantité presque égale de légumes frais, un peu moins de légumes secs. Les conditions de l'alimentation du Sud ne paraissent donc pas très heureuses, non seulement il mange moins que le Nord, mais sa nutrition est essentiellement végétale, tandis que celle du Nord est principalement carnivore : or on sait que, tandis que les viandes sont très bien assimilées, les aliments végétaux ne le sont pas bien.... il (le Sud) mange donc et assimile moins et cela aggrave ses conditions de nutrition insuffisan¹⁰

_____

(1) Nicefero-*Italiani del Nord italiani del Sud* p. 191.

Cette mauvaise nutrition est souvent cause de dégénérescence et représente un des premiers facteurs de la criminalité.

Celle-ci conserve encore cette brutalité et cette violence qui dans les pays plus en progrès. ont cédé la place à la fraude et à la tromperie.

Les *conditions intellectuelles* sont aussi très tristes. Les illettrés sont plus nombreux dans le Midi, que dans les autres régions de l'Italie, qui elle-même, dans la gradation de l'instruction chez les différents pays, est classée à la troisième place par M. Pétersilie (1). Dans le tableau suivant nous exposons la nomenclature des illettrés dans les différentes régions du Midi de l'Italie.

Illettrés pour cent habitants au-dessus de six ans.

Régions (2)	1872	1901	Diminu-tion
Abruzzes et Molises......	84,82	69,77	17,1%
Campanie...............	79,97	65,09	18,6%
Apulie.................	84,50	68,33	19,1%
Basilicate.............	88,00	75,39	14,3%
Calabre................	87,11	78,71	9,6%
Sicile.................	85,26	70,95	16,7%
Sardaigne..............	86,10	68,33	20,5%
Ensemble du royaume	68,77	48,49	29,4%

(1) Mo. « Analphabeten » dans l'*Handwörterbuch* de Conrad.

(2) Voir Colajanni. *Statistica e demografia*, vol. II, pag. 125. De Nobili, ouvrage cité p. 105 et suite. Niceforo ouvrage cité p. 210 et suite.

Il ne faut pas croire que les illettrés sont aussi nombreux dans les autres régions de l'Italie. Ils le sont beaucoup moins dans l'Italie Centrale et très peu dans le Nord : Ainsi le Piémont a seulement en 1901 17,69 illettrés pour 100 habitants au-dessus de 6 ans;la Ligurie 26,54 et la Lombardie 21,38.

Puisque la diffusion de l'instruction chez un peuple correspond à son état de civilisation et à son développement économique (1), on peut constater, en considérant les chiffres ci-dessus combien sont misérables les conditions du Midi.

« Un peuple illettré, dit M. de Nobili (2), est socialement et politiquement dans une condition inférieure : il ignore les premières nécessités de la vie sociale, il vit dans une espèce d'esclavage. Dans les périodes critiques, il ne voit aucun horizon nouveau, il ne sait pas lutter par des moyens légaux, ne sait pas influer, par une action éclairée et pacifique, sur les classes riches et sur les pouvoirs publics pour obtenir des conditions de travail plus humains, il ne réussit pas enfin à défendre son existence par une activité plus grande : il ne connait que la fuite. »

L'œuvre des dominations étrangères et de l'église, puissant ennemi de l'instruction populaire, les conditions climatériques et la superstition,

(1) Niceforo. Œuvre citée p. 221. Colajanni. Œuvre citée p. 128.
(2) Taruffi, de Nobili, Lori. Ouvrage cité p. 797.

ont augmenté l'action des mauvaises conditions économiques sur la grande ignorance des classes travailleuses.

Beaucoup de monde se méfie de l'école et la méprise en la considérant comme cause démoralisatrice et pouvant amener des malheurs.

L'action du gouvernement a été faible et en tout cas impuissante à vaincre tous les obstacles, et la loi sur l'instruction obligatoire est souvent restée lettre morte, soit faute de communications et de moyens de transport, soit par l'insuffisance de la surveillance des communes, dépourvues souvent du personnel et des locaux indispensables.

Il y a des écoles qui sont de vraies maisons de correction, car elles sont misérables, malsaines, exposées à toutes les intempéries, souvent installées dans de vieux couvents sans lumière et sans air, en opposition avec les règles les plus élémentaires de l'hygiène et de la pédagogie.

Nous avons jusqu'ici parlé des conditions de la vie économique, morale, intellectuelle de la population du Midi : examinons maintenant *comment elle emploie son activité au travail.*

Si on pense que l'Italie a une superficie totale de 28.500.000 hectares, dont bien 20.000.000 sont plus ou moins bien cultivés, et seulement 4 millions 634.000 hectares occupés par des rues, fleuves, lacs, terres et 3.772.000 incultes, on s'apercevra facilement que l'Italie est un pays éminem-

ment agricole. La population agricole était de
9 millions et demi en 1901, constituant 30% de la
population totale, tandis que la population industrielle est seulement de 20%·

L'industrie et le commerce, empêchés par le
manque d'instruction et d'initiative, par l'insuffisance de capitaux, par la timidité et la mobilité
de l'esprit de la population du Sud, ne sont pas
très développés dans cette partie de l'Italie, tandis que dans la Lombardie, le Piémont, la Ligurie,
la Vénetie, la Toscane, ils sont très florissants.

Dans le Midi, le climat est doux, la terre est naturellement fertile, et l'existence matérielle satis-
faite de peu, exige peu d'efforts. La vie à l'air libre, n'absorbe pas toutes les activités de l'esprit
comme dans les froids pays du Nord, et dévelop-
pe et affine le talent de l'homme méridional dont
l'esprit est naturellement agile et métaphysicien.

La principale occupation est l'agriculture, qui
est dans certaines régions la seule ressource de la
population. Elle pourrait très bien suffire à rendre la vie très commode, si elle était régulière-
ment développée et exploitée, mais malheureusement elle se trouve dans des conditions pitoyables, qui constituent la cause principale du malaise du Sud.

La question méridionale est donc une question
essentiellement agraire, puisque l'agriculture est
presque la seule ressource du pays. Les différentes classes sociales en tirent directement ou indi-

rectement, leurs moyens de subsistance, par conséquent le problème économique se confond avec le problème agraire.

La petite propriété y fait défaut, tandis que les propriétés très étendues sont encore nombreuses et accroissent le malaise agricole. En effet les grands propriétaires ne s'occupent pas de la culture de leurs terres; ils les louent à des grands fermiers qui ne s'occupent que du gain qu'ils peuvent faire en sous-louant les mêmes terres par petits lots aux vrais agriculteurs. Ceux-ci paieront ainsi un prix de location plus élevé et ne pourront pas apporter d'amélioration aux terres, étant dépourvus des moyens suffisants (1).

A ces grandes étendues de terre correspondent souvent des propriétés très fractionnées, qui ne suffisent pas aux besoins de ceux qui les possèdent (2).

Outre cette défectueuse répartition de la terre on remaque souvent l'absence de connaissances agraires, techniques, chez les agriculteurs, qui, n'ayant aucune instruction suivent toujours les méthodes traditionnelles. A cela s'ajoute encore *l'insuffisance des moyens d'irrigation*. Il y a des pays, comme l'Apulie, qui sont dépourvus presque complètement de fleuves. Pourtant les étés étant

---

(1) Voir Taruffi, etc. Ouvrage cité p. 368 et Lo Vetere. Il movimento agricolo Siciliano p. 34 ter, Palermo 1903.

(2) Voir Taruffi. Ouvrage cité, p. 315.

très longs et les pluies peu abondantes, il faudrait employer l'irrigation sur une beaucoup plus vaste échelle que dans le Nord de l'Italie, où elle est cependant très développée.

Les systèmes de culture sont comme partout au nombre de deux : la culture extensive et la culture intensive. Seulement, dans le Midi la première est plus répandue que la seconde, mais si l'une et l'autre se basent sur des principes surannés; en général, là ou la culture extensive prévaut, on cultive exclusivement des céréales, avec des instruments primitifs et l'on épuise la productivité de la terre cultivant du blé, de l'orge, du maïs, ou des fèves successivement, sans les faire alterner avec des plantes industrielles ou fouragères, et sans faire souvent usage de fumier et d'engrais. Cependant l'on fait souvent alterner les cultures (système des rotations agraires) (1) pendant les périodes qui varient d'un an à six, selon les pays.

Par exemple on a très employé en Sicile le système suivant : pendant la première année on laissait les terres en pâturage, pendant la deuxième année on y semait du blé, et pendant la troisième de l'orge. Souvent pendant la première année on renonçait à plusieurs mois de pâturage, et au commencement de février on jacherait les terres.

Dans les terres à culture intensive, qui généra-

---

(1) Voir Squillace. *La base economica della questione meridionale*. Palermo 1905, p. 57 et Taruffi, etc. Œuvre citée p. 480 et suite.

lement se trouvent à proximité des villes ou le
long de la mer, les rotations se succèdent avec
plus de régularité. A la culture des plantes légu-
mineuses et des céréales s'associe dans ces
champs celle des arbres à fruits, (jardins d'orangers,vignes), etc., et l'élevage des bestiaux. Beaucoup d'agriculteurs qui commencent à employer
les engrais chimiques sèment dans la première
année des fèves avec l'engrais chimique, et ensuite du blé pendant un ou deux ans.

Or, si cela a eu une utilité pour la plus grande
production du blé, c'est aussi la cause de malaise pour le pâturage car la quantité des terres laissées en pâturage est très petite. Ainsi par exemple, le pâturage qui dans la province de Catane
pouvait auparavant coûter 25 fr. l'hectare, à présent ne coûte pas moins de 60 fr.

Les instruments de culture laissent beaucoup à
désirer.

On fait encore le labour de la terre, avec la
charrue à clou et la houe ; la semaille à la main,
la moisson avec la faux et la faucille; le battage,
avec les chevaux et les bœufs.

Les machines commencent à 's'introduire, mais
lentement, du reste souvent on ne peut pas les
employer à cause des conditions défavorables de
la terre. Ainsi, par exemple, là où la terre est très
aride et compacte, on ne peut pas employer la
charrue perfectionnée qui ne glisse pas facilement.

Systèmes d'administration agraire.

Les différents systèmes d'administration agraire présentent aussi des défauts et sont souvent très oppressifs aussi bien pour les cultivateurs que pour la terre. Les formes des contrats agraires sont presque partout : la mise en valeur directe du sol (économia diretta), le fermage et le métayage, dans ses différentes combinaisons. La mise en valeur directe, qui pourrait donner des bons résultats, présente des désavantages produits par le manque d'une direction agraire et industrielle, technique et rationnelle et quand elle est appliquée dans la grande propriété, cause l'emploi d'une foule d'ouvriers agricoles, souvent mal payés et sans aucun intérêt pour la terre qu'ils cultivent.

Le fermage a comme caractéristique principale l'épuisement de la terre, et l'exploitation des cultivateurs, qui souvent sont obligés de restituer au propriétaire les semences et les secours avancés en denrées avec 20 ou 25 % d'intérêt.

Bien préférable est le métayage, car i. permet une meilleure répartition des risques et des bénéfices entre le propriétaire et le cultivateur, et il entretient l'intérêt de l'un et de l'autre pour la terre; il requiert du propriétaire un plus grand emploi de capitaux et une surveillance plus étendue et peut devenir une lourde charge pour le colon, qui doit payer souvent de forts intérêts pour

les secours reçus du propriétaire qui trouve encore souvent moyen de l'exploiter.

Une nouvelle forme de contrats agraires commence à s'introduire en Sicile et se rencontre aussi dans le *Nord*, dans les provinces de Milan, de
Bergame, de Bologne, etc.; c'est le *fermage collectif*.

Il a été introduit par des associations catholi-
ques, afin de supprimer l'intermédiaire des grands
fermiers entre propriétaires et cultivateurs, et d'é-
tablir entre la terre et le travail un rapport capable de donner la meilleure production possible.

Généralement les associés sont responsables envers les tiers, sans restriction; et entre eux, proportionnellement à leur participation au travail
et à la culture. Les terres sont réparties proportionnellement entre les familles des associés qui
travaillent chacun pour soi et sous leur responsabilité propre, après avoir payé un prix de location
à la caisse commune. Cela n'est pas une sous-
location, mais seulement une mesure administra-
tive, car chaque associé a une participation au
contrat général de location.

Ce fermage collectif (1) mérite, selon nous, le

(1) Il est employé déjà dans les provinces de Calta-
nisetta, Girgenti, Palermo et à Caltagirone, par les
démocrates chrétiens, dont le leader le plus ardent
est le prêtre Don Sturzo qui, avec son énergie et son
activité de fer a sû tirer de l'organisation des populations rurales des effets excellents.

plus large emploi possible, car il remédie à plusieurs inconvénients des « latifondi », éliminant la spéculation des grands fermiers, augmentant le sentiment de responsabilité et de solidarité des travailleurs et entretenant l'intérêt du paysan pour sa terre : favorisant le travail intensif et les progrès techniques par un meilleur emploi des bras et l'introduction plus facile des méthodes nouvelles de culture et des instruments perfectionnés; rendant enfin beaucoup plus facile la fonction bienfaisante du crédit.

Le Crédit.

En effet, les conditions du *Crédit* dans le midi sont pitoyables et constituent aussi une des causes secondaires du malaise. Le crédit personnel de l'individu envers l'individu, étant entravé par la méfiance qui résulte des mauvaises conditions économiques, il faut donc recourir aux Institutions de Crédit; à moins de s'adresser aux usuriers, qui constituent presque la seule source de crédit privé, et sont encore un des fléaux du Midi. Leur puissance maléfique est parfois très grande, car ne pouvant pas recourir aux sociétés de Crédit qui n'existent pas, ou requièrent des formalités longues et compliquées de garantie, ni à des particuliers dépourvus souvent de capitaux, ils restent les seuls maîtres de la destinée de beaucoup de ces malheureux.

Cependant leur champ d'action a été limité depuis quelque temps par l'introduction de l'or d'Amérique des émigrants.

Le crédit, dû le plus souvent à la Banque de Naples et à la Banque de Sicile, est d'une nature essentiellement agricole, car l'économie personnelle se fonde surtout sur l'agriculture.

Malheureusement les deux formes de crédit agricole : le crédit foncier et le crédit agraire n'ont pas bien réussi dans ce pays. Ainsi la première a été souvent cause de plus de malheurs que de bienfaits, car les propriétaires ne comprenant pas sa délicate fonction, ont employé l'argent qu'ils avaient emprunté aux banques à la satisfaction de leurs besoins personnels, ou pour leurs caprices, au lieu de les employer à l'amélioration de l'agriculture.

La deuxième, dernièrement réglée par la loi du 7 juillet 1901, surtout dans le but d'apporter le capital directement à la terre pour avantager la production, n'a pas non plus eu beaucoup de succès. Les causes sont diverses : les petites institutions de crédit rural, destinées à recevoir le crédit des grandes banques et à le répandre dans les diverses parties du territoire, font défaut; l'ignorance des paysans ne leur fait pas comprendre toute la valeur du crédit ; la complication des formalités pour l'obtenir; la limitation des emprunts, ne pouvant pas dépasser selon les cas, 1.000, 2.000 ou 3.000 fr., empêche ainsi la grande propriété d'en

profiter; la brièveté de l'échéance, (ordinairement
à un an et seulement dans les cas spéciaux, à trois
ans) oblige souvent le propriétaire à vendre hâti-
vement et dans de mauvaises conditions, en dimi-
nuant les avantages apportés par le crédit même;
l'incertitude de la production dérivant de l'influence d'éléments les plus différents, physiques et
météréologiques, et d'autres encore.

Conséquences.

De tout ce que nous venons de dire, relativement aux conditions du Midi, il résulte une répercussion dans l'organisme agraire et industriel;
des récoltes insuffisantes, aucun soin dans la mise en état des terres, qui s'éboulent facilement, de-
venant moins aptes à l'application des machines;
manque de culture technique, de direction et d'esprit industriel chez les propriétaires. C'est là la
désorganisation industrielle, commerciale, agricole; c'est le manque d'équilibre dans les rapports
qui doivent exister entre l'homme et la société,
entre le gouvernement et le peuple. Il y a une
lutte pour l'acquisition du bien-être, mais la lutte
n'a pas le même but, et les moyens ne sont pas
les mêmes. Chacun voit son malheur personnel et
cherche le remède souvent au détriment des autres.
Nous avons vu dans la première partie, que
l'émigration se produit, augmente et s'arrête sous

l'influence des conditions économiques sociales et politiques des pays d'émigration et d'immigration : et nous sommes venus à la conclusion que plus les conditions d'un pays sont favorables et plus l'émigration est faible, plus elles sont défavorables et plus l'émigration est étendue.

La réaction.

Etant données les conditions si mauvaises du Midi de l'Italie, que nous venons d'esquisser, il est clair qu'une réaction serait arrivée un jour ou l'autre.

L'action politique ayant été très faible, celle des particuliers très lente, et parfois nulle; la réaction a trouvé sa réalisation non pas dans les grèves ou les révoltes, mais dans l'émigration; surtout après la propagation des nouvelles de l'existence de pays où la vie est meilleurs que dans la mère patrie.

Bien que les conditions économiques et sociales du Sud laissent beaucoup à désirer, il n'est pas douteux que dans les vingt dernières années elles ont subi de *rapides améliorations*.

Nous n'avons exposé jusqu'à présent que les mauvais éléments de la situation du Mīdi. Il en existe cependant de bons et ce n'est pas parce qu'ils y font défaut que nous n'en avons pas parlé, mais pour faire mieux remarquer et comprendre la cause et la nature des phénomènes qui dérivent des mauvais.

Ce n'est pas pour dénigrer ces régions que nous n'en avons relevé que les défauts. Comme tout bon Italien, nous aimons trop notre patrie pour cela et nous nous empresserions de les exalter si cela pouvait y faire naître une émulation bienfaisante; mais, comme chez tous les peuples méridionaux, on n'y a que trop de tendances à se satisfaire à peu de frais, et ce ne servirait qu'à y endormir les activités par la fumée d'un faux orgueil et la vision d'un beau mirage.

En tous cas les conditions du Midi, nous le répétons, ne sont pas si mauvaises partout et on peut même remarquer que la situation y devient moins précaire.

Si aujourd'hui la nourriture des paysans se compose de poivre d'Espagne, d'oignons, de pommes de terre, de fèves et de pain, auparavant elle se composait souvent d'herbes des champs et des restes de la table des riches.

Si les écoles sont dans beaucoup de villes dans des conditions déplorables, antérieurement elles n'existaient même pas.

Si la charrue à clou et la houe sont encore des instruments employés pour le labour de la terre, on voit déjà fonctionner à côté d'elles, la charrue perfectionnée.

Si autrefois les prolétaires subissaient pacifiquement les oppressions et les vexations des riches, à présent ils ont souvent l'énergie de se révolter et d'aller chercher ailleurs des conditions plus favorables de la vie.

Tout cela indique que l'activité régénératrice n'est pas éteinte dans le Midi, et qu'il y a encore une vigoureuse énergie qui pousse ces peuples vers le progrès.

Certes dans les petites villes il y a une marche beaucoup plus lente que dans les grandes.

Quelques-unes de celles-ci n'ont rien à envier aux métropoles des pays plus civilisés; soit pour la propreté et la largeur des rues, pour les installations de lumière électrique, d'eau, d'égouts, pour les maisons très commodes, pour les hôtels très confortables; soit pour leurs moyens de communication et de transports.

En général partout on peut remarquer une tendance à bâtir, une augmentation des prix des marchandises, des terres et des loyers, un taux des salaires plus élevé, enfin une extension plus grande des besoins, qui tous, sont le signe certain d'une marche vers le progrès.

CHAPITRE III.

*Mouvement de la population — Mariages —
Naissances — Mortalité — Emigration.*

On remarque que la prospérité d'un pays croît
souvent avec le nombre des naissances. Nous voulons cependant étudier spécialement le mouvement de la population dans le Midi de l'Italie afin
de mieux constater le rapport d'action et de réaction existant entre lui et l'émigration.

Pour bien comprendre l'action que l'émigration
exerce sur un pays, il faut connaître la quantité
et la densité de la population et l'influence que les
mariages, les naissances et les décès exercent sur
le mouvement de la population.

Population

Selon les divers recensements, la population et
la densité du Midi de l'Italie ont varié comme suit:

| | | Population selon les recensements | | | | Population calculée | |
Régions (1)	Superficie en kilom.	31 déc. 1861	30 déc. 1871	31 déc. 1881	31 déc. 1901	31 déc. 1909	Densité 1901
Abruzzes et Molise . .	16.529	1.212.835	1.282.982	1.317.245	1.444.551	1.487.865	87
Campanie . .	16.292	2.265.830	2.754.592	2.896.577	3.166.448	3.258.815	194
Apulie. . . .	19.110	1.315.209	1.420.892	1.589.064	1.959.668	2.099.945	103
Basilicate. .	9.962	492.959	510.543	524.504	490.705	475.264	49
Calabre. . .	15.075	1.146.396	1.208.302	1.257.883	1.370.508	1.429.054	91
Sicile	25.740	2.392.414	2.584.099	2.927.901	3.529.799	3.574.424	137
Sardaigne . .	24.077	588.064	636.660	682.002	791.754	861.294	33
Royaume . .	286.587	24.449.822	26.801.154	28.459.628	32.475.253	34.269.764	113

(1) Ce tableau a été composé d'après les statistiques fournies par M. Colajanni. Ouvrage cité p. 25 et le Statesmanns Year Bock,

Entre 1861 et 1909, toutes les régions ont subi une augmentation de population, la Basilicate seule après une augmentation qui dura jusqu'en 1881 est entrée dans une période décroissante.

Cette augmentation de population est, selon nous, un signe de progrès économique. Plusieurs économistes en ont conclu que la densité de la population est un des principaux facteurs de l'émigration. Nous ne nions pas que la densité de la population ait parfois une action sur l'émigration, mais seulement quand un développement industriel et agricole ou une amélioration des conditions économiques en général, ne viennent pas à neutraliser ses effets.

En effet ce principe de l'influence prédominante de la densité de la population sur l'émigration se trouve en contradiction évidente avec la réalité des faits dans le Midi. L'Apulie, qui, avec une forte densité (103) devrait selon ce principe avoir une forte émigration, n'en a qu'un faible courant, tandis que la Basilicate qui, avec une faible densité (49), devrait avoir une faible émigration, en a une très grande.

Mariages

Le Midi présente une haute nuptialité, tandis que dans le reste de l'Italie elle est presque partout inférieure; ainsi dans le Piémont, elle est (en 1906) 7,3 par 1.000 habitants, dans la Lombardie 7,6 et dans Ligurie 6,9.

Nuptialité en 1906 par 1.000 habitants.

Abruzzes et Molise........................ 8,5

Campanie................................. 7,9

Apulie................................... 8,8

Basilicate............................... 8,8

Calabre.................................. 7,8

Sicile................................... 7,6

Sardaigne................................ 8,1

Royaume 7,6

Nous croyons que la cause principale de cette haute nuptialité est l'émigration.

Plusieurs économistes reconnaissent que la nuptialité est influencée par les facteurs économiques et sociaux et M. Colajanni (1) dit qu'elle a une grande importance comme signe du bien-être d'un peuple.

Or, lorsque dans une pays l'émigration a produit des effets bienfaisants, le fait de voir que beaucoup de gens ont amélioré leur position, donne en général aux autres l'espoir d'avoir eux aussi une bonne situation, et favorise ainsi l'augmentation des mariages.

En effet la Basilicate qui a subi une émigration tellement étendue que sa population absolue est considérablement diminuée, présente le coefficient le plus élevé de nuptialité (8,4) et la Sardaigne qui en général n'a pas eu une grande émigration, présente la plus basse nuptialité du Midi (7,5).

_____

(1) Ouvrage cité p. 107.

Naissances

Le phénomène de la naissance est, en rapport de l'émigration, très important.

Il permet le renouvellement de la population et remplace les vides laissés par la mort et l'émigration.

Le coefficient de natalité a été et se maintient encore très élevé dans le Midi de l'Italie.

Natalité dans le Midi de l'Italie

Régions	Moyenne 1900-1904	Années 1905	1906
Abruzzes et Molise	32,35	33,48	32,26
Campanie	31,82	32,38	32,06
Apulie	36,72	37,68	36,67
Basilicate	34,09	35,22	35,26
Calabre	33,58	35,33	32,25
Sicile	33,58	33,94	32,06
Sardaigne	32,05	31,72	32,31
Royaume	32,56		

Relativement à toute l'Italie, l'Apulie et la Basilicate ont le maximum de natalité, tandis que ce sont deux régions du Nord qui en ont le minimum, à savoir : le Piémont (28,54) et la Ligurie (27,18).

Cependant il existe une tendance à la diminution de la natalité, comme on peut le constater en comparant la moyenne de 1900-1904 avec celle des années 1905 et 1906. Mais cela n'a rien d'alarmant parce que, à cette diminution de la natalité, correspond une diminution de la mortalité. Du reste il semble maintenant démontré que le nombre des naissances est limité par la diffusion de la civilisation

Mortalité

Selon M. Cauderlier des conditions économiques favorables amènent la diminution progressive de la mortalité, tandis que les conditions défavorables l'entravent. En effet, dans les pays plus riches et civilisés on rencontre un coefficient minime de la mortalité, qui est ainsi le signe de l'état hygiénique et de la santé d'un peuple.

Dans le Midi de l'Italie le taux de la mortalité concomittamment aux misérables conditions de l'existence, est assez élevé.

(1) Mortalité par 1.000 habitants

Régions	Moyenne 1862-65	Moyenne 1902-06	Diminution %
Abruzzes et Molise	32.8	19.9	39.3
Campanie	30.3	22.0	27.2
Apulie	33.8	22.1	34.6
Basilicate	39.2	23.4	40.3
Calabre	32.8	20.2	38.4
Sicile	28.9	22.4	22.4
Sardaigne	32.8	19.9	39.3
Royaume	30.9	20.7	33.0

(1) Colajanni. Ouvrage cité p. 321.

Le coefficient de mortalité de l'Apulie est le maximum de toute l'Italie, tandis que celui de la Ligurie en est le minimum (18,1).

Malgré tout, on peut constater dans le Midi une forte diminution de mortalité, qui est sûrement la conséquence de l'amélioration des conditions économiques et hygiéniques de ce pays.

Ce qui nous frappe beaucoup c'est le haut P. % de diminution (40,3 p. %) de la mortalité dans la Basilicate, qui est le pays le plus pauvre, avec une très forte émigration. Nous croyons que la cause en doit être cherchée dans les bienfaits introduits par l'émigration.

Accroissement de la population

Quoique le coefficient de natalité soit en décroissance et le taux de mortalité soit relativement élevé, on peut tout de même constater un accroissement de la population.

L'augmentation moyenne annuelle par 1.000 habitants de 1901 à 1907, selon M. Colajanni (1) est la suivante :

Augmentation moyenne annuelle par 1.000 habitants dans le Midi de l'Italie

Abruzzes et Molise...................... 2,4
Campanie.............................. 2,1
Apulie................................ 7,5

(1) Ouvrage cité p. 721.

Basilicate............................... 7,0
Calabre................................ 5,2
Sicile................................. 2.5
Sardaigne........................... 10,6
Dans tout le royaume................ 6.3

Par conséquent il y a partout un accroissement; la Basilicate seulement présente une diminution de population, mais cela n'a rien d'anormal par suite de ses conditions économiques et sociales très misérables qui donnent lieu à une forte émigration et nous sommes sûrs que, lorsqu'elle les améliorera, il s'en suivra naturellement un arrêt dans l'émigration et consécutivement une augmentation de la population. En effet quelque chose de pareil est arrivé dans l'Italie du Nord, le Piémont, la Ligurie, la Lombardie et la Vénétie, qui jusqu'en 1900 on fourni à peu près les deux tiers de l'émigration italienne et avaient en même temps l'augmentation annuelle de population suivante :

Régions	Augmentation moyenne par an et par 1.000 habitants 1861-1900
Ligurie	10,1
Lombardie	8.0
Vénétie	9.3
Piémont	5.1

Au contraire de 1901 à 1909 leur contingent d'émigration s'étant réduit à un troisième de l'émigration totale, leur population à subi un plus fort accroissement.

Régions	Augmentation moyenne par an et par 1.000 habitants 1900-1907
Ligurie	15.3
Lombardie	8,6
Vénétie	12,7
Piémont	5.3

Emigration

L'émigration du Midi de l'Italie de 1876 à 1909.

Le Midi de l'Italie donne à présent le principal contigent des émigrés italiens, (46,6 p. 100 émigrants) (1).

Ce grand développement de l'émigration du Midi est un phénomène qui se produit seulement depuis les dernières années du XIX° siècle et continue sans cesse pendant le XX° jusqu'à nos jours.

En 1876 des 108.000 émigrants italiens 7.000 seulement étaient du Midi.

De 1876 jusqu'en 1886 c'est le Nord qui donne la contribution la plus importante d'émigrants (92.000) (2) celle du Sud étant de 27.000.

(1) Voir Relazione sui servizi dell' emigrazione per l'anno 1909-1910. Roma 1910 p. 2 et suite.

(2) Les chiffres des émigrants relativement aux trois périodes, que nous considérons, sont la moyenne annuelle de l'émigration.

Dans la période de 1887 à 1900, quoique l'émigration du Sud soit encore inférieure à celle du Nord, elle a presque triplé (86.000) tandis que celle-ci n'a pas même doublé (151.000).

Mais dans la période 1901-1909 l'émigration du Midi prend la première place (278.000), celle du Nord étant de 210.000 et le total de 597.000.

Les régions du Midi de l'Italie qui de 1876 à 1901 ont fourni le plus grand contingent à l'émigration sont : tout d'abord : la Campanie qui, sur un nombre total d'émigrants du Sud de 1.858.708 — en a fourni 596.378; en deuxième ligne la Calabre avec 310.363, et ensuite les Abruzzes et Molise avec 305.314. Les autres régions en fournirent un nombre plus restreint : la Sicile 263.167, la Basilicate 208.029, l'Apulie 65,140 et la Sardaigne 10.317.

Dans la période de 1902 à 1909 ces proportions changent : En huit années le total des émigrants est presque doublé, (2.267.486) auquel les différentes régions participent avec les quantités et dans l'ordre suivant :

Régions	Emigrants 1902-1909
Sicile	640.665
Campanie	562.311
Abruzzes et Molise	378.777
Calabre	355.070

Apulie 172.385
Basilicate 113.551
Sardaigne 43.727

Total 2267.486

Les chiffres effectifs annuels de l'émigration du Midi de 1876 à 1909 sont les suivants :

Années	Abruzes et Molisé	Campani	Apulié	Basilicate	Calabre	Sicile	Sardaigne	Royaume
1876....	375	3.165	339	1.102	902	1.228	28	108.774
1877....	574	2.891	405	1.125	1.266	767	20	99.213
1878....	1.436	4.487	503	2.441	2.143	1.065	16	96.263
1879....	2.162	9.373	558	5.766	3.777	888	23	119.831
1880....	1.935	9.698	471	5.182	2.952	884	16	119.901
1881....	2.952	10.970	379	4.920	1.551	1.143	68	135.832
1882....	4.735	14.107	790	7.786	10.522	3.215	205	161.562
1883....	9.043	15.903	1.021	7.058	9.546	4.040	148	169.101
1884....	4.975	7.830	632	5.081	4.723	2.420	119	147.017
1885....	6.210	13.125	872	10.018	10.908	2.186	208	157.193
1886....	10.515	17.578	806	11.524	9.672	4.270	265	167.829
1887....	13.409	22.129	1.348	12.128	13.171	4.653	138	215.605
1888....	13.147	22.134	2.144	9.354	15.021	7.015	82	290.736
1889....	10.103	14.479	2.707	8.316	12.331	11.308	100	218.412
1890....	12.842	21.647	2.744	9.062	11.757	10.705	104	215.954
1891....	12.250	20.272	1.944	9.304	11.225	10.130	88	293.631
1892....	9.045	22.259	1.675	7.327	10.013	11.912	66	223.667
1893....	13.367	34.514	1.899	9.005	18.998	14.626	89	246.751
1894....	9.709	19.880	2.470	7.250	13.351	9.125	107	225.323
1895....	17.760	32.097	5.503	10.440	18.378	11.307	150	293.181
1896....	20.587	41.208	5.806	10.963	18.965	15.432	2.510	307.482
1897....	12.591	32.604	3.270	8.529	15.557	19.109	2.760	299.855
1898....	15.151	32.057	3.387	8.052	15.153	25.579	58	283.715
1899....	17.522	34.414	3.653	8.906	17.713	24.604	73	308.339
1900....	22.932	49.070	4.936	10.797	23.328	28.838	694	352.782
1901....	59.021	75.587	14.707	16.588	34.437	36.718	2.182	533.245
1902....	50.192	84.493	15.175	14.096	35.918	54.466	3.382	531.509
1903....	46.349	70.518	15.788	13.402	33.990	58.820	2.436	507.976
1904....	32.159	50.863	13.848	11.856	35.482	60.662	4.512	471.191
1905....	58.929	84.316	21.350	17.009	62.290	106.208	2.801	726.331
1906....	58.032	89.769	33.762	18.098	57.081	127.603	6.672	787.977
1907....	50.490	76.143	29.712	15.088	47.229	97.020	11.050	704.675
1908....	20.174	37.134	16.260	10.126	30.552	50.453	6.575	486.674
1909....	53.443	68.075	27.490	13.975	52.516	94.833	5.630	625.637

Voyons maintenant le rapport proportionnel de *l'intensité de l'émigration à la population* de chaque région.

Dans la période de 1876 à 1900 les régions à émigration plus intense sont : 1° La Basilicate; 2° la Calabre, 3° la Campanie, 4° les Abruzzes et Molise; celles à émigration peu intense étant : 1° la Sicile, 2° l'Apulie, 3° la Sardaigne.

Dans la période de 1901 à 1909 ces proportions changent : les régions à émigration intense deviennent : 1° les Abruzzes et Molise, 2° la Calabre, 3° la Basilicate, 4° la Sicile, 5° la Campanie; celles à émigration peu intense étant: 1° l'Apulie, 2° la Sardaigne.

L'émigration du Midi de l'Italie pendant la

période 1876-1909.

Proportions par 1.000 habitants et par région

Périodes	Abruz. Molise	Campanie	Apulie	Basilicate	Calabre	Sicile	Sardaigne
1876-1880...	3.9	0.9	2.1	0.3	6.0	1.8	0.3	0.03
1881-1885...	5.4	4.2	4.2	0.5	13.4	6.3	0.9	0.2
1886-1890...	7.4	8.8	6.8	1.1	19.6	9.5	2.4	0.2
1891-1895...	8.3	8.9	9.0	1.5	17.2	10.9	3.5	0.1
1896-1900...	9.7	12.5	12.2	2.2	19.1	13.4	6.6	1.6
1901-1905...	16.8	34.4	23.2	8.2	30.4	29.1	17.2	3.8
1906........	23.5	40.0	28.1	16.6	38.4	40.5	35.6	8.0
1907.	20.9	34.6	23.7	14.5	32.1	33.3	27.3	13.8
1908........	14.3	19.7	11.5	7.8	21.4	21.3	14.0	7.7
1909........	18.3	35.9	20.9	13.1	29.2	36.7	26.5	6.5

L'émigration temporaire et permanente, et les
pays de destination.

Avant 1904 on distinguait dans l'émigration
Italienne, comme nous l'avons déja dit, l'émi
gration *temporaire*, composée des personnes qui
allaient travailler à l'étranger pendant une courte
période de temps, et *l'émigration permanente*,
composée de celles qui y allaient pour une période de temps indéfinie.

Cette distinction était vraiment peu opportune,
car il n'est pas possible qu'un émigrant qui va
dans un pays neuf, sans en connaître la langue,
les habitudes, et sans être certain d'y trouver des
conditions favorables de travail; sache avant de
partir, si son séjour à l'étranger sera prolongé
ou de courte durée.

Pour cette raison depuis 1904 la Direction Générale de la Statistique et le Commissariat de
l'Emigration adoptèrent la distinction « *d'émigration pour les pays transocéaniques* » et « *d'é-
migration pour l'Europe et le bassin de la Méditerranée* ». En général, on fait correspondre à
la première, l'émigration permanente et à la
deuxième l'émigration temporaire.

Il est bon cependant, de faire remarquer que la
désignation « émigration permanente » n'a qu'une
valeur tout à fait relative, car, si les émigrants
Italiens vont à l'étranger pour une période de
temps indéfini, ils ont toujours l'idée de retour-

ner dans leur patrie aussitôt qu'ils auront fait
une épargne suffisante. Les pays transocéaniques,
où les les émigrants se dirigent, sont principalement les Etats-Unis, l'Argentine et le Brésil,
mais il y a aussi un faible courant vers le Canada, le Mexique et quelques autres pays de l'A-
mérique.

En Europe, ils vont de préférence en Allemagne, en Suisse et en France; et en Afrique, en
Tunisie, en Algérie et en Egypte.

I · Émigration du Midi de l'Italie pour les pays transocéaniques, ou émigration permanente

Régions	Émigration 1876-78	moyenne 1896-98	annuelle 1905-07	Chiffres proportion- nels à 100.000 habitants 1905-1907	Chiffres effectifs	
					1908	1909
Abruzzes et Molise ...	626	14.27	49.349	3.409	23.262	47.122
Campanie	1.959	32.515	78.565	2.458	33.258	84.645
Apulie	52	3.253	23.885	1.181	13.041	23.520
Basilicate	1.292	8.369	16.316	3.453	9.748	13.025
Calabre	1.180	15.401	54.179	3.853	29.582	51.064
Sicile	290	19.122	103.817	2.893	45.813	90.226
Sardaigne	3	1.758	1.941	2.304	3.415	2.581
Royaume	20.812	167.412	458.307	1.370	238.370	398.916

2 'Emigration du Midi de l'Italie pour l'Europe et les autres pays du bassin de la Méditerranée, ou émigration temporaire

Régions	Emigration moyenne annuelle			Chiffres proportionnels 1905-1907 à 100.000 habitants	Chiffres effectifs 1908-1909	
	1876-78	1896-98	1905-07			
Abruzzes et Molise ...	169	1.838	6.471	447	5.912	6.321
Campanie	1.536	2.778	4.945	155	3.876	3.430
Apulie	363	901	4.390	217	3.219	4.070
Basilicate	264	812	416	88	378	351
Calabre	257	1.157	1.355	56	970	1.460
Sicile	730	918	6.660	186	4.649	4.607
Sardaigne	19	18	5.103	615	3.160	3.049
Royaume	80.606	129.605	281.355	841	248.304	226.721

L'émigration transocéanique prévaut dans l'Italie Méridionale, la Sardaigne exceptée, car celleci a une forte émigration européenne à cause de la proximité de la Corse. Au contraire dans le Nord prévaut l'émigration européenne. Cela provient non seulement du fait que le Nord se trouve en contact immédiat avec les grands centres de civilisation moderne, mais aussi du fait que la situation économique du Nord est meilleure que celle du Sud.

Sexe, âge et profession des émigrants.

Aussi bien, dans le Midi que dans le reste de l'Italie, l'émigration des femmes ne joue pas un grand rôle : ce qui vient à confirmer ce que nous avons dit, c'est-à-dire que l'émigration a surtout un caractère temporaire.

Si nous considérons la période de 1904-1906 nous constatons que la Basilicate présente la plus forte émigration de femmes (25,05 pour cent émigrants en moyenne) et la Sardaigne la plus restreinte (9,42). Quant à l'émigration des hommes elle est plus intense dans la Sardaigne (90,58) et moins étendue dans la Basilicate (74,95).

En général l'émigration des femmes est plus étendue dans le Midi que dans le Nord de l'Italie, où celle des hommes atteint le pourcentage le plus élevé du Royaume. L'émigration des en-

fants au-dessous de 15 ans est aussi minime. La
plus forte partie est formée d'hommes de 15 à
45 ans. Ce fait a soulevé de nombreuses craintes
et l'on a soutenu que cette sortie d'hommes ro-
bustes et forts est une perte d'énergie pour la nation, où restent les vieillards, les femmes et les
enfants. Nous renvoyons pour la critique de ce
principe à la première partie de cette étude, et
nous nous demandons maintenant si l'émigration
vaudrait à la nation les avantages qu'elle lui as-
sure à présent, si c'était seulement l'élément pas-
sif et épuisé de la population qui émigrait.

L'émigration par groupes de familles présente
une tendance à baisser. Elle était de **76 %** du total des émigrants de toute l'Italie à la période
1884-86, et, descendue à 40,77 % dans la période
1894-96, elle forme à présent seulement le cin-
quième de l'émigration totale.

Dans l'année 1909, on constate le plus haut
pourcentage en Basilicate (**32 %** du total des émigrants), en Sicile (**30,5**), en Campanie (**28,6**), le
plus bas dans la Sardaigne (**11,8**).

Nous donnons ci-dessous la statistique de l'émigration du Midi par sexe et par âge :

L'émigration du Midi de l'Italie par sexe et par
âge de 1904 à 1909.
Proportions pour 100 émigrants dans chaque
période de temps.

Régions	Hommes Nombre moyen annuel				Femmes Nombre moyen annuel				Mineurs de 14 ans Nombre moyen annuel			
	1904-06	1907	1908	1909	1904-06	1907	1908	1909	1904-06	1907	1908	1909
Abruzzes et Molise..	83.94	81.46	81.29	84.83	16.06	25.83	25.80	27.30	15.16	13.49	14.65	13.50
Campanie.	75.50	74.17	74.20	72.70	24.50	18.54	18.71	15.17	9.62	11.68	11.57	8.15
Apulie ...	85.80	86.25	81.53	83.60	14.20	13.75	18.47	16.40	9.51	11.02	9.75	11.07
Basilicate.	74.95	75.90	73.51	74.08	25.05	24.10	23.49	25.92	14.69	15.20	19.16	14.72
Calabre...	83.64	81.14	82.29	81.54	16.36	18.86	17.71	18.46	9.83	10.31	10.43	12.27
Sicile.....	75.77	74.37	76.10	76.37	24.23	25.63	23.90	23.63	15.13	14.54	16.12	14.99
Sardaigne.	90.58	92.93	92.23	91.67	9.42	7.07	7.77	8.33	5.70	4.93	5.31	5.60
Royaume	82.30	81.52	82.71	81.16	17.70	18.48	17.29	18.84	10.59	10.25	9.96	10.29

Quant à la profession des émigrants, celle d'agriculteur dont le pourcentage proportionnel (34.69 % dans la période 1901-1903 (1) est du reste le plus élevé dans l'ensemble du Royaume, prévaut dans le Midi.

Dans le Nord les émigrants sont des maçons; des tailleurs de pierre et des terrassiers. Si nous considérons l'émigration de 1909, nous constatons que la Basilicate donne le pourcentage le plus élevé d'agriculteurs (65,56 pour cent émigrants) et ensuite la Calabre, la Campanie et la Sicile. Les Abruzzes et Molise et la Sardaigne fournissent le pourcentage le plus élevé du Midi pour les terrassiers et les journaliers. Les émigrants de professions libérales sont très peu nombreux; le maximum est fourni par la Sardaigne (0.66 %).

---

(1) Colajanni. Ouvrage cité p. 386.

Emigration par profession et sexe pendant l'année 1909, proportions par 100 émigrants.

Régions	Agriculteurs pasteurs etc.		Maçons manœuvres		Terrassiers journaliers etc.		Ouvriers menuisiers etc.		Professions libérales, médecins etc.		Professions inconnues	
	Hommes	Femmes	Hommes	Femmes	Hommes	Femmes	Hommes	Femmes	Hommes	Femmes	Hommes	Femmes
Abruzzes et Molise..	38.85	46.02	5.54	2.51	47.32	18.58	4.92	6.94	0.19	0.34	3.18	25.61
Campanie..	51.04	40.77	7.69	0.31	22.23	9.63	10.74	15.42	0.22	0.37	8.08	33.50
Apulie......	35.46	9.75	14.63	0.72	28.35	5.16	11.68	14.63	0.17	0.14	9.71	69.60
Basilicate..	65.56	60.68	4.68		14.21	3.18	12.11	7.72	0.18	0.04	3.26	28.38
Calabre.....	57.20	46.08	7.76	0.71	22.29	17.47	7.67	5.76	0.14	0.06	4.94	29.92
Sicile.......	41.74	14.00	8.72	0.39	28.22	2.36	12.44	16.93	0.21	0.12	8.67	66.20
Sardaigne..	30.61	2.58	7.45		33.91	2.01	20.26	2.58	0.66	0.28	7.11	92.55
Emigration totale du Royaume	36.18	26.56	11.61	1.41	35.12	13.55	10.26	14.47	0.37	0.32	6.44	43.69

Le retour des émigrants.

Pour bien juger des effets économiques de l'émigration il faut voir si tous les émigrants restent pour toujours à l'étranger ou s'ils reviennent après quelque temps.

L'émigration italienne étant temporaire ou permanente seulement d'une manière relative, la plupart des émigrants reviennent dans leur pays dès qu'ils ont constitué un petit capital.

La statistique de ceux qui reviennent ainsi n'est pas très digne de foi, à cause de l'imperfection des moyens de relèvement (1), mais en général, on peut admettre qu'elle varie entre 40 et 50 % par an pour toute l'Italie.

Pour la même raison on ne peut pas bien établir quelle est la proportion des émigrants qui retournent dans l'Italie du Sud.

Le Commissariat de l'Emigration, faisant la comparaison entre le nombre des émigrants revenus dans la période 1905-1906 et celui de ceux qui sont partis en 1901-1902, relève que la proportion des rentrées est de 41,7 pour cent émigrés dans le Midi, tandis qu'elle est de 74,6 % dans le Nord.

Pour l'Italie Méridionale, les retours sont donc plus restreints et moins fréquents et cela prouve, une fois de plus, le caractère prédominant d'émi-

(1) Relazione sui servizi de l'émigrazione per l'anno 1909-1910 p. 25 et suite.

gration permanente en ce pays. La Basilicate et les Abruzzes et Molise ont relativement aux autres régions du Midi, le plus petit pourcentage de retour (28,4 %).

En tous cas quoique l'Italie du Midi occupe la dernière place dans la répartition des émigrants qui reviennent, il ne faut pas s'en alarmer, si l'on considère le fait qu'elle reçoit, après quatre ans, plus des deux cinquièmes de ceux qui en étaient sortis.

CHAPITRE IV

Causes de l'émigration.

L'émigration étant en rapport très étroit avec les conditions de la vie d'un pays, rechercher les causes de l'émigration dans le Midi de l'Italie, c'est rechercher les différents éléments générateurs de son grand malaise.

Ayant déjà eu l'occasion, en parlant de l'état des conditions économiques et sociales du Midi, d'en montrer plusieurs, nous tâcherons maintenant de les grouper selon la prédominance de l'élément économique, social, intellectuel ou politique.

Causes économiques.

Une fois donné le pourcentage très élevé des émigrants agriculteurs, qui dans quelques régions va jusqu'à 65,56 % (Basilicate), il est évident que l'émigration a son fondement dans les conditions de l'agriculture.

La première cause de l'émigration doit donc être cherchée dans l'état de misère des agriculteurs en général, journaliers, métayers, fermiers, petits propriétaires. La plus grande partie des émigrants, interrogés sur la raison de leur départ pour l'Amérique, ont répondu le plus souvent : « qu'ici on ne peut pas vivre; car dans nos habitations nous vivons comme des bêtes ». Les salaires sont très bas; il y a quelques années, le salaire d'un paysan variait de 60 centimes à un franc 25 par jour, augmentant dans les périodes de grand travail, telles qu'à l'époque de la moisson, jusqu'à 2 fr. 50 au maximum. Les capitaux font défaut; et la position des petits propriétaires est rendue très difficile par l'augmentation des prix.

Quoique les causes soient en général de même ordre, c'est-à-dire économiques, elles diffèrent selon les différentes régions.

Ici c'est la pauvreté du sol, la propriété trop étendue, là le grand morcellement de la terre, le phylloxera, la maladie des orangers, ou celle des oliviers, ailleurs c'est la malaria, le manque d'irrigation, de viabilité, de forêts, de moyens de transport, d'habitations, ou encore la grande agglomération ou la mauvaise nourriture.

L'industrie enfin n'existe pas dans le Midi où elle est très peu développée, soit par défaut de capitaux, soit par concurrence des autres pays de l'Italie et de l'étranger.

Causes sociales.

Des causes sociales, celles qui ont la plus grande influence sur l'émigration du Midi sont l'absentéisme et le paupérisme.

Quant a celui-ci nous savons déjà combien est misérable la condition des populations rurales et urbaines, qui souvent, n'ont pas même une hutte pour s'abriter.

L'absentéisme est aussi un grand fléau qui cause bien du mal et pousse beaucoup de monde à émigrer. Les grands propriétaires, ne s'occupant pas directement de leurs terres et en confiant l'exploitation aux grands fermiers, négligent de leur apporter une amélioration quelconque. D'autre part les fermiers ont surtout intérêt à gagner le plus possible et vexent de mille manières les agriculteurs, qui finissent souvent par sortir du joug en émigrant.

A côté de ces causes internes, il ne faut pas oublier une cause externe, très puissante elle aussi, *le besoin d'immigrants de l'Amérique* et l'influence de ses conditions. L'Amérique ayant un grand nombre d'entreprises à exploiter, a grand besoin de bras et par suite cherche à provoquer et à favoriser l'émigration.

La demande d'hommes a été très pressante, bien supérieure à l'offre et par conséquent les taux des salaires ont été très élevés. Il est évident que toutes les personnes du Midi, inoccupées, mal employées et mal récompensées, venant à connaître un tel état de choses ont été très alléchées.

En effet l'Amérique a absorbé presque tout le courant de l'émigration du Midi, moins les quelques individus qui émigrèrent en Europe ou en Afrique.

Causes intellectuelles.

Les conditions intellectuelles du Midi de l'Italie ont beaucoup influé sur l'émigration, mais cela a donné lieu à des discussions.

Quelqu'un a soutenu que les régions qui ont le nombre le plus élevé d'illettrés fournissent l'émigration (1) permanente, la plus abondante; un autre (2) a dit que l'instruction qui n'est pas accompagnée d'une amélioration économique, favorise l'émigration directement et indirectement.

Nous croyons que les deux idées ne se contredisent qu'apparemment et en réalité, se complètent l'une l'autre.

Un peuple qui se compose d'un grand nombre d'illettrés, se trouve dans une évidente infériorité par rapport à celui où l'instruction est plus répandue; car n'ayant pas de connaissances étendues il ne sera pas dans la possibilité de faire

_____

(1) De Nobili. Ouvrage cité p. 797.
(2) Colajanni. Ouvrage cité p. 710.

des progrès et d'améliorer ses conditions économiques, sociales et politiques. Par conséquent
dès qu'il s'aperçoit, pour une raison ou pour
une autre, qu'il pourra dans un autre pays, trouver des conditions plus avantageuses de vie, il
sera fortement attiré vers ce pays. Le manque
d'instruction pourra augmenter beaucoup et rendre aléatoire l'émigration, faute de notions préci-
ses sur les pays d'immigration ou l'incapacité de
bien apprécier les nouvelles qui en émanent.

Au contraire, un pays où l'instruction prévaut
sur l'ignorance, se trouve dans des conditions
bien meilleures que les autres parce que l'instruction avec l'augmentation des connaissances
et le développement des sciences, produit nécessairement, une amélioration dans les conditions
de la vie des habitants. Or, on peut observer que
les nations où les individus ont atteint un certain degré de bien-être n'émigrent pas beaucoup
(France, Belgique, Allemagne).

Mais puisqu'il peut arriver qu'au progrès intellectuel ne corresponde pas le progrès économique, l'instruction réveillant la conscience individuelle, provoquera l'augmentation des besoins,
qui, n'étant pas satisfaits, accentueront le malaise
et pousseront les individus à émigrer.

L'instruction en facilitant encore les progrès
techniques et en répandant la civilisation, favorise les communications et les relations avec les
autres nations, et tend à unifier de plus en plus

les mœurs des divers pays (1). Par conséquent
l'attachement à la patrie et aux habitudes devient
plus faible et les hommes s'expatrient facilement
sous l'influence des lois de l'offre et de la demande (2). Dans le Midi de l'Italie, l'ignorance et
l'instruction en même temps ont influé sur l'augmentation de l'émigration. Car l'ignorance a empêché la population d'améliorer sa situation et a
augmenté la contagion psychique de l'émigration, et l'instruction, mal réglée et dirigée, n'a
pas eu tous les heureux résultats qu'elle promet-
tait. Au contraire, elle a produit une quantité de
déclassés ou de semi-illettrés (3).

Causes politiques.

Le sentiment patriotique, formé surtout par
les idées fournies par la littérature et l'art, unifia
l'effort de tous les Italiens pour se rendre indépen-
dants et obtenir ainsi l'Unité Nationale. Par suite
on fit une législation unifiée correspondante, dans
le but d'accroître le progrès dans les régions où
les conditions économiques et sociales étaient
déprimées. Mais cette seule loi ne pouvant pas
correspondre aux besoins et aux conditions sociales si différentes du Nord et du Midi, elle pro-

(1) Voir Malthus *Essai* p. 349.
(2) Voir Say. Ouvrage cité p. 223.
(3) Voir Bolton King et Okey. *Italy to day* p. 233.

duisit des effets contraires, en exagérant même les malheurs existants.

A cela il faut ajouter la mauvaise administration. des villes, les impôts fiscaux très lourds, les charges (contributions) communales insupportables (1).

L'impôt sur les immeubles dans les villes où la population est très agglomérée, est nécessairement plus dur. Les paysans ne pouvant pas dormir dans leur champ : soit faute de maisons, soit à cause de la diffusion de la malaria, sont obligés d'habiter dans une agglomération, et leur misérable hutte se trouve frappée d'impôt.

Tout cela ne peut que pousser des milliers de personnes à chercher des conditions de vie meilleures.

Causes accidentelles

A côté des causes *considérées jusqu'à présent,* il y en a d'autres qui, quoique n'ayant pas la même importance et n'agissant pas constamment, ont souvent une grande influence sur l'émigration des habitants du Midi. Ainsi nous pouvons citer *l'influence des lettres* des émigrants à leurs parents et amis, qui, donnant des renseigne-

---

(1) Nous savons de deux petites villes en Sicile, San Michele di Ganzeria et Piazza Armerina, où les taxes communales sont presque aussi élevées que les taxes fiscales.

ments sur les conditions de travail, sur les salaires, etc., deviennent bientôt l'objet de discussions et de comparaisons. Ces nouvelles envoyées p.., des personnes connues, sont généralement acceptées avec la plus grande bonne foi supérieure à celle que la propagande des journaux (très peu lus, du reste) où les informations officielles, peuvent obtenir.

Dans «l'Enquête parlementaire sur les conditions des paysans dans les provinces méridionales et dans la Sicile (1) » on dit en parlant de la Basilicate: « L'influence des lettres, l'exemple des personnes de la même ville, agissent à présent puissamment, plus même que les conditions économiques, qui aujourd'hui sont sans doute meilleures que celles des temps qui ont précédé (2) ».

L'épargne de ceux qui ont émigré aide souvent à l'émigration d'autres personnes, car en envoyant des pays d'immigration, de l'argent ou simplement des billets de passage « prépaids » on fournit les moyens de partir à ceux qui n'en avaient pas. Si donc les conditions de travail à l'étranger restent supérieures à celles de la patrie, on peut dire que l'augmentation de l'épargne des émigrants, apporte une augmentation dans l'émigration.

---

(1) Vol. 9 1909.
(2) Voir vol. 5, p. 82 et suite.

La multiplication des grandes lignes de navigation, la diminution des prix de passage, les tremblements de terre (qui depuis quelques années affligent presque sans cesse plusieurs régions du Midi), les alluvions, l'inconstance et souvent le manque de pluies, les mauvaises récoltes sont toutes des causes qui favorisent aussi l'émigration.

CHAPITRE V

Effets de l'émigration.

L'exposition des causes de l'émigration du Midi de l'Italie suffit à nous prouver que ce phénomène n'a rien d'artificiel et de pathologique (1).

Le paysan sur la sollicitation de parents ou d'amis, qui lui envoient souvent son billet de passage, va en Amérique parce qu'il y trouve des conditions meilleures de travail pour améliorer sa fortune. Il n'est pas alléché par un faux mirage, il n'est pas guidé par un préjugé, mais par la vi-

(1) Cabrini p. 66. Bodio p. 265. *Discussion devant les deux Chambres Italiennes des modifications apportées à la loi sur l'émigration du 31 janvier 1901 dans* le Bollettino dell'Emigrazione n° XI 1910.

sion exacte de ses intérêts. L'émigration du Midi
est donc une manifestation normale de la vie économique et sociale de ce pays, elle est un **remède
qui fonctionne contre un mal et pas un mal à soigner.** Nous avons démontré dans les chapîtres II
et III de la partie générale de cette étude, comment l'émigration dans de telles conditions, est
toujours productrice d'effets bienfaisants.

Voyons maintenant, s'il en est ainsi dans le
Midi de l'Italie.

*Opinions des habitants du Midi sur les effets de
l'émigration.*

Dans le Midi, (selon les réponses que nous
avons obtenues à notre questionnaire, et les ap-
préciations des journaux et des revues), il y a
deux courants opposés d'idées au sujet des effets
de l'émigration : l'un est pessimiste, l'autre opti-
miste.

Voilà l'opinion générale : « L'émigration, dit
un grand fermier et propriétaire, a apporté au
Midi jusqu'à présent des effets bienfaisants. Autrefois le nombre des travailleurs était trop considérable, et par conséquent, l'offre des bras étant
abondante, la main-d'œuvre était si mal récom-
pensée qu'un malheureux ouvrier ou paysan ne
pouvait pas nourrir sa famille. Dès que l'Amérique a ouvert ses portes aux émigrants, les habitants du Midi poussés par la misère, ont vaincu

leur attachement au sol natal et ont commencé à
s'expatrier pour aller à la recherche du bien-être.
Dès lors la vraie misère a presque disparu. Un
grand nombre de familles qui ont envoyé quelques-uns de leurs fils en Amérique, en ont reçu
de grosses sommes d'argent, qui les ont aidé à re-
lever leur situation économique. Beaucoup de
journaliers sont devenus des travailleurs pour
leur propre compte, faisant augmenter ainsi la
valeur effective et locative de la propriété foncière. Les propriétaires y ont gagné parce que les
fermiers peuvent leur payer avec plus de régularité un prix de location plus élevé, et les ouvriers
industriels aussi parce qu'ils peuvent mieux vivre et même quelquefois se mettre à leur compte.
Il y a cependant des personnes qui en ont souf-
fert, ce sont les petits propriétaires et les petits fermiers, qui doivent payer davantage le travail des
journaliers. Mais ils remédient à cela en employant
des machines agricoles perfectionnées qu'ils se
mettent à plusieurs pour acheter.

Il y a des pays où les ouvriers sont presque
tous émigrés, et où les terres restent incultes;
mais ces pays sont en nombre négligeable et sont
en général ceux qui sont entourés de « latifondi »
et dont les habitants, n'ayant aucun attachement
à leur terre, émigrent facilement.

Cependant un péril menace sans cesse les propriétaires : qu'une famine survienne et les
paysans ne tarderont pas à émigrer sans satis-

faire leurs obligations et en laissant leurs terres incultivées.

Un grand commerçant et industriel dit: que : « l'émigration a apporté et apporte au Midi des avantages sérieux et presque aucun mal. Les crimes ont diminué, leurs auteurs étant des gens dans de mauvaises conditions économiques, qui à présent préfèrent émigrer.

L'émigrant du Midi, qui n'oublie jamais le beau soleil de l'Italie, à peine a-t-il mis de côté quelques épargnes, retourne dans son pays et consacre ses capitaux à l'acquisition de terres ou de maisons. L'émigration a causé une augmentation de salaires, qui de 80 centimes ou 1 fr. sont montés à 2 fr. par jour et même plus. Ainsi le paysan, qui autrefois ne pouvait nourrir sa famille et était obligé de recourir à l'usure ou aux vols, devient maintenant un bon père de famille ».

Un grand propriétaire et entrepreneur industriel dit que « l'émigration apporte en même temps au Midi des avantages et des désavantages. Elle est avantageuse pour le prolétaire et sa famille, qui dans l'émigration trouve des ressources économiques; pour les travailleurs en général restés dans leur patrie, qui ont obtenu des salaires deux fois plus élevés qu'auparavant; à toute la vie économique du pays par l'introduction de capitaux étrangers qui servent au développement des industries.

L'émigration est au contraire désavantageuse

aux entrepreneurs et aux fermiers, qui devant
faire des dépenses supérieures à celles qu'ils
avaient prévues, subissent souvent des déficits et
font faillite; et aux propriétaires, dont beaucoup
de terres restent incultivées à cause du manque
de bras. Mais il n'est pas à douter que les avantages l'emportent sur les désavantages car c'est
surtout la classe des travailleurs, représentant
les 4/5e de notre pays qui en bénéficie ».

Un vice-consul anglais en Sicile arrive à peu
près aux mêmes conclusions.

Un petit propriétaire et fermier interrogé dit
que « la hausse des salaires l'a obligé à abandonner la spéculation agraire, et à se limiter à la culture de ses terres. L'argent d'Amérique ajoute-t-il
est seulement un soulagement pour ceux qui y
sont ».

Un autre se préoccupe aussi beaucoup de la
hausse des salaires et de la perte des ouvriers in-
telligents qui émigrent.

Un propriétaire croit que « l'émigration est un
avantage positif pour les ouvriers qui se sont
ainsi délivrés de leur état de servage. Elle est très
désavantageuse aux propriétaires, qui ne peuvent
plus trouver d'ouvriers affectionnés, qui s'intéressent à leur travail. Tous pensent à émigrer.

« Ceux qui reviennent ne veulent plus faire les
travaux en usage dans le Midi, car ils les trouvent plus pénibles que dans les autres pays. Le

propriétaire doit payer beaucoup sans savoir s'il en recueillera quelque chose ».

Un avocat soutient que « les effets mauvais de l'émigration sont plus grands que ses bienfaits, qui sont plus apparents que réels. Le dépeuplement presque complet de quelques régions et le manque de travailleurs prouvent que la meilleure partie de la nation s'en va... Chaque travailleur qui émigre représente pour la nation une perte d'énergie et de force productrice, qui ne peut pas être compensée par les naissances... et pour cela l'émigration est une saignée, une mutilation de l'agrégat social, un vrai désastre. (! ! !)

« Les envois d'argent ne sont qu'un bénéfice très relatif en comparaison des capitaux et des hommes perdus, des privations et des souffrances, des émigrants....

« Ceux qui restent ne sont pas non plus avantagés, car à la hausse des salaires correspond la hausse des loyers et du prix des vivres... pas d'avantage moral non plus : en effet, la prostitution des femmes et des filles des émigrants augmente, et de même le nombre des délits commis par des mineurs ».

On voit bien, par la contradiction de ces jugements, qu'ils ne correspondent pas en tout à la réalité.

Ils sont souvent dictés par l'intérêt individuel, par le préjugé et souvent par l'ignorance qui fait

confondre les effets de l'émigration avec ceux de
la dépression économique persistante.

Les prolétaires voient en l'émigration une ré-
surrection et une libération de leur vieil esclavage,
tandis que les propriétaires à cause de l'augmentation des salaires croient en général que l'émigration est une ruine.

En général, ce sont ceux qui se plaignent, en
voyant partir tous ces hommes, qui autrefois, cul-
tivaient leurs champs pour un salaire dérisoire,
presque jamais supérieur à un franc par jour. Ce
sont les grands « latifondisti » qui voient souvent
abandonner leurs terres épuisées. Mais la faute
est la leur. Ils sont restés inertes et apathiques
vis-à-vis du progrès, qui se produisait ailleurs
dans les méthodes et dans les moyens de culture,
dans les formes d'association et de prévoyance
sociale. Ils sont restés immobiles et indifférents
au mouvement constant, quoique lent et graduel,
vers la lumière du progrès de cette armée de gens
sans forme et sans couleur, de ces paysans qui
moins que des hommes, étaient considérés comme quelque chose entre la bête de somme et la
machine. Aussi quand cette classe de misérables,
fatigués d'une vie sans ressources, trouvèrent
dans l'émigration un moyen d'échapper à tant de
privations, les propriétaires obligés de payer de
plus hauts salaires se sentirent ruinés et seulement s'aperçurent de l'utilité d'une réforme

dans les méthodes de culture et dans l'ordre habituel de la vie économique et sociale.

Leurs cris ne doivent pas alarmer; s'ils se ruinent c'est leur faute, et non pas celle de l'émigration.

Du reste « les écoles dit M. De Molinari, sont inévitables dans toutes les entreprises et elles ont leur utilité finale, en ce qu'elles signalent les écueils qu'il faut éviter et la route qu'il faut suivre ».

Nous renvoyons aux chapitres II et III de la partie générale où nous avons suffisamment prouvé le défaut de base des idées pessimistes sur l'émigration, qui dérivent des mêmes principes dans le Midi que dans les autres pays.

Nous voulons maintenant prouver que tout ce que nous avons dit en général est vrai aussi pour le Midi, et signaler en même temps les immenses bienfaits que l'émigration a apporté au Midi de l'Italie.

Effets démographiques.

Nous avons déjà démontré comment *l'émigration n'est pas cause d'une diminution de la population*, or nous pouvons constater qu'il en est ainsi dans le Midi.

En effet en comparant l'excédent des naissances sur les morts avec l'excédent des émigrants sur les immigrants pendant l'année 1906 on obtient les résultats suivants: (1)..

Régions	Excédent des naissances	Excédent des émigrants	Gain	Perte
Abruzzes ...	17.852	10.622	7.230	
Campanie ..	31.781	28.517	3.264	
Apulie	29.560	11.919	17.641	
Basilicate ..	5,592	8.239		2.747
Calabre	16.921	11.855	5.066	
Sicile	34.334	50.658		16.324
Sardaigne .	10.325	984	9.341	
Royaume	374.108	174.927	199.181	

Il y a une grande augmentation dans toutes les régions à l'exception de la Basilicate et de la Sicile, qui se sont trouvées dans des conditions spéciales très misérables (2). Cela a jeté une grande alarme chez quelques économistes (3), mais nous ne la partageons pas.

La sortie des personnes est déterminée non par des causes artificielles, mais par le malaise de la vie.

Or il est préférable dans de telles situations, de bien employer à l'étranger les activités qui pourront ainsi apporter à la patrie des avantages plus

(1) Colajanni. Ouvrage cité p. 397.

(2) Cissotti. Sulla. Questione méridionale p. 13.

(3) Colajanni. Ouvrage cité p. 398. De Nobili. Ouvrage cité p. 747, 891. Combe de Lestrade. Revue économique internationale, 30 août 1907, etc.

grands que ceux qu'elles pourraient lui valoir en
y restant inertes. Au lieu de crier contre l'émigration il faudrait diriger tous les efforts à l'amélioration des conditions très déprimées de ces
pays,ce qui s'accompagnerait d'un arrêt de l'émigration et d'un naturel accroissement de la population.Ainsi nous avons vu qu'en Irlande,quoique
la population pendant la période 1841-1907 ait diminué de 8.205.000 à 4.378.568, à présent que les
conditions économiques sont en voie d'amélioration, l'émigration a commencé à se faire plus restreinte.

*On se plaint que la force militaire de l'Italie ait
diminué* de 200.000 soldats, pendant une période
de 10 ans, par suite de l'émigration. Ce sont des
préoccupations inutiles, car ce n'est pas à cause
du défaut de sentiments patriotiques que les hommes émigrent, mais pour des motifs économiques.

Les peuples méridionaux, quoique ignorants,
ont un fort sentiment de l'honneur et un amour
très vigoureux pour leur patrie, et ce sont des
éléments précieux qui empêchent toute assimilation avec les habitants des pays d'immigration. Et
nous sommes certain qu'en cas de péril la plus
grande partie viendrait aider la patrie. Un empêchement à l'émigration ne ferait qu'augmenter le
nombre des insoumis. Du reste les nations modernes n'existent pas seulement pour s'occuper
de leur défense, mais de leur développement moral et matériel.

Dans le Midi *la préoccupation d'une diminution de la population agricole*, et par conséquent du nombre de bras disponibles pour la culture de la terre est peu sérieuse. Si dans les périodes de travail intense (moisson, battage, etc.), des propriétaires se plaignent du manque de travailleurs, nous avons bien raison de croire, eu égard aux conditions de l'agriculture dans le Midi, que cela arrive non parce que les paysans font réellement défaut, mais parce que les salaires qu'on leur offre sont dérisoires. Certes si les conditions de travail étaient avantageuses, tout le monde les accepteraient et elles pourraient même donner lieu à une immigration, par suite du jeu de la loi de l'offre et de la demande.

De larges étendues de terres, dit-on, sont laissées incultivées, à cause du nombre insuffisant des **paysans.**

Cela n'est pas ! Les travailleurs existent, mais ces terres ne sont pas en conditions d'être cultivées, parce que leur produit n'est pas suffisant à couvrir les travaux et les dépenses de culture. Du reste les terres abandonnées sont le plus souvent loin des habitations, dépourvues de moyens de viabilité et en général de tout aménagement nécessaire à la culture, et nous sommes sûrs qu'une fois améliorées, elles trouveront des cultivateurs.

Effets économiques.

Les avantages économiques apportés par l'émigration aux émigrants et au Midi de l'Italie sont remarquables.

· L'envoi de grosses sommes d'argent dans le Midi prouve encore une fois que son émigration a un caractère tout à fait économique.

Le professeur Lorenzoni (secrétaire de la Sous-Commission d'enquête sur les conditions des paysans dans la Sicile) calcule qu'en 1907 les envois d'argent en Sicile s'élevèrent en tout à 106 millions de fr. Le Commissariat de l'Emigration se basant sur les recherches de M. Lorenzoni pour la Sicile, parvient à la conclusion que le total des envois d'argent dans le Midi est de 365 millions par an (1) tandis que pour toute l'Italie il est de 500 millions.

Donc plus de la moitié des envois totaux d'argent en Italie, va dans le Midi, concourant ainsi à la nourriture des familles des émigrants, aux paiements des impôts, au développement de l'industrie et à l'amélioration de l'agriculture.

Les épargnes sont augmentées. Il y a des petits pays de quelques milliers d'habitants où les caisses d'épargne ont des dépôts qui surpassent le million M. Nitti (2) dit que la propriété de la rente publique dans le Sud s'élevait en 1902 à plus

---

(1) Relazione. Citée p. 394-396.
(2) La Ricchezza d'Italia 1904.

de 70.000.000 tandis qu'en 1876 elle était seulement de 54.000.000.

Si cette augmentation de capitaux n'a pas donné lieu à des avantages supérieurs à ceux qui se sont déjà produits, c'est seulement parce que trop souvent on les a laissés inactifs dans les banques et les caisses d'épargne, beaucoup de régions n'offrant pas des conditions assez sûres de placement; la Basilicate par exemple, où les émigrants achètent souvent pour y bâtir leur maison, des terres près de leur petite ville, à des prix exorbitants à cause de la supériorité de la demande sur l'offre (1). Plusieurs sont contents de cette amélioration précaire de leur fortune, d'autres retournent en Amérique pour y faire de nouvelles épargnes (2).

La cause de ces achats désastreux résultent du désir habituel de vivre en ville, et encore plus de l'impossibilité pratique de s'établir à l'écart, faute de moyens de communication et de viabilité, ou de la malaria.

En tous cas ces achats de terres favorisent la division de la propriété (3) et une bienfaisante substitution des propriétaires des terres. En effet l'augmentation des salaires rend toujours plus difficile la condition des petits propriétaires non cultivateurs, qui sont souvent obligés de vendre

(1) Il y a des pays où le prix des terres a presque triplé.

(2) Relazione citée p. 47.

(3) Colajanni, ouvrage cité p. 98.

leurs terres et de se consacrer à une autre profession, cédant ainsi leur place à des propriétaires
cultivateurs, qui sont dans des conditions meilleures pour tirer de la terre de plus grands profits.

Les partants, mauvais consommateurs quand
ils étaient dans le Midi de l'Italie, deviennent au
contraire par suite de la prospérité de leurs affaires dans le pays d'immigration, des consommateurs très importants et ouvrent des *débouchés
nouveaux au commerce et à l'industrie* de leur
pays d'origine (1).

L'émigrant du Midi perd difficilement ses goûts
et ses habitudes, et par conséquent même dans
les pays d'outre-mer il sent le besoin des produits
nationaux.

Ainsi une augmentation des échanges est dé-
montrée par la statistique des lettres, cartes pos-
tales, mandats-postes, etc.

Régions	Nombre de pièces de correspondance par un habitant	
	1891-1892	1901-1902
Abruzzes et Molise	5,85	6,83
Campanie	13,20	23.21
Apulie	6,25	8,09
Basilicate	4	6,15
Calabre	5,22	7,16
Sicile	7,55	10,89
Sardaigne	6,71	10.22

(1) Voir Chandèze. L émigration (L'Intervention des
pouvoirs publics au xixᵉ siècle). Paris 1898.

Le commerce italien en profite beaucoup. Les exportations d'Italie aux Etats-Unis de 100.147.000 francs en 1892 s'élevèrent dans l'année 1908-1909 à 246.439.000 francs (1).

Les exportations en Argentine de 20.535.000 fr. en 1892 s'élevèrent à 134.340.000 francs en 1909. Donc dans la courte période de 17 ans les exportations italiennes pour les Etats-Unis ont plus que doublé et pour l'Argentine sont devenues plus de cinq fois plus importantes.

Puisque, en général, on exporte des marchandises de consommation populaire, pâtes alimentaires, fromages, légumes, vins, tabacs, coraux, étoffes; il est évident que la cause essentielle de cette augmentation est l'émigration. Et puisque les émigrants du Midi prévalent dans ces pays sur ceux du Nord de l'Italie, il est évident qu'ils consomment des marchandises auxquelles ils étaient habitués dans leur pays d'origine, et que le Midi est la partie de l'Italie qui bénéficie le plus de ces avantages commerciaux (2).

L'émigration a aussi exercé une *influence très bienfaisante sur la marine*, en la rendant plus nombreuse, plus rapide et de plus grand tonnage (3).

_____

(1) Voir les échanges commerciaux de l'Italie avec l'Etranger de 1862 à 1910 dans la « Rivista Commerciale d'Oriente-Venezia-Aprilé 1911.

(2) Bolton King. Italy to day, p. 318.

(3) Voir I progressi dell'Italia in un cinquantennio. Rivista Commerciale d'Oriente, Aprilé 1911.

Aussi malgré la concurrence des marines étrangères dans le transport des émigrants, elle a réussi depuis 1907 à les dépasser.

Pourcentage des émigrants transportés en

Amérique par la marine italienne et les marines étrangères.

Années	Marine italienne	Marine étrangère
1905	46,3	53,7
1906	45.6	54.4
1907	52.1	47,7
1908	72.5	27.5
1909	63.5	36.5

Entre les effets économiques de nature indirecte, de l'émigration, nous pouvons citer : l'intérêt plus grand que prennent les propriétaires à l'amélioration et à la production de leurs terres, et la *hausse des salaires*.

Mais nous faisons remarquer que surtout dans ce dernier cas, il s'agit seulement d'une influence indirecte de l'émigration, et précisément comme conséquence de l'amélioration qu'elle apporte aux conditions économiques, sociales et morales du pays. Les salaires des paysans ont doublé en dix ans, et même ceux des ouvriers ont triplé, mais cela surtout parce que les besoins ont augmenté, parce que les prix des produits ont monté. Ceux qui craignent une hausse excessive des salaires causée par l'émigration et empêchant la production, sont dans l'erreur. Il est évident que si 2 fr. 50 par jour étaient un salaire bien suffisant à tous les paysans du Midi pour nourrir leurs familles, ils ne partiraient pas pour l'Amérique; de plus si l'offre des bras avait diminué à cause de l'émigration, la demande étant de beaucoup supérieure, les paysans pourraient s'imposer aux propriétaires et prétendre à des salaires supérieurs à ceux qu'ils ont à présent, et qui à cause de l'augmentation générale des prix ne suffisent pas à faire vivre le paysan et sa famille (1).

Effets moraux et politiques.

Quant à la morale des émigrants et de ceux qui restent dans le Midi, l'émigration produit sûrement des effets bienfaisants. L'usure diminue, les classes pauvres sont traitées avec plus d'humanité, les vexations ne sont plus tolérées; et les émigrants s'affinent au contact des peuples plus civilisés.

Cependant on se plaint de ce que l'émigration augmente la corruption des émigrants, de la prostitution de leurs femmes qui restent dans leur pays natal, des adultères et des naissances illégitimes. Cela est partiellement vrai, mais la proportion de ces cas n'est pas alarmante. L'émigrant

(1) Voir De Nobili. Ouvrage cité p. 787-792 et De Luca. Ouvrage cité p. 99-105.

du Midi est sobre et économe, très attaché à sa
famille et à sa patrie. Il ne se laisse pas facilement corrompre par les vices des grandes métropoles; il pense surtout à travailler, à gagner plus
et à dépenser moins pour retourner dans sa patrie avec des capitaux. La prostitution des femmes, et l'adultère pourraient se produire en grand
nombre dans le cas où les familles restées dans
le pays natal, ne se trouveraient pas dans de bonnes conditions économiques, ou si le mari émigré
restait pour un temps indéfini à l'étranger. Or
cela, comme nous l'avons déjà démontré, n'a pas
lieu; car les émigrants du Midi envoient de grosses sommes d'argent presque tous les mois à leurs
familles, et l'émigration a un caractère de plus
en plus temporaire. De tels cas, du reste, ne sont
pas très fréquents, et sont presque négligeables
relativement aux grands déplacements causés
par l'émigration et eu égard aux autres bienfaits
même seulement moraux qu'elle produit. Il n'y
a personne qui n'admette l'influence de l'émigration sur la *diminution des crimes* dans le Midi.
Elle a obtenu contre le brigandage, et l'homicide
des effets que la police n'aurait jamais pu provoquer. En Calabre, en Basilicate, en Sicile, dans
les Abruzzes, le nombre des délits violents a diminué, soit à cause des conditions économiques améliorées, soit par la diminution des désœuvrés, soit
par le contact des gens plus civilisés des autres
nations.

Politiquement aussi les avantages de l'émigration sont très importants. L'émigrant, en contact avec les classes ouvrières qui prennent en Amérique et dans les grandes nations modernes, une grande part à la vie publique, retournant dans la mère patrie, montre moins d'indifférence pour le mouvement politique. et administratif, et donne une plus grande valeur à la liste électorale (1).

Effets physiologiques, hygiéniques et intellectuels

On a dit que l'émigration est la cause de dégénérescence physique des Italiens (2) qui revenant dans leur patrie y répandent la tuberculose, la neurasthénie, la syphilis, etc. Or nous croyons que ce sont des préoccupations exagérées. La mortalité dans le Midi, nous l'avons dit, est en diminution; de plus l'émigration avec ses bienfaits économiques a apporté de grandes améliorations à l'hygiène et par conséquent des empêchements à la propagation des maladies. Les « américani (ainsi sont appelés dans le Midi ceux qui reviennent d'Amérique) ayant été en contact avec des populations plus raffinées, emportent dans leur pays natal des principes hygiéniques, qui leur manquaient.

---

(1) Relazione citée p. 51.
(2) Raseri-Influenza dell'émigrazione per l'estero nello stato demograficoe sanitario della popolazione del Regno. Propaganda Sanitaria N° 11 1907.

« Beaucoup d'émigrants revenus dans leur pays
l'origine (écrivent plusieurs Maires), en donnant
des informations au Commissariat de l'Emigration) bâtissent sur les terres achetées, une mai-
sonnette destinée à l'habitation et bien différente
de la hutte malsaine où des hommes, des femmes et des animaux vivaient dans un mélange im-
moral et antihygiénique; dans les nouvelles cons-
tructions, propres et souriantes, se manifeste
presque toujours une conscience plus claire des
besoins hygiéniques et moraux de la vie civile. »

En outre, l'émigrant, parti grossier et ignorant,
avec des idées très étroites par suite de l'influence d'éléments plus civilisés et plus instruits,
revenant dans sa patrie, est plus vif, moins rus-
tique, plus soigné, il a appris parfois à lire et à
écrire et en général à parler un peu la langue
du pays où il était. Il a appris la valeur et la nécessité de l'instruction, ayant été souvent exploité
à cause de son ignorance et il pousse ses enfants
à fréquenter l'école.

En conclusion l'émigration est aussi pour le
Midi de l'Italie la cause de grands bienfaits. Elle
a augmenté le sentiment de liberté individuelle.
en soustrayant les prolétaires aux vexations, elle
a amélioré la façon de vivre de ses peuples, elle
a fait affluer de gros capitaux en Italie; elle y a
introduit de précieux éléments de civilisation en
renforçant les sentiments de perfectionnement,
de liberté, d'épargne, etc. Les autres remèdes n'a-

vaient encore rien pu faire pour résoudre la vieille question du Midi, l'émigration, au contraire,
en secouant tout le monde, lui a fait faire un
grand pas.

Ce grand mouvement de déplacement de gens a
attiré l'attention du gouvernement italien sur le
Midi, autrefois assez négligé, et l'a obligé à se bien
conduire et à venir en aide a ces régions désolées.

En même temps les énergies assoupies de ces
régions ont été stimulées par la sortie de forces
surabondantes, les personnes qui autrefois ne
sentaient pas le besoin de travailler sont obligées
maintenant d'avoir une occupation, ainsi, l'on a
d'un côté une forte incitation au travail, et de l'autre côté une augmentation des forces vives. « L'é-
migration n'est donc pas pour nous une saignée,
mais un remède corroborant, non une crise dangereuse, mais une fièvre d'accroissement comme
celles qui viennent dans la jeunesse, et desquel-
les le corps sort plus fort et plus fait.

« C'est le besoin fatal du travail fatigant qui
pousse l'émigration des Italiens et dans cet effort,
dans cette résistance des muscles à la fatigue, repose une grande partie de la richesse future de
notre pays » (1).

_____

(1) Mosso. L'émigrante. Nuova Antologia, 16 juillet
1905.

Vaut-il mieux pour le Midi que son émigration
cesse ?

L'émigration étant le produit de facteurs démographiques, économiques, sociaux et politiques de ce pays, nous croyons qu'elle est nécessaire et qu'elle ne doit pas cesser. Naturellement
il serait désirable que toutes ces forces, qui ai-
dent à la formation de la puissance des autres nations soient employées dans la mère patrie, mais
jusqu'à ce que celle-ci offre les conditions nécessaires à cet emploi, il est toujours préférable de
les voir utilisées par l'émigration que rester inac-
tives.

CHAPITRE VI

La protection de l'émigration

Quoique l'émigration du Midi de l'Italie soit un phénomène tout à fait normal et avantageux, on n'a pas su en utiliser tous les bienfaits et elle a été souvent cause du malheur et de la misère de beaucoup d'émigrants. Et cela à cause de l'ignorance des émigrants méridionaux et de l'exploitation que leur font subir toute une foule d'agents d'émigration dans leur pays natal, et de « padroni » et « banchisti » dans les lieux d'immigration.

L'ignorance a empêché souvent les émigrants d'agir avec discernement, de bien choisir les lieux d'immigration, de se comporter plus civilement dans les pays d'outre-mer, de savoir bien employer leurs épargnes et a donné lieu à des sentiments de répugnance chez les Américains, qui les ont souvent considérés comme « undésirables » (1).

C'est en profitant de leur ignorance et de leur bonne foi que les agents, les padroni et les banquiers les exploitent. Les premiers connaissant les lieux d'immigration, et étant en relation avec les compagnies de navigation, les ont poussé à émigrer, leur faisant faire des rêves dorés, se chargeant de leur procurer le billet de passage, et de faire les démarches nécessaires auprès des autorités compétentes; les deuxièmes en leur faisant de fausses promesses de travail; et, les derniers en les trompant dans l'administration de leurs dépôts et dans les envois d'argent à leurs familles

La protection directe. La protection de l'Etat.

Or si l'Etat n'a pas le droit d'entraver ou de stimuler l'émigration, il doit la protéger, afin d'empêcher que ses forces hétérogènes ne viennent à

---

(1) Les raisons de cette répugnance américaine sont en général les suivantes : Les émigrants du Midi sont pauvres, illettrés, « unskilled » avec un bas « Standard of life »; ils sont trop prolifiques, font concurrence au travail des indigènes ; ils soustraient aux Etats-Unis de grands capitaux, car ils sont des oiseaux de passage et ne s'assimilent pas.

Voir les argumentations très intéressantes apportées par. M. Colajanni contre ces plaintes. **Ouvrage** cité p. 473 et 491.

en amoindrir les bienfaits; afin de cultiver chez les émigrants le sentiment national et de mieux mettre en valeur les avantages sociaux, économiques et politiques que le pays tire de cette grande force d'expansion et de libre conquête.

Avant 1889, il n'y avait pas en Italie de lois sur l'émigration si ce n'est celle du 20 mars 1865 (art. 64), dont quelques dispositions statuaient sur les obligations imposées à ceux qui voulaient établir des agences publiques; dispositions appliquées spécialement aux agences d'émigration, selon l'avis du Conseil d'Etat.

La première loi sur l'émigration date du 30 décembre 1888, et fut confirmée par le Décret Royal du 10 janvier 1889.

Cette loi fut bientôt critiquée et fit sentir le besoin d'une plus large protection des émigrants, et de réformes dans les concessions des Agences. La loi du 31 janvier 1901, œuvre de notre maître Luzzatti et de M. Pantano, y pourvoit en instituant le Commissariat de l'Emigration, rattaché au Ministère des Affaires Etrangères, et dans lequel on concentra tout ce qui se rapportait aux services de l'émigration.

Dans les ports d'embarcation on créa des Inspecteurs d'émigration pour la surveillance, la tutelle et la visite des bagages des émigrants et des immigrants, pour l'inspection des asiles d'émigrants, pour recevoir les réclamations, visiter les vapeurs, etc.

Cette loi donnait aux communes la faculté de constituer des Comités pour donner les renseignements nécessaires à ceux qui désiraient émigrer, et les mettre à l'abri des exploitations.

Elle instituait aussi des Commissaires du gouvernement à bord de chaque navire transportant des émigrants, pour y surveiller l'hygiène et la manière dont sont traités les émigrants, et même leur donner des conseils amicaux.

Dans les pays d'immigration elle établit aussi d'accord avec les gouvernements, des offices de protection et d'information. Elle créait des Inspecteurs ambulants pour informer le Commissariat des conditions de l'émigration italienne et en même temps supprimait tous les intermédiaires malhonnêtes entre l'émigrant et l'armateur, établissant pour cela des sous-armateurs spécialement autorisés; et défendait toute provocation à l'émigration. Enfin elle fixa la garantie que les armateurs autorisés devaient fournir, et leur responsabilité.

Les effets de cette excellente loi, presque universellement appréciée, furent merveilleux, se manifestant principalement par une remarquable amélioration dans les conditions des transports maritimes et par une protection mieux comprise dans les pays d'immigration où furent aussi créés et subventionnés des patronages, tandis que l'on instituait des fonctionnaires spéciaux pour la tu-

!elle des emigrants et des offices pour l'assistance
légale des émigrants.

Mais étant donné le grand nombre des émigrants, et l'impossibilité de satisfaire à toutes les
nécessités de l'émigration, des abus sont restés
impunis, et beaucoup d'intérêts ne sont pas sauvegardés. L'exploitation des émigrants est toujours très active et trouve de nouvelles formes
pour surprendre leur bonne foi; et la surveillance
à l'intérieur et dans les ports d'embarcation est
trop restreinte, le manque presque complet de Comités communaux s'y ajoutant encore.

A l'étranger aussi, les Patronages et les autres
institutions n'ont pas pu satisfaire à leur tâche
très compliquée, surtout à cause de la difficulté
de trouver partout des éléments aptes au bon
fonctionnement de ces institutions. Le nombre
des Inspecteurs et des Attachés au service de l'é-
migration est resté très étroit et par conséquent
disproportionné aux besoins des émigrants.

Le petit nombre des Consulats, dont la charge
est déjà très complexe, rend difficile l'assistance
de nos travailleurs qui en ont un besoin constant
à cause de leur ignorance.

La loi du 17 juillet 1910, s'attache à la satisfaction de ces besoins et tend à mettre l'administration de l'émigration en mesure de mieux remplir
son office auprès des émigrants et des immigrants: à mieux organiser l'administration du
Budget de l'émigration, à améliorer le service du

recrutement, et à faciliter la réacquisition de leurs
droits de citoyens aux émigrants qui auraient dû
se faire naturaliser à l'étranger à cause des nécessités indispensables de la vie. Cependant il reste
encore beaucoup à faire. Quoique le gouvernement mérite des louanges pour les progrès faits
dans la protection matérielle des émigrants on
doit constater qu'il a fait très peu pour leur protection intellectuelle. La protection matérielle des
émigrants n'est que le remède de leurs maux
symptomatiques, elle fait fonction de palliatif,
mais n'en combat pas directement la racine qui
réside dans l'ignorance des émigrants, spécialement des méridionaux. C'est elle qui est la cause
de tous les inconvénients qui empêchent les méridionaux de tirer de plus grands bienfaits de l'é-
migration, qui les fait souvent mépriser des américains et les force à se faire naturaliser (1).

L'effort de l'Etat devrait être double dans cette
question : répandre l'instruction dans l'Italie du
Sud, conserver et défendre la culture et la langue italienne chez les émigrants à l'étranger.

Mais cette instruction doit avoir des bases bien
solides, elle ne doit pas seulement diminuer les illettrés, mais créer un idéal, stimuler des senti-

(1) Voir Locatelli. L'Italia che non c'è dans le « Se-
colo » de Milan du 6 février 1911, aussi Bevione. Gli
Italiani Nella Republica Argentina dans le « Giornale
d'Italia » de Rome, 7 février 1911.

ments, vaincre l'ignorance technique. Elle ne doit pas seulement faire naître des besoins, mais doit aussi fournir les moyens de les satisfaire et faciliter le passage de l'école à la vie.

L'Etat doit donc exercer toute son activité sur ce point, il doit faire sentir l'affection et les services de la patrie aux émigrants, afin de les tenir ainsi, de loin, liés et attachés à elle.

La protection privée.

Etant données la grande complexité du phénomène de l'émigration et la grande diffusion dans le monde des émigrants italiens, l'Etat ne peut tout faire par lui-même; les particuliers aussi doivent protéger les émigrants.

A cet effet, plusieurs sociétés privées se sont constituées en Italie et dans les pays d'immigration et ont prêté une aide très efficace à l'œuvre d'assistance des émigrants italiens.

En Italie le plus grand nombre de ces associations se trouvent dans le Nord, où la « Società Umanitaria » de Milan, qui s'est aussi occupée de l'émigration des provinces méridionales a pris une grande extension. Cependant dans le Midi il y en a aussi quelques-unes, comme par exemple le « Comité Communal pour l'émigration », de Naples, et la « Société de Patronage pour les émigrants », de Palerme, dont l'œuvre a été d'une grande utilité.

Plusieurs associations existent en *Amérique*.

A New-York il y a : « La Società di protezione »
qui a un bureau de renseignements, un service
de guides et des agents pour s'occuper du débar-
quement des immigrants; « l'Istituto di benefi-
cenza » qui se charge du logement des immigrants
pendant les premiers jours, donne des secours de
médecine, et d'argent, etc.; « la Società di S. Raffaele » qui donne assistance aux immigrants sans
argent, ou qui attendent leurs parents, recùeille
les orphelines, etc.; « l'Investigation Bureau » qui
accorde l'assistance légale aux immigrants et pré-
vient les fraudes qu'on leur fait;et le « Labour Bureau » qui cherche gratuitement l'occupation de
la main-d'œuvre italienne.

A Boston il y a la « Società di S Raffaele »; à S.
Francisco de Californie, un Comité de secours et
de patronage pour les immigrants italiens; à Pitts-
burg, une caisse de prévoyance pour secourir les
immigrants en cas d'accidents du travail, ou de
mort.

Dans l'Amérique du Sud on remarque : l'Uffi-
cio di protezione de Rio Janeiro, qui est peu actif; à St. Paul il y a une « Società di patronato per
gli émigranti » et « l'Hospedaria » où logent pen-
dans les premiers jours les immigrants, et où se
trouve un bureau de renseignements et de placement; l'hôpital italien « Umberto 1 »; enfin à Buenos-Ayres la « Società di patronato e di rimpa-
trio » qui est très inactive.

Mais en général, l'œuvre de ces Institutions, qui sont toutes subventionnées par le Budget de l'émigration, est très limitée faute de moyens ou très faible, et aurait besoin d'une plus grande activité et d'un plus large développement.

La protection indirecte.

Mais l'œuvre de protection ne s'arrête pas ici. Il y a encore une protection indirecte de l'émigration qui est celle que l'Etat ou les particuliers exercent non pas sur des manifestations immédiates, mais sur les conditions générales, économiques et sociales du Midi.

Le but principal de cette nation est l'amélioration de la mauvaise situation du Midi, car aux progrès économiques sont intimement liés les progrès intellectuels et moraux et en prenant conscience de leur dignité de citoyens d'un pays libre et civilisé les émigrants méridionaux se trouveront dans de meilleures conditions pour tirer tout le parti possible de l'émigration et échapper aux pièges des exploiteurs. Ainsi les lois spéciales pour le Midi, la loi de 1904 pour la Basilicate, celle de 1906 pour les provinces méridionales, continentales et pour les îles, et d'autres encore faites à l'occasion des tremblements de terre, s'occupent de l'assainissement, de la construction des routes, de la diminution des impôts; règlent les contrats agricoles et prennent des dispositions pour favoriser la propriété foncière; instituent des chaires ambulantes d'agriculture et des Institutions de crédit agraire; et donnent des subventions à l'instruction élémentaire.

Mais la plus grande partie de ces remèdes sont restés lettre morte, soit parce qu'ils ne sont pas souvent bien adaptés aux conditions réelles du pays, soit parce qu'on a employé pour leur mise en action des fonctionnaires, les Préfets par exemple, qui sont déjà surchargés par leurs autres occupations. Il faudrait peut-être mieux nommer des Commissaires spéciaux qui puissent exercer une action éclairée et énergique.

A cette action du gouvernement s'ajoute encore l'initiative privée, dont l'exemple très important est « l'Associazione Nazionale per gli interessi morali ed economici del Mezzogiono » sous la présidence honoraire de M. Pasquale Villari. Ces buts principaux sont de coopérer à l'instruction de nouvelles générations et de recueillir et bien employer la force économique, créée par l'émigration, en constituant une Société pour l'achat de terres, et leur répartition par petits lots à ceux qui reviennent de l'étranger. —

La « Società Dante Alighieri » dont le principal but est la propagation de la langue et de la culture italienne a aussi produit de grands bienfaits (1).

_____

(1) Voir Colajanni : La Dante e gli emigrati anafalbeti.

Mais toutes ces institutions sont inférieures aux besoins; il faudrait que ces initiatives se multiplient dans tout le Midi de l'Italie, et que l'œuvre de l'Etat et des particuliers soit aussi aidée par les émigrants eux-mêmes. Quand ceux-ci seront bien organisés (1), alors seulement ils pourront bénéficier de l'assistance de l'Etat et des particuliers et devenir une force vive et réelle qui pourra peser sur la politique des pays, natal et d'immigration, qu'ils pourront aider, faisant ainsi augmenter leur importance.

Il faut donc que les forces sociales soient bien organisées, qu'on lutte avec uniformité de moyens et de but et que l'intérêt général soit supérieur à l'intérêt individuel.

(1) Voir Quaglino. Discussion sur le projet de loi cité p. 97-104.

CHAPITRE VII

L'accord international

L'émigration est un phénomène d'une grande importance internationale, car elle intéresse non seulement l'Etat où elle se produit, mais aussi l'Etat où elle se dirige. Il est vrai que les « nations ont le devoir moral de s'aider et de se secourir mutuellement dans la mesure de leurs forces (1). mais cela n'empêche pas que dans un phénomène si complexe, comme l'émigration, il ne se produise de nombreuses questions, (situation légale des émigrants, droits et devoirs des autorités des différents pays à leur égard, etc.) dont une solu-

(1) Bonfils. Droit Inter. Publ. p. 17.

tion équitable n'est pas possible sans un accord international.

Dès 1856, M. Duval sentait la nécessité de ces accords, mais jusqu'à présent, cela n'a été mis en pratique qu'en très peu de cas (1). Ce fut l'Institut de Droit International de Gand, qui dans le Congrès tenu à Copenhague en 1897 s'occupa du problème et rédigea un projet de réglementation internationale de l'émigration, dont le rapporteur fut le prof. Olivi aidé par le prof. Heimburger. Ce projet, en proclamant la liberté d'émigrer et d'immigrer, détermine les personnes auxquelles l'émigration doit être défendue; règle la surveillance des autorités dans le mouvement migrateur et fixe les conditions rigoureuses à satisfaire pour pouvoir exercer les opérations de l'émigration, les conditions de validité du contrat de transport et toutes les formalités à cet égard; les devoirs et les obligations des armateurs envers les émigrants; les suites à donner à leurs réclamations par des commissions d'arbitres instituées à cet effet. Les Etats seraient obligés de suivre les principes de ce projet, tout en étant libres, du reste, de fixer

---

(1) L'Italie a déjà eu quelques traités, mais seulement avec des pays où se dirige une faible partie de son émigration ; ainsi par exemple : le traité de 1889 avec la République de Saint-Domingue ; du 16 octobre 1890 avec la Bolivie ; de 1890 avec le Mexique et de 1893 avec le Paraguay.

dans leurs législations nationales les règles qu'ils croiraient les plus favorables de l'émigration (1).

Quoique ce projet ait réussi à attirer l'attention des Etats, il a le tort de n'avoir pas suffisamment considéré la protection des émigrants, dont il ne s'occupe qu'à l'art. 34 où est établie la seule obligation des Etats de destination de protéger les émigrants.

Cependant ce problème de la tutelle des émigrants dans les pays de destination est de la plus haute importance et mériterait d'être résolu le plus tôt possible.

Il faudrait que les pays de destination garantissent matériellement et moralement l'intégrité physique et patrimoniale des immigrants qu'ils protègent, l'exécution des contrats conclus entre nos immigrants et les indigènes, qu'ils punissent quiconque trompe les immigrants, qu'ils accordent à ces derniers les mêmes conditions de travail qu'aux nationaux, la même assistance en cas d'accidents du travail (2), et tous les moyens nécessaires pour faire valoir leurs droits.

---

(1) Voir Dupuis. L'Institut de Droit International Session de Copenhague (août 1897). (Revue Générale de Droit International Public. T. VI p. 762.

( ) Le 15 avril 1904, une convention a été signée entre la France et l'Italie pour assurer dans chaque pays, aux travailleurs appartenant à l'autre pays, des garanties de réciprocité analogues à celles que les

Nous croyons que la réglementation de cette matière dans une Conférence internationale serait
d'un grand avantage pour les immigrants et pour
les pays.

———

traités de commerce ont prévues pour les produits du
travail

Un autre traité a été passé entre les deux pays le
9 juin 1906 concernant les accidents du travail.

TABLE DES MATIÈRES

"Suffering is not a punishment for sin, nor is it God's response to human evil.

It can be understood only and exclusively in the light of God's love, which is the ultimate meaning of everything that exists in this world."

John Paul II

Dissociative Identity Disorder (DID):
Formerly known as multiple personality disorder, DID is characterised by the presence of two or more separate personality or identity states that take control of an individual's behaviour. Each identity may have its own unique patterns of thought, feeling, and behaviour.

This novel is a complete product of the author's imagination; all events, places and names are invented, accidental or randomly selected and have little to do with reality.

Table of Contents

Prologue

Ever since I got here, I have been unable to keep track of time. Although at first, I was still able to count the days, when the days started to mix with the nights and the nights with days, I became completely lost.

Losing consciousness, sometimes from pain, sometimes from exhaustion. Beaten, starved and humiliated. Only, I knew why I was here. It was supposed to be a guarantee that Edward would pay off his debts.

I thought that we were not in the United States. In fact, I was certain that I was somewhere in Mexico. But it made no difference to me then; captivity is captivity, no matter where you are.

My biggest worry was not knowing if I would get out of this alive at all. Having developed a strange tolerance, I noticed that my mind could disconnect from my body at moments when the pain became unbearable.

I noticed then that I was able to wait out this time as if in a sleep state, or leaving my own body standing somewhere nearby and only waking up when it was all over.

As an 18 year old boy, I could not have expected to find myself in such a terrible situation, and what's more, it was through no fault of my own.

The fact that I was not a saint and had already done a lot of evil in my short life, but it was not in my nature to humbly repent for another person's sins, so I tried to fight and oppose my tormentors with all my might, which only enraged them.

Days passed by, and I was losing hope, sitting in a dirty and dingy basement somewhere in the middle of nowhere, where the devil says *goodnight*.

I waited for any sign that someone was looking for me, that someone missed me. Images of my family home and friends who did not know what was happening to me appeared in my head. Each attempt at rebellion ended with more wounds, and I sank deeper and deeper into despair.

I knew one thing, however, that if I ever managed to escape from here, I would be a different person.

The fear and pain that had become my everyday life carved deep marks on my soul.

I suffered because of my brother's debts, but the thought of my freedom gave me the strength to survive.

At one point, I managed to free myself from the bonds that had been loosened after countless attempts to break them.

I jumped up at one of the men present and knocked him out with a surprise punch, then took his gun. Then, a spark of hope lit up in my mind.

This will be the moment when I get out of here, I thought naively.

When three armed men burst into the room, my hopes for freedom were dashed faster than they had appeared.

Especially when I realised that human life had no meaning for them, they were unscrupulously willing to sacrifice their own companions just to achieve their goal.

I was convinced of this when, in an act of desperation, I fired two shots at the previously overpowered kidnapper, to which the other three reacted by noticing the opportunity of my inattention, using it to attack me and finally disarm me.

At that time, I still thought that these were my memories of those events, even though I remembered them as if through a fog, but my perception of reality had changed. I just didn't know it yet.

I will never forget the day when I was unexpectedly released, the feeling of relief in my body and soul when my wounds were dressed in the local hospital.

It was then that I realised that the extraordinary pain tolerance I had previously thought about was nothing more than a slow stage in the splitting of my consciousness, a defence system that allowed me to survive it, the memories of fighting my captors were not my memories, and behind all of them was, *The other one.*

1

Gary, what have you done?

"(...) And here there is nothing, but trembling, but words found out of nothingness - oh, you still have a part of that wonder, which will be the whole content of eternity."

18 years later.

January 9, 1982, Texas, El Paso, Time: 06:99 a.m.

BOOM!!! BOOM!!! BOOM!!!

I heard banging on the front door. It sounded like it was coming from miles away.

BOOM!!! BOOM!!! BOOM!!!

"OPEN UP, POLICE!!!"

I was uncertain if this was just a dream. I slowly opened my eyes; I was feeling dizzy, and my head hurt terribly. I was sitting in an armchair in the living room, and I must have spent the whole night here. I fell asleep in the same position I was in last night, with a joint in my hand and a bottle of whiskey on the table.

Ed? it crossed my mind; at the same time, I looked around for my older brother. We were together yesterday, but I think he went home when I lost consciousness. At least that would make sense.

BOOM!!! BOOM!!! BOOM!!!

The noise reached my ears again; I started to realise that I was already awake.

"What's going on?" I asked myself, straightened myself up and stood up. Then I noticed that my things were stained with red liquid.

This discovery made me start to look around myself vigorously, and yes, my pants and white shirt were dirty with some substance that I did not recognise yet, which would soon turn out to be blood.

"What the fuck?" I asked myself.

After those words, my eyes fell to the floor, where I saw the handle of a revolver on the right side of the chair. Immediately, I leaned down to get a better look and recognised it as my father's old Colt Pocket M1849.

I was completely disoriented and I did not remember anything.

I had no possible way to explain what could have happened.

Making matters worse, Ed had disappeared, and I had no way to even find out why I was sitting there covered in what looked like blood. My father's gun was lying on the floor, and probably heavily armed officers were knocking on my door.

Gary?

The only explanation that came to my mind at that moment.

Gary, what the fuck did you do?

The strangest thing about all of this was that it was not the stains, the gun, or even the police at my door that concerned me the most. These factors are among my top concerns, but my clothes were my primary concern. I wasn't wearing them yesterday. Of course, I could have changed while drunk and didn't remember, or Gary had decided to change clothes, although that was unlikely.

Was it Gary?

It was the only explanation I could think of.

What the fuck have you gotten me into again?

BOOM!!! BOOM!!! BOOM!!! BOOOOM!!!

With one last bang, the lock on the door gave way, giving me no more time to think.

"POLICE!!! ON THE GROUND!!! GET ON THE GROUND!!!! HANDS ON YOUR HEAD!!!"

"STEWARD JOHNSON, YOU'RE UNDER ARREST FOR MURDER!!"

Despite the deafening noise and the adrenaline pumping through my veins, I couldn't tear my eyes away from the details of that surreal scene. The officers, as if in slow motion, surrounded me, and the handcuffs were tightened around my wrists.

For a moment, I had the overwhelming feeling that this was all just a nightmare. The moment they led me away, I felt cold drops of rain running down my face. In the driveway, I noticed the flashing lights of police cars, which were unpleasantly painful for my eyes.

In the distance, I could see the silhouette of a neighbour who was watching the whole event with interest from outside his window. I was being led to the police car when I noticed a Ford passenger car pull up to the house, and a man in a black suit and raincoat got out.

2

The morning after the murder.

"Sometimes we are faced with truths for which there are no words."

At the same time, a Ford sedan pulled up to the Johnson's house, parked between the illuminated police cars of the law enforcement officers at the scene. A moment later, a man dressed in a black suit and raincoat got out.

It was Michael Williams, a thirty-five-year-old detective who had arrived at the suspect's house with his partner.

Michael took his first steps on the muddy ground, mud splashing up to his shoes. That night, it was raining heavily and had been pouring down mercilessly for the past few hours, turning the streets into paths of a rushing river.

The detective headed toward the house without waiting for his partner, Paul Mendoza, who was just getting out of the vehicle.

When he was a few metres from his destination, he noticed the police officers exiting the vehicle, along with Steward. The handcuffed man walked between two tall police officers, keeping his head down.

However, as he passed Michael, he looked up, and their eyes met. The detective had the impression that the man looked disoriented as if he had not expected the visit of the officers at all or had just been shaken out of a deep sleep.

Michael knew Steward because he was not a person who led a quiet and peaceful lifestyle, which often got him into trouble with the law.

This time he must really gone overboard Michael thought.

However, the detective also had a lot of sympathy for the mentally unstable man. He knew that most of his troubles if not all, were due to his second personality, which existed in his mind. The man named Gary was created in Steward's consciousness as an alternative to situations in which he felt threatened. The phenomenon began when Steward, still a teenager, was kidnapped as security for a debt owed by his older brother, Edward, to a dangerous loan shark and gangster.

Steward was 18 years old at the time. He was beaten, starved, and tortured for two weeks before Edward managed to get $20,000. He regained his freedom but never recovered. While in the hospital after the traumatic events, doctors diagnosed the teenager as suffering from a split personality.

When asked his name, he introduced himself as Gary, another time as Steward. It was noted at the time that Gary could be crazy, if not dangerous, and manifested himself when Stewart felt threatened.

The diagnosis of specialists was unanimous: *Dissociative Identity Disorder*. An arbitrarily created self-defence system in the mind of a vulnerable person.

It was an unexpected turn of events, but not hopeless. Steward began treatment immediately after leaving the hospital, taking medications to help his condition and attending therapy.

Despite everything, he didn't manage to keep Gary under lock and key all the time, so Gary gave vent to his explosive nature at every opportunity.

Michael was aware of all this, but the law is the law, even if it's not easy to deal with someone who may not be one hundred per cent responsible for their actions, apart from being in the same body.

In this situation, the case was clear: a few hours earlier, two people had been brutally murdered (three, counting the baby of a pregnant woman), and Steward had been seen at the crime scene. In Michael's mind, there was now the dubious pleasure of collecting evidence of guilt.

"What do we have?" he asked as he entered the house.

"We are waiting for the forensics team, but in general, the case is simple," one of the uniformed officers answered.

"There lies a revolver, his clothes are stained with blood, and he drank and smoked marijuana," he added, pointing his finger at the place where Steward had been sitting until recently.

The detective came closer, and it was exactly as the officer had described. There was only one conclusion:

Steward was intoxicated with alcohol and drugs, something threw him off balance, and Gary took over, and went on a murderous rampage. Michael thought.

"Was there anyone else here?" he asked.

"I am not aware of anyone."

"Okay, I'll ask Steward at the interrogation," Michael added, thinking out loud.

"Do you think Gary could have done something like that?" Paul asked, standing behind his partner.

"It's hard to say, so far everything seems to indicate that."

"We've known for a long time that he's a lunatic, but I didn't expect he could be capable of murder," Paul added.

"Me neither, but we won't learn anything more here. We'll see what Steward tells us." Michael replied.

"Yes, if we`ll be able to talk to him."

"He should calm down by now. If not, we'll get the nurses to give him some medicine."

The detective stepped back towards the door and glanced outside. The rain continued, and large drops pelted loudly on the roofs of cars and the ground, creating an irritating noise. Michael looked towards the ground. To his right was a wooden shoe stand.

The man crouched down next to it. There were four pairs of shoes, three sports shoes and one hiking shoe. Michael took each of them in his hand and, after a moment, frowned thoughtfully.

"Look here," he said suddenly to his partner.

"What's that?"

"See?" he asked. "All these shoes are completely dry," added the detective.

El Paso police department, an hour later.

I had been waiting in the interview room for over thirty minutes. Dressed in an orange uniform, I knew I wouldn't be getting out of here anytime soon.

My previous clothes had been given to be analysed to see whose stains they belonged to. Personally? I had no idea.

All I remember was that Edward was with me at our parents' house the night before.

We had a few beers, smoked a few joints, and then Ed opened a bottle of whiskey, and then nothing.

The next memory was being woken up by the officers and being arrested, but that didn't really explain anything.

What was I doing that night? I don't know. However, I think Ed could shed some light on this. But before I made the first phone call, I had to make a statement and to do that, I needed someone to talk to, and apparently, no one was in a hurry to come over.

Minutes passed.

Despite the circumstances, I felt calm, not because I had nothing to worry about, quite the opposite. I simply agreed to take antidepressants so I could be myself.

I couldn't let Gary get active, and I needed to hear for myself what really happened and what my options were.

It was almost 9:00 pm.

Only now, the door opened, and two men in suits entered. I recognised the first one. I had met him before, after Gary started a fight in a bar or on the street, and I ended up in a police cell for the night.

I can't say that it was not my fault. Because I knew that I shouldn't drink alcohol while taking medication.

I was warned about the consequences, in which I might not be able to control my second consciousness while under the influence of stimulants.

But what could I do? I'm just a person with a passion for parties and going out on the town.

Like my brother Edward, we never shied away from alcohol and having a good time, even though it often ended with injuries, visits to the hospital and even the police station.

I looked at the second policeman, but he was not familiar to me.

Lightly brown in complexion, quite tall with short, black hair styled in a gel style, suggesting him to be someone of Latin descent.

Probably Mexican. I thought.

The first one was Michael, a tall and well built man with light hair, a typical American. Both gentlemen sat down in chairs in front of me. It was time for me to find out why I was here.

"It's January 9th 1982, one minute before nine o'clock," he said after pressing the record button on a small tape recorder placed in the middle of a table.

"Mr. Steward Johnson, I'm Detective Michael Williams. This is my partner, Detective Paul Mendoza."

"Yes, I know who you are," I answered and looked at the other, who, in return, stared at me attentively.

"Of course, we've already met," Michael said. "Steward, do you know why you were arrested?"

"I was told that there was a murder."

"Yes, you are currently suspected of the murder of Thomas Jones and his girlfriend, Katy Joys." He answered with a serious voice.

"Thom and Katy?" I said under my breath, surprised. Of course, I knew those people.

Thomas was a good friend of Edward's, not so much mine, but we used to play poker together.

I recognised Katy as well, mostly by sight, because we used to meet up often around town.

But I had no quarrel with them and certainly no reason to hate them. As a result, Gary did not perceive any responsibility or threat to harm those individuals.

"Could you tell us where you were last night, between three and five in the morning?" Michael asked.

"From what I know, I was at home, I fell asleep in the armchair, and you woke me up in the morning," I answered truthfully.

"Was there anyone with you who could confirm this?"

"My brother Edward was with me yesterday, but I don't know what time he left because I had too much to drink and blacked out, but you can ask him."

"Your brother has been notified and should be on his way here now; we will talk to him when he gets there," Michael replied.

"Steward, do you remember leaving the house in the middle of the night? For example, to go to the gas station for cigarettes?" Until now, silent, Paul joined the conversation.

"No, but I know what you're getting at. The nearest gas station to my house belongs to Thomas' family. I wasn't there yesterday."

"Or maybe Gary?" Paul added.

"No, I mean, I don't know," I thought out loud. "But I doubt it. He appears in stressful situations. Nothing like that happened yesterday."

"As you`ve said, you're not 100% convinced? So, it's a possibility?" Michael asked.

"I'm not sure," I confessed. "Can you finally tell me what the fuck happened?!"

"Thomas and Katy were shot at a gas station; we have an eyewitness who saw your Ford pickup leaving the scene," Michael replied.

"We also secured a revolver in your house, which will be analysed soon, along with your clothes," Paul added.

"There will also be surveillance footage of the incident, so if you want to confess, now is the best time to do it," Michael said while looking me straight in the eye.

I wasn't sure what to say or even if I should have said anything else. Maybe I should have asked for a lawyer.

"Steward, we know about your condition, and it can be considered a mitigating circumstance, but you must tell us if Gary did it, maybe you can avoid the death penalty," Paul added.

"She was pregnant, Steward, six months," Michael said.

It was bad, and I knew it was bad. No matter what I said at that moment, it wouldn't have made my situation any better.

At best, I would get a life sentence. At worst, the death chamber awaited me. But that was not what worried me the most. My biggest problem was that deep down, I felt I was innocent. But how could I defend myself?

I had no arguments in my favour. Maybe Ed would be able to clear me of the charges? Or should I have accepted the punishment with honour and accepted that this time, Gary got me into such trouble that there was no way out?

For a moment, I felt like confessing, but I couldn't say it with a clear conscience. I decided I must deny it.

"It's really sad what happened, but neither I nor Gary did it," I replied.

"Is that your final answer?" Michael asked.

"Yes, now please call a lawyer for me," I added, thus ending the interview.

"Of course, as you wish," Michael said. "The time now is 9:23. Mr Steward Johnson asks for a lawyer. At this point, the interview is over." He added and turned off the recording.

Both detectives got up from their seats and headed for the exit.

Michael opened the door and let his partner go first, staying behind him. Then he turned to me and said:

"Good luck, Steward, you're going to need it." After those words, he closed the door behind him.

I was alone in the room. All I could do was wait for the uniformed officers, who would probably have been here in a moment, to escort me to my cell, alone with my thoughts. I wondered if Ed was here. If so, would they have let me talk to him? I wanted to see my brother, even though things weren't always going well between us. He was the only family member I still saw after our parents died. My new family would soon be my cellmates unless Gary turned everyone against me again.

3

The trial.

"The reason for the existence of all politics is to serve man."

A week later.

January 23, 1982, El Paso County Courthouse, 2:30 p.m.

My trial had begun two days ago, and since then, my court-appointed attorney had been trying to prove that my alleged actions were taken during a fit of insanity.

But I still did not consider myself guilty and had no intention of acting like it, which apparently only irritated the jury and the judge. Part of me could understand their point of view, which was that I was arrogant and did not know how to accept the consequences of my actions. Only in this situation was there also my point of view, which nobody apparently wanted to understand.

Because how could I admit to doing something I didn't recall doing?

And deep down, I knew I couldn't have done it. But here, no one's sentiments or personal feelings mattered. What mattered were the facts, of which there was indeed no shortage whatsoever.

Of course, none of them were in my favour.

The prosecution side had all the aces in the case, and there was no doubt that they were so undeniable and solid that there was no way to undermine them.

They were the revolver from which the lethal shots were fired, my clothes from which DNA samples were taken, and the gunpowder traces that remained after a gunshot.

The prosecutor also had a recording from a CCTV camera located in the petrol station building. It was no surprise that the laboratory results matched the blood samples of the injured people, clearly indicating me as the main culprit.

The same was true regarding the revolver. Only my fingerprints, matched cartridges and residue from the shots fired.

But the biggest surprise for me was the recording from the camera. Presented on a medium-sized TV, the quality left much to be desired.

Despite everything that was going on with the man who looked a lot like me, he was dressed exactly as I had been that fateful night, and he was wearing a baseball cap that only left half of his face visible.

But it was enough to acknowledge the resemblance, as the distinctive moustache was clearly visible.

Since I am a tall man, five feet nine inches or 180 centimetres, with light brown hair and a large moustache of the same colour. The camera from this place was positioned to have a view of the first part of the gas station.

In other words, you could see who was entering and leaving, and on the right, the cash register and the person behind it.

That was why the recording from that time showed a man, in my opinion, very similar to me, who entered the interior after being let in earlier by Thomas using the electric button that unlocked the front door.

The man entered, headed towards the cash register where Thomas was with Katy, extended his right hand, holding a revolver, and fired two shots.

He then went behind the counter and emptied the cash register of money, took Thomas by the arm, and together they disappeared into the back room.

This was the moment when Thomas was forced to open the safe located in the store, and immediately afterwards, he died from a shot in the head at close range.

In the last part of the recording, the killer could be seen quickly leaving the scene of the crime, and in the distance, he was seen heading towards a Ford pickup truck parked just outside the building. Mainly, four shots were fired in a manner resembling an execution. The motive was a planned robbery because it happened on a Sunday, and the safe contained the entire week's earnings, which were traditionally deposited in the bank on Monday.

Given these facts, I could be certain that it could have been Gary who acted on impulse and was unable to plan ahead because I was in control 90% of the time. However, this explanation was not sufficient in the face of such strong evidence against me.

On top of that, there was the eyewitness who claimed to have seen me get into my car and drive away from the station.

Plus, the fact that Thomas Jones wouldn't let a stranger in at 3 am, and we knew each other, after all. All this made me doubt, at times, whether I was in the wrong here.

Gary could be insane, and I knew it, and the evidence before me made me believe that I might, indeed, be guilty. But since it was too late for me to suddenly confess to anything, I decided to wait, because the verdict was due in just a few minutes from that point. The jury deliberated for six hours before it reached a decision.

The time for the verdict was announced at 9:00 a.m. the following morning. I, of course, spent that time in the city jail, getting used to the idea that I would soon be changing my current cell to a place in a maximum-security prison for the most dangerous criminals.

The sergeant came to me thirty minutes before nine in the morning, announcing that it was time to go to court. We arrived there a few minutes before the scheduled start, and the courtroom was already almost filled with the public.

Many people were curious about the sentence I would hear. There were those who sincerely wished me the death penalty, for example, the families of the victims, and others probably wanted life imprisonment. I didn't think there was anyone among them who believed in my innocence.

Because how could anyone think that when I began to doubt it myself?

Perhaps only Edward and his girlfriend Stacy wanted a pardon for me, which, of course, bordered on a miracle.

As they, during the hearing and trial, both spoke favourably of me. Edward testified that he was with me the night of the murder but left after midnight and returned to Stacy's apartment, who later confirmed his story.

They also said that whatever happened, I was not legally responsible because of my long-standing mental illness.

My therapist and the doctor, who diagnosed me with this rare condition 16 years ago, also weighed in on the matter. All of this was certainly noted, but it was given little attention because of the seriousness of my actions and my criminal record.

It was almost nine o'clock, the jury had already taken their seats, and only the judge was missing. I was sitting next to my lawyer, and I felt the eyes of the victims' families piercing my soul. Even though my back was turned to them, I knew they were staring at me intensely, and I could feel a dose of hatred emanating from them.

It was an irrational feeling that could be compared to the sudden impression of being watched in a crowded place.

You don't see a specific person, but your sixth sense tells you that's exactly what you're seeing. Although given the circumstances, it was perfectly justified.

I was the bad guy that nobody liked.

Subjected to public humiliation and judgment, which was the main point of the show.

"All rise, the court is coming!" the orderly announced at exactly nine o'clock. After these words, I stood up from my seat along with the others.

At that moment, the presiding judge appeared in the doorway of the back room, dressed in a long, black robe. It was Logan Smith, a 50 year old man known for his sharp temper and abrasive nature. When I found out who the person in charge of my trial was going to be, I knew I was fucked.

And that wasn't even my statement because that's exactly how my lawyer summed it up, and I had no reason not to believe him.

Logan took his seat, allowing the others to sit down as well. The man put on his glasses and picked up the papers in front of him, tapping them on the desk so the pages would line up equally, and said:

"I am resuming trial number twenty-three, State of Texas versus Steward Johnson. I ask that the jury foreman stand up."

A black woman dressed in a black, elegant suit stood up from the end of the first row, being the closest to the judge.

"Yes, Your Honour." She announced.

"Excellent, the defendant, Steward Johnson, please stand up."

I did as I was told. My lawyer stood with me.

"Mr Johnson, you have been charged with two counts of aggravated murder and one count of involuntary manslaughter, as one of the victims, Katy Joys, was pregnant at the time of the incident," the judge said, giving me a reproachful look.

"I now ask that the verdict of the jury be read." He added, turning to a woman in the first row who had been waiting the entire time.

At that moment, the entire courtroom held its breath; there was complete silence, and no one dared to even cough so as not to drown out the reading of the verdict.

It was like a collective paralysis. For the next few seconds, people sat with their eyes wide open, their ears pricked up, and the buzzing of flies from across the room could be heard in the air. I stared at the woman with my heart in my throat.

I promised myself I wouldn't get nervous, but in these circumstances, I couldn't do anything about the fear that was taking over me. I guess only a 100% sociopath would be able to stand there unmoved.

"We, the jury of the State of Texas, USA," the woman began to speak. "Have unanimously found Steward Johnson guilty..."

Guilty was the last word I heard over the sounds of the audience's joy before I lost consciousness. From that moment on, I did not know what happened next, although I would find out relatively soon.

"...of the charges against him, and we sentence him to death." The presiding judge finished.

Steward had been standing motionless until now. However, when the verdict was read, his face and posture began to change.

His eyes took on a hostile expression, pressed by the eyebrows that were lowering. The wrinkles on Steward's forehead began to appear so quickly that it seemed that the man was ageing by the second.

Up until now, his posture, straight and impeccable, had hunched forward so much that you could hear the stitching of his suit stretched to the limits of its capacity around the back. The transformation took place before the eyes of the judge, who watched the man in disbelief.

Thanks to this, he understood that from this moment on, he was no longer dealing with Steward Johnson because Gary, who was furious, had just appeared before him.

In a split second, Gary grabbed the chair right behind him and threw it at the unsuspecting security guard standing next to the judge.

"I'LL FUCKING KILL YOU!!!" he shouted in a hoarse voice, then jumped over the table in front of him, grabbed a pen with his left hand and rushed towards Logan Smith.

"AAAAAA!!! OH MY GOD!!!" people screamed in terror.

This situation caused panic among the gathered. Some quickly jumped towards the exit, while others remained in their seats, not knowing how to behave.

Edward grabbed Stacy's hand, and they both left the room.

Fortunately, the security guard who had been hit with the chair earlier quickly recovered, and then, thanks to the help of two others, placed in different parts of the room, they effectively overpowered Gary.

But it didn't come easy for them. Although Steward Johnson was a tall man, he was not as heavy as any of the guards present.

Gary, nevertheless, seemed to be exceptionally strong. It was only after several minutes of struggle that three men managed to subdue the convict's urges.

They managed to handcuff him and quickly led him out of the room, thanks to which the situation was brought under control. The entire incident was observed by Michael Williams, who also could not believe what he saw.

The detective's special attention was drawn not only by the fact that Gary had taken control of Steward in front of dozens of people but also by the fact that he had proven how dangerous and crazy this personality was.

There was one more detail that the observant man noticed in these circumstances, and to his surprise, he realised that he was beginning to have serious doubts, not only about Steward's guilt in the murders but also about Gary's guilt.

4

Doubts.

"Work cannot be treated - never and nowhere - as a commodity, because a human being cannot be a commodity to another."

10 minutes later.

Michael left the courthouse and headed to his car. His mind was racing with all sorts of thoughts. On the one hand, he was impressed by the incident involving Steward, or rather, Gary.

The detective had never seen someone lose control so much before. Yes, he had experienced outbursts of aggression from people under arrest, but this was a whole other level of fury. On the other hand, he had noticed something even more disturbing, but before he could confirm his suspicion, he needed to get some physical evidence.

At that point, the man decided to go to the Johnson house before it was handed over to Edward as the last member of the family.

It was a procedure that allowed the police to secure a place to gather evidence during the trial.

Now that the trial was over, the property was to be returned to its owner within the next 24 hours, and Michael had a feeling that he should take one last look at the place.

It was 9:40 a.m. when the detective started the engine of his *Ford Fiesta* and joined the traffic.

It was a nice sunny morning. The temperature hovered around 9°C. Dressed in a warm coat, Michael headed towards the nearest telephone located on the street.

He drove along *E Overland Ave* and turned onto *S Mesa St,* at the end of which there was a public telephone.

Michael stopped the vehicle at the booth and got out, a moment later dialling the number to Paul Mendoza.

"Detective Paul Mendoza." The partner answered.

"Hi Paul, this is Michael, it's over, Steward got a gas chamber."

"Uuuu... that's tough. Well, I didn't expect a different verdict..." Paul replied. "...and you, are you surprised?"

"Not necessarily, but that's not why I'm calling you. I want you to do something for me."

"What's up?"

"I need you to get some footage of Steward Johnson..." Michael began to explain.

"...we know that he was involved in many bar fights, see if any of these places caught it on camera."

"Do you have anything specific in mind?"

"No, look through his records. I'm sure you'll find something there," Michael replied.

"And what are you doing?"

"I'll go to his house while we still have access there. I think we missed something."

"You've got to be kidding..." Paul was surprised. "...The investigators spent two days there. We were there for a good few hours, too. What makes you think you'll find something now?"

"I don't know, I just want to go there, do what I asked you to. I'll join you later."

"Okay, let me know if you need anything else."

"I will," Michael said and hung up.

The detective left the phone booth and went back to the car. A moment later, he was driving directly to Steward's house.

15 minutes later.

Michael pulled the car into the Johnsons' driveway and wasted no time in heading inside.

The front door was covered in yellow police tape with large black letters: *POLICE LINE DO NOT CROSS.*

The house was secured, with no signs that anyone had entered. The tapes were supposed to be removed that day, but Michael preferred to leave them intact, so he opened the door and slipped through.

The first thing that immediately hit the detective's nostrils after entering the room was the unpleasant smell of dried blood mixed with remnants of alcohol, burnt tobacco, and marijuana.

Someone's going to have to work hard here to get this thing up and running, he thought.

The lounge was the first room to be found on the right side of the entrance to the house.

Michael remembered it well because he had been there twice with Paul. Apart from the minimal remnants of the forensics work, everything looked the same, undisturbed.

A large sofa stood by the window to the right, a table in the middle, and two single armchairs on either side.

A piece of furniture was placed at the end of the room, on which stood an old black-and-white television, which no one probably used.

The detective knew that after the death of Dorothy Johnson, Edward and Steward's mother, only the younger son lived in the estate.

Edward, on the other hand, moved in with his girlfriend a few miles away.

Michael, aware of these facts, expected that all the items found in the house would belong to Steward.

However, he remembered that Edward was also there on the night of the murder, so no one was surprised that his fingerprints were everywhere. But that was not the reason he had come there.

He was not interested in what was already known to everyone, and his intuition told him that something else was hidden from the eyes of people who had been there before. The man slowly walked through the living room, looking at the mess that reigned there.

Empty beer cans were strewn about, cigarette filters in both the ashtray and the table and the wooden floor, leaving burn marks in places, an empty bottle of whiskey and, of course, the bloodstains next to the armchair where Stewart was found.

Michael scanned every cubic inch again as he made his way to the stairs on the other side of the room.

When he finally got there, he went up to the first floor, the second time he had been there since the investigation began.

The first time, he had only looked around for a few minutes because he saw no reason to spend any more time there.

Because everything he needed at the time was on the first floor, and there was so much evidence that the main question of the investigation was not *Who?* but *Why?*

This time, the detective decided it would be good to see the conditions in which Steward lived. He wondered if there were any visible traces of two men or just one, especially since the scenes from the morning courtroom brawl were still fresh in his mind.

The intention of this undertaking was to bring into focus the character of Steward Johnson as a person with a split personality and to see which of these two dominated the man's private life.

Michael, therefore, paid special attention to distinctive clothing, gadgets, magazines, music tapes, posters, etcetera.

The small single-family home had three rooms and a bathroom upstairs.

The first room on the detective's left was a large bedroom once owned by Stewart's parents. To his right was Edward's room, and across from Steward, at the end, was the shared bathroom.

Michael could only tell by glancing into each room. Each one had some detail that immediately gave away its owner.

The parents' bedroom looked untouched. Everything was tidy: the bed was made, barely a trace of dust, and family photos were neatly arranged on the dresser and nightstand.

At first glance, it was obvious that Steward had taken great care of this room.

He must have loved his parents very much to be so sentimental. The detective thought.

However, the same could not be said for Edward's room.

Even though the place was practically empty, it was so messy that one could tell that someone had moved out in a hurry, leaving some of their belongings behind, and never returned to clean up the space they had occupied.

"Apparently, Steward didn't care about this room," Michael stated.

The last and most important room was Stewart's; it was where the detective wanted to spend the most time.

But once inside, he quickly found that he didn't see anything out of the ordinary.

Yes, there were a few VHS tapes with different movie themes, from comedies to thrillers, stacked on top of each other next to the VHS player and the small TV set on the dresser opposite the bed.

But that was completely normal for anyone who liked watching movies. Other than that, the wardrobe looked uniform.

In the dresser were stacked jeans of various colours, mostly dark blue and black, black and white T-shirts, underwear, and socks. In the closet, Michael found hanging plaid shirts, several belts, a couple of denim jackets and winter jackets, and three baseball caps.

There was no indication that the man had trouble deciding what style of clothing was right for him.

Maybe Gary isn't so different from Steward after all. Michael thought.

This was a rather disappointing discovery, especially since the detective was becoming increasingly interested in the topic of multiple personality disorder and was hoping to uncover some anomalies.

All that remained was the man's bed and a small nightstand next to it. Michael walked over and opened the first drawer.

Inside were several letters addressed to Steward and his parents; some of them were unopened. Michael also found the man's wallet there, containing several dollar bills, a driver's license, and a small bag of marijuana.

This also didn't surprise the detective, as there were small pieces of dry green leaves visible in several places, including on the dresser and nightstand.

The question remains: did he smoke because he liked using drugs, or did he smoke to feel calm? the detective wondered.

The second drawer turned out to be empty. When he opened the third and last drawer, his eyes met orange tubes with pills inside, eight of them. Michael took one in his hand and saw that it was a sedative prescribed by the pharmacy under the name of Steward Johnson.

Each one had the man's name and surname on it. They only differed in the content.

It turns out that Steward takes strong psychotropic drugs to control himself. He drew conclusions.

The detective put the tube down, closed the drawer behind him and left the room.

As he reached the stairs, he heard the telephone on the ground floor start to ring.

A coincidence? he thought.

He quickly went downstairs and went to the phone, standing next to the long sofa.

RING...!! RING...!! RING...!! RING...!!

For a moment, he doubted whether it was a good idea, but he answered.

"Michael?" a man's voice asked immediately.

"Paul?" he was surprised.

"It's a good thing I caught you there, listen, I talked to the owner of the bar, The Three Gringo's on Sixth Street..." Paul began to explain. "...two weeks ago, Steward was arrested by the uniformed officers there, the guy has the video and agreed to show it."

"Great, when do you want to meet him?"

"He said that even today, he's at the bar all day, we can go right away."

"Go ahead, we'll meet there," Michael replied, looking at the dark brown throw on the couch he was standing next to.

"Okay, how long will it take you?"

"I should be there in an hour."

"Do you know where this is? Do you need the coordinates?"

"I know, don't worry, I'll see you there."

"Okay, see you later," Paul replied and disconnected the call.

Michael put the phone back on the cradle and frowned, looking at the couch carefully. Memories of previous visits to this place flashed through his mind.

Quickly reviewing the images in his memory, he noticed that he didn't remember the bedspread being tampered with in any way. That could only mean one thing.

"No one has touched it before." He stated, and without thinking twice, he grabbed the material and ripped it off the sofa in one swift movement.

When he carefully examined the entire piece of furniture, there seemed to be nothing noteworthy about it.

Except two barely visible holes, one next to the other, were visible almost in the middle, but then again, it was an old piece of furniture, so who could be surprised? But his trained detective eye and instincts told him otherwise.

He stepped closer and inserted his index finger into one of the holes.

He then withdrew his hand, straightened up, and pushed the sofa away hard, so that it moved a few inches, revealing two holes in the wooden floor.

They were in the same place as the cracks in the sofa that had been there a moment ago.

Michael crouched down next to them.

Oh shit, are those, bullet holes? he thought in disbelief.

The discovery itself and the fact that no one had noticed it before were not enough because the holes were not empty.

The detective quickly got up from the floor and went to the kitchen to find something that could help him dig deeper.

After a moment, he found a butter knife and decided that it would be enough.

He returned to the spot and carefully began to pry the barely visible bullet from the hole from all sides.

It took several minutes, during which he turned the cutlery clockwise in the wood, before he finally managed to extract the first cartridge and then the same with the second one.

15 minutes and a few uncomfortable leg cramps later, he had what he had come for, something that had hidden itself from view but could not hide itself from Michael.

He put his discovery in a clear plastic bag and excitedly left the house, eager to share it with Paul.

20 minutes later.

It was almost eleven o'clock in the morning when Michael pulled up to the bar, "The Three Gringo's" on Sixth Street.

As he approached his destination, he noticed his partner's car parked on the street, and a moment later, Paul himself was waiting for him in front of the building.

Well, the conversation is obviously over. He thought.

The man stopped the car and got out, then walked over to his partner.

"Do we have anything?" he asked a few steps away from him.

Paul extended his hand in response, holding a black VHS tape without a wrapper.

"Yeah, the owner was very helpful..." he said, nodding his head towards the bar. "...he knows Steward well and knew immediately what incident I was talking about.

When I arrived, he was already waiting for me with this recording." He added again, showing the tape more clearly.

"Excellent, we'll look at it in the office. I have something too..." Michael replied and reached into the pocket of his coat. "...I found them in the Johnsons' house, under the sofa." He added, taking out a plastic bag with two cartridges.

Paul frowned in surprise.

"Are these...?" he began to ask when Michael immediately interrupted.

"I think so. In fact, I'm 99% sure that these are the two missing cartridges from Steward's revolver."

"And you found them in the house?"

"Exactly, it looks like he fired the shots indoors," Michael replied.

It's strange that the techs didn't find them. Paul wondered.

At the same time, he took the bag from Michael and held it higher, towards the sun, to get a better look at it.

"They had no reason to move the furniture; everything they needed was right in front of them. They secured what was visible, hence the oversight." Michael explained.

"Yeah, that makes sense." Paul agreed.

"Well, we've got our hands full, let's get back to the station, I have another theory I need to check..." Michael suggested.

"...I'll tell you what it is if my guess is confirmed."

"Okay, let's get going."

Both officers returned to their vehicles and, a moment later, were on their way to the police station.

Upon arrival, Paul headed to the conference room, where there were televisions with HVS players.

"I'll join you in a minute, I'll just stop by the evidence room for a moment," Michael said and headed in the opposite direction.

Paul, on the other hand, walked a dozen or so metres and, at the end of the corridor, entered a large room where team meetings usually took place.

Then, without wasting time, he walked over to the television, set against the left wall of the room, turned it on, and inserted a tape into the player.

After a few seconds and a few annoying bars on the screen showing the poor quality of the video, the image appeared.

Paul sat down in a chair, and his eyes were met with the view from the bar's camera, mounted on the ceiling so that it cast a view behind the staff. Michael returned then, carrying yet another tape in his hand.

Hearing the door opening, Paul looked in his direction.

"Another recording?" he was surprised.

"Yeah, I need something to compare it to," Michael explained.

"Okay, turn on the one next to it," Paul pointed to the other TV set.

"Do you have anything yet?" Michael was curious.

"Not yet, I just started."

"Okay, let me know if you spot anything," Michael replied, stepping closer to his partner.

"Sure."

Michael sat down next to Paul, and both men watched intently for Stewart's familiar face on the screen.

This was no easy task, given the crowded room on a Saturday night.

The number of people and the poor quality of the recording made Michael feel like he was looking for a needle in a haystack, except that each blade of grass was constantly moving in all directions and was hard to see.

It could drive even the most patient person crazy.

Paul was also uncomfortable with this, and after the first few minutes, he started to get a headache. The officers were not about to give up, though, knowing that a breakthrough was imminent.

And so, it happened during the 15th minute of surveillance.

Although they did not see Steward right away, something bad was happening as people started to run in different directions in obvious panic and fear.

"Look…" Paul said, pointing at the person. "…there he is."

"That's it, the man himself."

In this shot, Stewart, or by then Gary, could be seen struggling with a man.

For the next 60 seconds, the two men punched each other, then Steward grabbed a beer bottle and smashed it over his opponent's head, causing him to fall to the ground.

The space between the two brawlers quickly cleared out as the crowd of frightened customers fled the scene.

"Stop," Michael said suddenly.

Paul carried out the order just as the screen showed two men attacking Steward.

"Rewind to the moment with the bottle," again, the partner obediently began to carry out the instructions while Michael also started the tape he had brought.

"Who do you think we see here, Steward or Gary here?" asked Paul.

"Gary, no doubt, I saw what he's capable of today in the courtroom, you wouldn't believe it."

"Yes, I heard, quite a scandal. I almost felt sorry I wasn't there to witness it, hehehe..." Paul laughed.

"Okay, got it," Michael said, stopping his player where he wanted it.

"What the fuck?" said a surprised Paul.

"Do you see that?"

"Well, I`ll be damned," Paul's eyes opened wide.

On the TV to the right, opposite Michael, there was now an image of a murderer firing shots moments after entering a gas station, holding a gun in his right hand.

On the other side, Paul's TV shows Steward or Gary swinging an empty beer bottle at his opponent.

"Just as I thought, I noticed it in court today..." Michael said suddenly. "...the guy's left-handed."

5

The First Night.

"Conscience is a matter of fundamental importance to every man. It is his inner guide and is also the judge of his actions."

I woke up after 16 hours of sleep in the prison hospital. As I looked around with still sleepy eyes, I noticed the depressing state of the room I was in.

Dirty, shabby, once-white walls with dirty stains of an unidentified substance here and there, bars on the windows, and the smell of chemicals in the air.

My first instinct was to vomit, but fortunately, it passed after a while.

Thirty minutes passed as I lay on an old hospital bed, chained to it, waiting for the guards. It was more of a clinic, but for some reason, they called this place a hospital.

I was there because I had been given a heavy sedative directly into my bloodstream after Gary had almost murdered Judge Logan Smith in front of everyone.

I also learned this from the prison guards shortly after I regained consciousness and was trying to figure out where I was.

They told me at the time that I had apparently "Put on quite a show."

I didn't remember any of it, but maybe that was for the best.

Because who likes to hear people tell you about what they did the day before without realising it?

It's like hearing stories after a night of heavy drinking, when people were dead drunk and did unspeakable things, and then the next day, someone reminded them of it.

It was completely unacceptable, and that's how I felt in this case.

As always, when Gary caused trouble, I had to answer for it.

But that wasn't the worst because I realised that after such a display, the slightest hope that someone would look at me favourably disappeared.

If anyone had an ounce of sympathy for me, it was gone; by now, there was no trace of it.

Well, not the first time, but at least probably the last time. I thought.

The time for sentiments was over. Now, I was on death row.

There was no room for weakness here. The situation was clear; I had been sentenced to death, and soon, I would be led to the cell where I would spend the last days of my life.

A moment later, I heard footsteps coming from the corridor, the clinking of metal keys bouncing off each other, and the voices of men approaching.

They were the guards I was waiting for.

I can't say I was in a hurry to get to my cell, but nothing worse could have happened to me, and the hospital room itself gave me the creeps, so I didn't mind leaving it.

"Mr. Johnson, I see you're ready," the first guard said, right after arriving.

"Well, I guess I won't be more ready than that," he replied.

"Hahaha, Joker, I like that." The second man added.

"I think you know what is happening, or are there any questions?" the first asked.

"Yes, when's dinner?"

"Uuuu... Mr. Johnson, if I were you, that would be the last thing on my mind," the second said with a serious expression on his face.

"First, we need to familiarise you with your accommodations and the rules here." The first added.

The rules that apply. I thought ironically.

Did they think I was an idiot? I was sitting on death row.

There were no rules here. The greatest fringe of society locked in one crowded place, although I had never been here, I had an idea of what such a place might look like.

Don't get killed. The only rule that applies to prisoners. At least, that's what I thought at the time, but that, too, would soon change completely.

"Here's your new clothes." The first guard said suddenly while placing a plastic bag with orange things inside on my bed.

"Change, and we'll pick up the rest of the things you'll need on the way," the second one added.

"We've already completed the registration process, so from now on, you are officially our new resident," the first man added.

Okay, the time has come. I thought as I slid off the bed.

At the same time, one of the guards approached me to free my hand from the handcuffs, making the process of changing clothes easier for me.

After a few minutes, I was standing in my prison uniform, ready to go.

I gave the guards my temporary clothes, namely the suit pants and white shirt I had worn during the trial.

The guards put them in a bag to go with the rest of my belongings in case I ever needed them again.

Which I sincerely doubted.

They handcuffed me again, and the three of us headed down the hallway toward the entrance gate to this part of the building.

"It is our duty to inform you that due to your condition, you will receive medication once a day. Every morning, you will be asked to visit a nurse who will give you the tablets and supervise you to take them." One of the men said suddenly.

Yeah, my meds. I'm not convinced that's a good idea. I thought.

I was taking pills to keep Gary in check. They were supposed to relax me and calm me down so my other personality wouldn't come out.

The fact was, Gary got me into trouble every time he took over, but he was in my head for a reason. He was there to protect me, though his visits often had the opposite effect.

Despite this, I felt I needed him more than ever, even though I never expected to.

"And by the way, your case is fascinating," the second guard unexpectedly spoke. "I've heard of split identity, but I never thought I'd meet such a person," he added excitedly.

"You wouldn't talk as if it concerned you," I replied shortly.

"Probably not," he admitted.

We reached the gate, which the guard opened with one of the many keys attached to his belt.

"But tell me, how does it manifest itself?" the man inquired.

"Have you always been like this, from birth? How did it happen?" he bombarded me with questions.

Oh, god damn it! I thought.

That was all I needed, a curious guard.

"It's a long story, maybe I'll tell you sometime," I replied.

"Alright," he agreed to leave me alone.

I didn't feel like confiding in a stranger.

The story of how Gary had appeared in my subconscious was long, incredibly personal, and difficult to understand.

Because not everyone was able to accept the fact that my own brother could have caused me to become this way. Not directly, of course, but because of his actions, I was kidnapped and tortured for two weeks until he paid off a debt.

For a long time, I resented him for letting it happen. But over time, Ed proved to me that he was trying to make up for and compensate for my suffering.

For years, he had helped me cope with my new reality. In a way, I forgave him, but I never forgot. In any case, it was none of those guards' business.

We stopped for a moment in front of the guardhouse, where I was given a sheet, basic personal hygiene products, and two rolls of toilet paper, and then we moved on.

"Let me give you some personal advice, you're white, so join your own people once you're inside," the second man said suddenly. "I guess I don't have to tell you what kind of people you'll be hanging out with from now on.

The prison is generally divided into three groups: the Mexican Mafia, the Black Guerrilla Family, and the Aryan Brotherhood."

The guard spoke as we walked to the second gate, behind which was the prisoner's housing block. This is where I was to be alone with the rest of the criminals.

With one swift movement, the man opened the lock, and I was inside. We were on the first floor, and my eyes met a huge room with separate barred rooms downstairs and upstairs.

Almost everything was painted in yellow, and on the ground, floor were a few tables and a guardroom.

I would probably feel fear, maybe even panic, but despite this, being under the influence of sedatives, I remained calm.

Loud laughter, shouts, and curses from the people inside reached my ears. The rooms were locked, so as I walked toward my destination, I could feel the eyes of the people inside.

"YO!! HEY!! HEEEEY!!! HEY YOUUU!!" I heard to my right.

"New guy?!" someone shouted from a distance.

"NEW GUY!!" another added.

Then, a terrible roar from the people inside echoed through the entire block.

"AAAAAUUUUU!!!! FRESH MEAT!!!!!"

The men were screaming, laughing, clapping, and jumping around like wild monkeys locked in a cage.

"Welcome to the Allan B. Polunsky Unit," one of the guards whispered in my ear.

A moment later, we reached my cell, accompanied by overwhelming screams.

"We are here, get inside." The second one ordered.

I did as I was told and heard the gate slam shut behind me.

"Put down everything and turn around, back to the gates," the guard added.

After these words, I put the things I had taken from the guardhouse on the lower bed and approached the gate.

"Stretch out your hands."

"Join the Aryan ones, if you want to survive here even a week, take my advice." The second one said as my hands were being uncuffed.

"Good luck." I heard another as they were leaving, and I was left alone.

Then, reality began to dawn on me. My heart was picking up speed.

The medicine will wear off soon, I thought. *I am afraid to think what will happen if Gary shows up here.*

6

The prison reality

"Being a man of conscience means demanding from yourself, rising from your own falls and constantly converting again."

The next day, 06:59 a.m., January 25, 1982.

After only a few minutes of sleep the night before, two guards came to escort me to my first meeting with the nurse.

Throughout the night, I could hear the voices of my fellow prisoners.

I lay on the bed with my eyes wide open, listening to what they were saying.

Fortunately, it turned out that I was not sharing a cell with anyone else, which allowed me to calm down a bit after the lights went out.

However, the echo of quiet whispers combined with the occasional screams and laughter made me shiver at times.

I felt the gravity of this place, especially as it slowly became my reality.

Even though I spent a week in a detention centre, it didn't feel like a real prison, and there was no way I could mentally prepare myself for such a huge change, no matter how hard I tried to get used to spending time locked up.

The atmosphere of aggression, evil, and violence hung in the air, reaching me through the cracks in the bars along with the cold temperature of the unheated space.

The drugs in my system had long since worn off, and the only thing keeping me from losing control of myself was the fact that I was safely separated from the others by thick bars.

Just before seven in the morning, I heard the clank of a key turning in the lock and the creaking of the metal parts that made up the entrance mechanism to my cell, rubbing against each other.

At that sound, I lifted my head to see who had come.

Two men I hadn't seen before were standing in front of the entrance.

Apparently, the guards who worked with me yesterday finished their shift, and new ones have appeared in their place. I thought.

"Stand up and come forward with your hands out in front." The first one was ordered.

I did as I was told, after which I was handcuffed and led out of the cell.

"Down the stairs." I heard behind me as we walked along the metal balcony.

Then again, I felt the gazes of the others staring straight at me, and I tried with all my might to ignore them.

We went down the stairs, and I closed my eyes for a moment, trying to control my nerves. There were more cells on the ground floor and more prisoners, which meant more curious glances my way.

I knew Gary would take over at any moment; all it took was a little more nervousness and stress for it to happen.

I didn't want that, so I walked forward for a while, led by the guards, with my eyes closed.

When we got there, I was led into a small room with a few chairs lined up next to each other, and I sat down in one of them.

"The nurse will see you in a moment," one of the guards said, and they both left the room, leaving me alone.

I observed the surroundings, anticipating the next event. To my left, behind glass, sat a woman dressed in a prison uniform, locked alone in a small guard room.

Across from me was a white door, behind which a nurse was probably on duty. All of this was watched by a camera mounted on the ceiling in the left corner.

A few minutes passed before the white door opened, which immediately caught my attention.

I looked in that direction and my eyes met with a large man with light brown skin, obviously of Hispanic descent, dressed in an orange uniform.

I immediately noticed that he was at least a head taller than I, which made him seem monstrous from my perspective.

He must be at least six feet tall. I thought.

A man with a shaved head, a carefully trimmed beard and moustache, tattoos all over his body and face, with the build of a bodybuilder, gave me a sinister look that sent shivers down my spine.

Unable to maintain eye contact, I looked along his body and noticed that his hands were also handcuffed.

This was Luis Ramirez, the leader of the Latino gang in that part of the prison, but I didn't know it at the time.

I felt a slight sense of relief that he was handcuffed, because the two guards behind him only reached his shoulders and had no chance of stopping him if he wanted to attack me.

At the same moment, I felt that I was starting to lose consciousness, but it was not a state in which I would close my eyes and fall.

This was a manifestation of Gary's desire to activate. Fortunately, it did not last too long.

The guards escorted the giant to the door, where he was taken over by those waiting behind it.

The whole thing took only a few seconds, and then I regained control of myself.

That was a close call, I thought.

I meant that if he had been in this room for any length of time, Gary would have undoubtedly appeared.

I knew full well what he was capable of, so I was certain that he would have most likely thrown himself at the man without a moment's hesitation, seriously injuring him.

Gary knew no limits. He didn't care who his opponent was, what he looked like, or where he came from.

The only thing that mattered to him was the level of threat and neutralising it as quickly as possible.

"Next, please." The woman called from inside the room.

At these words, the guards approach me, and I move with them towards the white door.

"Mr. Steward Johnson?" the short, middle aged nurse reads my name from the patient list.

"That's right," I confirm.

"Please sit down," indicating a chair next to the desk.

"Thank you, I'll stand," I replied.

The guards approach me, sensing danger.

"However, I will insist..." the woman replies, looking at me suspiciously. "...sit down"

There is no point in being stubborn, so I sit down politely.

"Well, I have read your medical history, and I must admit that this is an unusual case..." she says, looking at me over the thick notebook.

"...Dissociative Identity Disorder, or colloquially known as Split Personality Disorder, is a very rare disease."

"Can you tell me something I don't already know?"

"Who is your other personality, or is that also what I'm dealing with now?"

"His name is Gary, and no, he isn't here right now," I answered honestly.

"Excellent, can you tell me under what circumstances Gary is most likely to become active?"

"Stressful, and in circumstances where my safety may be at risk."

"I understand, I'm afraid that in this place there will be many opportunities for that, which is why I have two sets of strong sedatives prepared for you," she says, walking over to the medicine cabinet. "Don't worry, I won't give you anything you haven't taken before."

Okay, at least I can be sure that I know how I'll feel after them, I say to myself in my mind.

"Here…" she handed me a small cup with two pills inside.

"…please swallow them," she added, pushing a plastic cup of water towards me.

In one movement, I pop the pills into my mouth and swallow them.

"I don't need a drink." I answered after consuming the pills.

"Okay, now you're going to sit in the waiting room for twenty minutes to let them work, we don't want any episodes in that time, do we?"

I answered that question with silence.

"We don't have the best conditions here to take care of someone with your disorder, but I can promise that I will do everything in my power to take care of you."

She said, looking at me with a pitying expression on her face.

She seemed sincere, which made me start to feel a little sympathy for her.

"See you tomorrow, Mr. Johnson."

"See you," I replied and stood up from my seat.

The guards lined up behind me on both sides, and we headed for the exit.

Stopping in front of the white doors, one of the guards opens them, and I find myself in a small waiting room again.

"Next, please." I hear the nurse's voice behind me, and then my eyes land on another man in orange clothing, waiting for his turn; he also looks gigantic.

A black, bald prisoner of my height, very muscular and with a serious expression on his face, stood up and looked at me.

I thought then that his eyes seemed empty, without any expression except hatred for the whole world.

Maybe it's because he's been here a long time and has lost hope of ever getting out. I thought.

Prison changes people. I had no doubts about that.

The only question that remained in this situation was how much prison would change me and whether, in a few years, or maybe even months, the last spark of hope for improving the situation in my eyes would not fade, and its place would also be taken by a feeling of hatred.

It was eight o'clock in the morning, time for my morning meal.

I had been in the cell for over 30 minutes, and the pills I had taken earlier were already taking full effect, making me feel slightly dizzy. I usually didn't eat breakfast, but here I had to adapt.

Roll call began promptly at eight in the morning, and all the cells were opened, and the prisoners had to line up in front of them.

This made it easier for the guards to check the number of people and then escort everyone to the canteen.

I left the room, barely able to walk. I would have preferred to stay inside, but it was out of my hands.

I stood next to the men from the neighbouring cells, and they stood next to the men from the next cells, and then the next, until we reached the end of our floor. Then, at a signal from the guard, everyone started heading for the stairs.

Being roughly in the middle of the row of strangers, I had to be careful not to step on anyone's foot, because that could have ended badly for me. Most of these people looked extremely menacing.

The omnipresent tattoos, scars on their faces and arms, and athletic builds reminded me of a meeting of depraved bodybuilders. The atmosphere was saturated with testosterone and inflated male egos. The malevolent stares and hatred towards each other hung in the air, filling the building with a depressing mood.

I must be very careful. I thought as I walked a few metres.

A moment later, I found myself in the prison canteen. It was here that I noticed how divided the prison was.

Being a person on the upper floor, I got there when most of the seats were already taken. This allowed me to recognise the men who were similar in groups. The Blacks sat in their own group, as did the whites and Latinos.

I figured there were 100s of people, with a few guards posted in the corners of the room.

You could say that each group had their own section of the canteen, and no one got in each other's way.

I also noticed the men I had met earlier during my visit to the nurse. The difference was that the first one, obviously of Latino descent, must have been an important person among his own people.

He was sitting in the middle of the table, and his colleagues seemed to be listening attentively to what he was saying.

The second, a black man, sat on the corner of the table among his companions, eating his meal in concentration. At the very end were the whites.

The Aryan Brotherhood. I thought.

Most of them had shaved heads, some had large moustaches, beards, and all had visible tattoos. Swastikas, the initials AB in a clover, crosses, the inscriptions SS and the number 666, which is commonly considered the sign of the devil.

These were the ones the guard mentioned when he took me back to my cell.

I started thinking about how I could join them. I had to face the truth: there was no way I could serve my sentence without support and not expose myself to additional problems.

I took the food and found an empty spot at the table. My tray was filled with what was probably supposed to be oatmeal.

A grey pile of seeds, glued together into one solid pancake that could be cut with a knife, two slices of buttered toast, and a glass of milk. It was the prison, cheap version, of breakfast, but people were eating anyway. I thought there were two reasons.

First, there was no hope for anything better, and second, a more likely explanation, they didn't care as long as they were filling their stomachs.

I personally had no appetite, even with a juicy burger and fries in front of me, that's how the drugs affected me. For the first few hours after taking it, it was hard to swallow anything.

However, in this situation, since my next meal was in a few hours, I had to force myself to eat something.

Sitting facing the room, everything was in sight. To my right was a group of Latinos, to my left were blacks, and finally, White men.

I ate a bite of oatmeal, discreetly observing them. Everyone was talking feverishly and stealing glances at each other.

This didn't look good. I thought.

I immediately thought that there was going to be a bigger fight. You could read it in the faces of the menacing-looking men.

"Oh, what a shit," I said to myself under my breath after swallowing a portion of oatmeal.

At this point, I was sure of three things: first, I couldn't take sedatives here because they made me too groggy.

Second, I was going to witness a fight in the prison any day now.

Third, the food here had to be healthy because it tasted disgusting, and anything that wasn't tasty had to be healthy.

Two hours later, 10:05 a.m.

Michael arrived at the police station with the intention of engaging in a serious discussion with the chief.

He was haunted by the feeling that he had made a mistake.

The sense of injustice that may have befallen Steward Johnson had tormented the detective since he discovered the inconsistencies that came to light after his conviction.

The two missing bullets from the revolver he found in the house, the tape recording that revealed the man was left-handed, and the dry shoes that were completely out of keeping with the circumstances of the murder on a rainy night.

All of this made Michael almost completely convinced that he had approached the investigation from the wrong angle.

Instead of gathering evidence against Steward, which ultimately contributed to his being sent to death row, he should have focused on finding third parties involved in the case.

But it was too late to fix the mistakes, and Michael knew it.

The detective also knew that the arguments he was going to present to the chief were not enough to convince him to reopen the investigation.

All the circumstantial evidence he had at his disposal at that point, he could have easily refuted himself in a way that would not have shed any other light on the matter and in no way indicated that Steward could have been framed by anyone.

Two bullets on the floor, he went crazy in the house and fired blindly.

Left handed Steward has two personalities, and only one of them is left handed.

Dry shoes, he simply didn't wear any that night, and the shoes he was wearing were left somewhere in the house.

Also, the part of the money found wasn't serious evidence, since he could have hidden the rest somewhere and come back for it later.

In other words, it wasn't much, but it was enough to catch Michael's attention and plant a seed of doubt in his mind.

The previous night, the area had been snowed on heavily, and the temperature had dropped below 3°C.

The sun was high in the sky that day, and it was pleasantly cool. The detective, dressed in a black coat, arrived at police headquarters a few minutes before 10:30 a.m., where Chief Stan Anderson was waiting for him.

Michael had called ahead to make sure the chief would make time for him, and agreed to meet promptly at 10:30 a.m.

The detective entered the building and glanced at the clock on the wall behind the officer on duty.

10:26 a.m.

Excellent. He thought as he walked over to his desk.

"Detective Michael Williams, I have a meeting with my commander," he said, showing his badge.

"Come on in," the officer responded, pointing to the hallway behind him.

The man moved forward without answering. He knew this place well and knew exactly where he would find the chief's office. After a few seconds, he stood in front of the elegant brown door and knocked several times.

"Come in!" he heard in response.

At this signal, Michael pushed the door, and it gave way, opening inwards.

"Commander," he said after entering.

"Good morning, Detective..." Stan Anderson replied from behind the desk, glancing at his watch as if to make sure Michael hadn't arrived too late. "...please." He added, indicating one of the two chairs in front of him.

"Thank you."

The detective sat down.

"So, what brings you here?" the commander began the conversation.

"Yes, sir..." Michael gathered his thoughts. "...There's no easy way to say this, so I'll get straight to the point..." he paused for a moment as the commander fixed him with a watchful gaze.

Stan Anderson was a 57-year-old police officer with a distinguished record and accomplishments in his line of work. He had been an excellent detective before he was promoted to commander. After that, he lost some of his detective instincts, overwhelmed by bureaucracy and paperwork behind a desk.

However, he knew at that moment that the matter must be serious when one of his subordinates bothered to talk to him face to face.

"...I have reason to believe that an innocent man has been sentenced to death." Michael continued.

The commander's already wrinkled face gained additional wrinkles, especially on his forehead, his face taking on a serious and focused expression as he listened to the detective.

Indeed, this can be an extremely delicate and sensitive situation unless the detective has made a mistake.

"Please explain," he replied shortly.

"Of course, sir, the case from January 9th, a double murder with particular cruelty at a gas station, the victims, the owner of the boarding house and his concubine in an advanced pregnancy..." Michael recited from memory. "...the accused, Steward Johnson, 34 years old, identified by an eyewitness, a number of evidence were found in the apartment confirming the guilt..." he told the story and could see from the face of the commander that he was analysing every sentence he said in detail.

"...the revolver from which the shots were fired, the remnants of scattered gunpowder after the shot, the clothes stained with the victims' blood, some of the stolen money, and the surveillance footage also seem to confirm that Steward is on their trail."

"Forgive me, detective, I thought you came here to argue about this man's innocence? So far, everything you've said has undoubtedly presented his guilt."

"That's right, commander, because I was responsible for collecting this evidence and then presenting it in court," Michael replied.

"So, you did a great job, the culprit was convicted, so where do these doubts come from?"

"Not exactly, commander..." the detective gathered his thoughts again, this time to present a different point of view.

"...my doubts began when I discovered strange and inconsistent circumstances in this case, unfortunately, it happened too late, after the trial was over."

"I understand. What are these circumstances?"

"First, the convict suffers from a disorder commonly known as a split personality and does not know whether he actually committed the crime.

"Second, the surveillance footage shows the man firing the gun while holding it in his right hand, while the convict's other personality is left handed..." Michael noticed that he had caught the attention of the commandant.

"...third, I found two cartridges fired into the couch in the apartment, which were stuck in the floor, which may explain why the convict had gunpowder residue on his clothes, there is also the matter of the missing money from the robbery and the fact that I did not find a pair of shoes in the apartment that he could have been wearing that night, because it was raining heavily and all the shoes were completely dry, several hours after the murder..." he explained in detail.

"...as you can see, commander, I would like to file a motion to reopen the investigation."

The commander took a deep breath, clearly struggling with his own thoughts, not quite knowing how to interpret this.

On the one hand, in the first part of the conversation, he had heard a series of serious and hard evidence that he could not ignore.

On the other hand, the very fact that the detective deeply believed in the irregularities, to the point of deciding to present them, made the man want to consider them more carefully.

"I'll be honest with you, detective," the commander finally said.

I'm counting on it.

"From an investigator's point of view, I understand what you're saying..." he began to answer.

"...I have no doubt that you are a good detective, and I agree that something may not be entirely clear, but I would like to emphasise that this is my personal opinion, although as commander, I cannot agree to your request." He replied, much to Michael's disappointment.

"Of course." He said quietly.

"Mr. Williams, I don't have to tell you what the costs are if you reopen a previously completed investigation."

Michael looked up at his commander, expecting this to be another obstacle he wouldn't be able to overcome.

The budget issue for such an operation would be huge.

A dedicated team of officers would be required to focus exclusively on identifying any potential third parties involved in this crime, even though their existence is uncertain.

Each of these people would have to be paid for their time with public money, and in the end, there was no guarantee that it would be used in a useful way, and Michael knew that well.

Worse, the detective was not 100% convinced that he was right, which caused a mental block that prevented him from having a certain discussion with his commander.

The only thing he could do in this situation was to silently listen to his superior's final answer.

"Yes, sir."

"As I said, I think you're a really good detective, so you can probably guess how weak your arguments are." The commander looked at the man once again.

"Yes, sir."

"Don't get me wrong. I personally think there's something to it, but I also have superiors, and I can tell you right now that they won't agree to open an investigation based on circumstantial evidence, especially since the verdict has already been reached"

"I understand, sir."

The conversation was coming to an end, and Michael wasn't particularly devastated by her failure.

Mainly because he hadn't expected success, which somewhat set him up for an adverse reaction.

To quote Maya Angelou: "Hope for the best and prepare for the worst."

"Thank you for your time," Michael replied and turned to leave when he heard something behind him.

"But there's nothing stopping you from conducting your own, quiet investigation."

The detective turned to the commander.

"Yes, sir, that's exactly what I intend to do." He replied and smiled at the man knowingly.

7

The will to live.

"Freedom cannot be simply possessed, but must be constantly won, created. It can be used well or badly, in the service of a true or apparent good."

The next day, 06:58 a.m., January 26, 1982

I spent the rest of the previous day in my cell. I was afraid of what might happen in the walking yard that afternoon, and the looks from my fellow prisoners were unsettling.

I was new, no one knew me here, so I aroused curiosity.

But I didn't want to engage in conversation with anyone, because I knew where it could lead.

I expected questions like:

"What were you sentenced for?" or "How many years did you get?"

But contrary to popular belief, prisoners don't ask themselves this question.

In most cases, this information reaches the appropriate people before a new prisoner arrives, and those who have committed particularly heinous crimes simply try to keep them a secret and avoid the topic like the plague.

My self-preservation instincts had been neutralised by the strong medical supplies, and any correlation would not be a sensible idea in such a state.

Because in the event of immediate danger, I would not be able to defend myself since Gary would remain in a dormant state.

I decided not to make that mistake again.

Although I was afraid of the situations I might find myself in due to Gary's impulsive nature, I decided that I could not keep him locked up if he wanted to survive the reality of prison.

The people here were tough, and there was no place for cowards and wimps.

I did not consider myself a person who was easily intimidated. I had been through a lot in my life, including situations where I had to show strong character.

However, compared to the other men here, I could tell that I looked rather puny.

Most of the ones I had seen so far were gigantic.

They obviously spent a lot of time here working out and gaining more and more muscle mass.

I was intimidated by this fact, but Gary didn't care.

So, I decided to stop taking sedatives.

It was almost seven in the morning when I heard a key turning in the lock of my cell. It was time to take my pills.

Two guards escorted me to the white nurse's door, just as they had done the day before, where they had left me in the waiting room.

I already knew that I was not the only person in the centre who needed regular medical attention.

Because, almost exactly as punctual as the morning before, a large Latino man whose name I did not yet know emerged from the centre.

This gave me the idea that the next person to come after me would be a black man, just like the day before.

"Mr. Johnson, please come in," said the kind nurse, looking at me from the room.

I stood up and walked over to her, escorted by the guards.

"Please sit down. How are you feeling today?" she asked caringly.

"Fine, thank you," I replied without conviction.

"How are your new surroundings affecting your mental health? Were there any episodes with Gary yesterday?"

"No." I replied shortly.

I appreciated that she was concerned about my health, or maybe it was just supposed to look like.

Because it was unlikely that she would be particularly concerned about me after one meeting.

Either way, it was quite nice, and I appreciated her commitment.

"Remember, if something happens, you can always ask the guards for help."

"Yes, I will," I said, without even thinking about it.

If there was one thing I knew about prison, it was that you don't talk to the guards. There's nothing worse than being called a *snitch*.

If I got that label, it would stay with me for a long time, exposing me to mutilation by fellow prisoners at almost every opportunity, and I couldn't allow that. So, I ignored that advice.

"Okay, here are today's pills and a cup of water..." she said, handing me two glasses. "...please swallow them."

"I don't need a drink," I replied, taking only the cup with the pills.

In one movement, I put them in my mouth and hid them under my tongue, while tilting my head back to look like I was swallowing them.

"Okay, see you tomorrow."

"Goodbye," I replied and stood up.

Two guards approached me and escorted me back to the waiting room.

"20 minutes, gentlemen..." I heard the nurse instruct behind me. "...so, the pills can start working."

"Yes, ma'am," one of the men answered.

The white door opened, and a familiar figure appeared before my eyes: a Black guy. As I expected, he was next in line.

The man stood up and gave me a hostile look. However, I ignored it as the medicine slowly began to dissolve under my tongue, leaving an unpleasant chemical aftertaste in my mouth.

It completely caught my attention.

At that moment, I could think of nothing else but getting this disgusting substance out of my mouth as soon as possible. I sat down on a chair, and when I was sure that no one was looking at me, I faked a sneeze. I covered my mouth with my hand as if I didn't want to spread germs and spat out the pills.

Then I deftly hid them behind the elastic waistband of my pants, fastening them tightly so that they wouldn't slip out, and then discreetly spat out the remaining chemical taste. Making sure not to swallow any of it.

Some might say that this was careless on my part. However, I considered it pure self-preservation. A fact that would prove true over the next 60 minutes.

Time: 07:24 a.m.

I returned to my cell and waited for breakfast. Remembering yesterday's scenes, when the divided groups of men in the mess hall exchanged ominous glances, I wondered if the scores between them had already been settled or if the conflict was still ongoing.

I will choose the second answer.

This was a prison for dangerous criminals, and as you can probably guess, there was no such thing as *settled scores*.

There were always some conflicts. If you managed to take care of one thing, another one would appear and so on and so forth, endlessly.

The clock struck 8:00 a.m., and the cells opened. I went out onto the metal balcony to get in line like the rest.

"TURN RIGHT AND DOWN THE STAIRS!!" one of the guards from the ground floor ordered.

I did as I was told and walked forward, looking at the back of the man in front of me, then I heard a whisper behind me.

"Be vigilant in the canteen."

"Why?" I asked without turning around.

"Just be careful."

It seemed that my neighbour in the next cell decided to warn me.

Of course, that didn't explain anything, but this wasn't the place or time for explanations.

I had no choice but to take the stranger's words seriously and keep my eyes wide open.

Fortunately, my mind wasn't clouded, my instincts were working properly, which would soon save not only my life.

I reached the mess hall, where, as before, the groups were already divided, and there were only a few seats left.

I looked at the person who had spoken to me earlier. It turned out to be a black guy. What I could tell about him was that he stood out from the others in terms of his bearing and demeanour.

He was not as tall as the others and clearly looked worried about being out in the open. I thought then that he must be relatively new here as well.

However, after receiving a portion of his morning meal, he sat down with his companions, as did the other prisoners.

So, he's not new enough to have not been recruited yet, I thought, carefully observing the room from my seat.

I managed to sit down again facing the room, from where I had a good view of almost everyone present.

People were eating and talking, some were joking and laughing.

For a moment, I had the impression that everything looked completely normal, considering the circumstances, which lulled my vigilance a bit.

There is no indication that an incident will happen here. I thought.

My naivety was a mistake, and what seemed like a calm atmosphere was nothing more than the calm before the coming storm.

I noticed the real tension only when I watched the guards, who seemed to be particularly vigilant.

None of them were standing in their place, as they had been the day before. The men were constantly walking around and carefully observing each prisoner.

There were eight armed prison guards in all, all looking as if they were expecting to have to intervene at any moment.

This sight made me realise the seriousness of the situation, and my vigilance, once again, began to work at full speed.

Less than 10 minutes later, my attention, and everyone else's, was drawn to the sound of shouting to my right.

They were Latinos, and there had clearly been a misunderstanding between the two men.

"FUCK YOU, PUTO!" one of them said.

"FUCK YOU BITCH! I'LL FUCK YOU UP!!" the other shouted, jumping off his seat.

"HOW DID YOU FUCKING CALL ME?!?! YOU'RE FUCKING DEAD!!!"

With that, the men began punching each other. Within seconds, two guards were on them, trying to pull them away from each other.

The rest of the group also stood up, and a mass brawl broke out between them and the guards.

Food, cups, plastic trays, plates, and cutlery started flying.

"AGAINST THE WALL!!"

"EVERYONE AGAINST THE WALL!! NOW!!" One of the guards gave an order while the other pressed the alarm button to call for reinforcements.

At this point, six of the eight armed men were tearing at the fighting prisoners, while the other two were keeping everyone else on their toes as they moved to the other side of the room, away from the brawl, to prevent the chaos from spreading.

I watched the event, keeping my composure. My safety was not in immediate danger, so Gary felt no need to reveal himself.

I slowly made my way to the left side of the mess hall, blending into the crowd, following the guard's directions.

The entire time I watched the prisoners' fight, I couldn't shake the feeling that none of them had any intention of seriously injuring their men.

Having been in countless fights, I had plenty of experience. While Gary usually finished the fights that started, I had personally witnessed how it usually went.

At this point, I was looking at about 40 well built men fighting, plus six guards, none of them with a single wound that was bleeding.

Normally, under these circumstances, there would be a bloodbath here, but it wasn't.

It seemed suspicious to me, and I was right. This was a diversion.

I understood this the moment I noticed a man from that group, who, under the cover of chaos, was approaching the rest of the prisoners unnoticed. At first, I had no idea what the purpose of this was.

He could have just as easily not taken part in the fight and gone to stand by the wall like the others. But when I saw a split second of light glinting off something metal, he was trying to hide in his right hand, I knew that wasn't his intention.

He looked like he was walking straight at me, and everything happened at lightning speed.

The last thing I remembered before Gary woke up was his gaze. He was looking in my direction, and I thought he was going to attack me.

But as it turned out, his real target was standing right behind me.

"MOVE!! FAST!! AGAINST THE WALL!! EVERYONE AGAINST THE WALL!!" The guard shouted in a panicked voice, waiting for backup.

Meanwhile, the Latino gang member was discreetly approaching the men on the other side of the room.

His gaze was fixed on one of the Aryan Brotherhood leaders, who, along with the others, was slowly moving along the canteen wall toward the exit.

The armed prisoner was so focused on his target that he almost didn't notice the Steward standing in his way, but he was watching him from a distance of a few metres. Then the man with the large red moustache took a fighting stance.

His back was bent forward in such a way that he looked slightly shorter but much broader in the shoulders. The Latino caught his eye as his face changed from confused to a sinister smile.

Gary loved these situations; he knew exactly what to do and was not afraid of anyone.

This sight surprised the gang member a little. However, he had a job to do, and he was not going to stop at anything that could ruin his plans.

He was ready to kill anyone who got in his way. Especially since the person who had been on the blacklist for a long time was now standing just a few metres away from him and he could almost smell his blood. The man knew that he could not waste such an opportunity, because the second one would not appear.

In case of failure, the Aryan Brotherhood would double the protection of the bosses, and they would almost certainly want revenge.

But if he succeeded, their morale would drop, they would become weaker, and he would gain great respect among his own.

It's either now or never. He thought and exposed the blade of his homemade knife more.

"FASTER!! GET OUT!!" The guard shouted.

At that moment, the large double doors from the back opened, and a special unit armed with shields and pepper spray rushed in to suppress the riots.

At that signal, the man confidently moved forward; from now on, only a few seconds remained until the end of the chaos.

Seeing this, Gary grabbed the first prisoner he came across with his left hand and pushed him towards the knifeman with such force that he almost fell completely on him.

However, he nimbly dodged to the right side, avoiding a collision with the person flying towards him, who, after a while, fell on his stomach.

When the unaware Latino was passing the human shield, he looked ahead and saw a flying fist emerging from behind.

Gary, immediately after making his first move, jumped at the attacker and struck him with his left hand. It lasted only a few seconds and was intended to give the opponent no time to think. And it worked.

The left hook landed squarely on the man's jaw, which cracked, indicating an almost certain break. The attacker staggered on his feet, stunned by the powerful blow. But thanks to his muscle mass and apparently extensive experience in one-on-one duels, he managed to maintain his balance.

There was only one word in his mind: kill.

Then, in a quick movement, he delivered a knife blow, aiming for Gary's throat.

But he had expected such retaliation. He leaned to the left and grabbed his wrist with his left hand, twisting it painfully until he let the object slip out of his hand.

"AAAAA!!!" The attacker howled in pain, but he was not going to give up.

Taking advantage of the opportunity, Gary reached for a makeshift knife to gain an advantage in this fight. It was a mistake.

Because then he felt the man's knee, painfully hitting his front teeth.

Gary threw his head back after the blow. But he managed to get the knife.

The enraged man rushed at him, grabbed him low by the knee and knocked him down on his back. This turn of events made Gary angry.

Lying on his back with a strong attacker sitting on his stomach, preparing to punch him in the face mercilessly. Gary delivered the first knife blow to his ribs, then another and another.

"AAAA!!!" he shouted again.

The other prisoners watched as additional reinforcements of guards ran to the fighting men.

They pulled the bloody Latino man off Gary, then handcuffed both, then escorted them to the infirmary.

That day, Steward would learn that, thanks to Gary's intervention, he had gained both grateful friends and mortal enemies.

8

Role within the organization.

"It will still be beautiful, despite everything. Just put on comfortable shoes, because you have your whole life to go through."

Two days later, January 28, 1982. 5:45 p.m.

Edward Johnson was at his concubine, Stacy Brook's, apartment at Pebble Hills Park, getting ready for a trip to Mexico.

Steward's brother had a lot to do that day.

First, he met a real estate agent in the morning, with whom he made arrangements for the sale of the Johnsons' house at Horizontes del Sur.

Then he had to make his way to El Paso International Airport, where he met a man who gave him a package intended for his boss.

After that, Edward drove the package, which probably contained cash, to a safe location, and his last task was to drive to San Antonio with his companions.

"They'll be here soon; do we have everything?" he asked.

"Yes, passports, cash, everything is there," she replied.

"Remember that we probably won't be back here for the night, take whatever you need for yourself until the next day, I don't know, underwear, cosmetics, whatever you want," Edward said, standing by the window, looking out for the familiar vehicle.

"Just worry about yourself..." Stacy replied suddenly. "...I hope this time you won't go crazy like last time, and stay in some casino, all night." She added.

Edward looked at her furiously. He hated it when she reminded him of his passion for gambling.

But Stacy knew what she was talking about, because the man could often lose up to several thousand dollars at once.

It was enough for him to enter a place where you could gamble, after one or a few beers and the world ceased to exist for him.

Then he would fall into such a trance that no forces could tear him out of this state, until finally his wallet was empty, and he was forced to stop.

This caused a lot of trouble not only for Edward but also for Stacy.

However, since they both joined the Aryans gang, their fate had changed, and Stacy wanted it to stay that way.

"You don't tell me what I can and cannot do!" Edward said as he entered the kitchen, where the woman was.

In response, she looked at him with pity.

"You know very well that if it wasn't for me, you would have been in prison a long time ago or buried somewhere in the desert," she replied.

"Yeah, I know, I'm just joking," Edward walked up to her, grabbed her by the waist and pulled her closer to him. He then kissed her passionately; the woman didn't resist.

The dysfunctional relationship between them made perfect sense.

Edward, 36, a compulsive gambler and Stacy, 33, a heroin addict.

She kept him from losing his temper at the casino or anywhere else where money could be spent, and he kept Stacy from completely losing herself to addiction.

They lived together, supported each other, and now made money together. Managing to function this way for five years.

BOOM, BOOM, BOOM!!

There was a knock on the door.

"They're here," Edward said and started walking towards it.

When he opened it, he saw two men dressed in jeans, t shirts and long sweatshirts that covered their numerous tattoos.

They were neatly combed and shaved so as not to arouse suspicion.

"Come on in, we'll be leaving in a few minutes." He said.

"Do you have cash?" one of them asked.

"Yes, it's here..." he answered and started walking to the kitchen.

Stacy was standing next to a table with clear packages wrapped in ten thousand dollars.

"... a hundred thousand," he added.

"Okay, take them and come to your car. We need to hide this." The second man spoke up.

"Sure, Stacy, start packing," Edward replied and handed the concubine a black backpack.

"She's staying," the first man said suddenly.

The woman and Edward threw him a surprised look.

"But, why...?" Stacy asked. "...that's not what we agreed on."

"Well, plans have changed," he replied.

Stacy turned to Edward, looking for an answer in him.

"Don't worry about it, stay and I'll be back tomorrow with the money," he reassured her.

The woman was not happy with the turn of events, but there was nothing she could do about it. Orders came from above, and she knew it well.

Despite everything, Edward still had his share of the expedition, so the payout was certain.

The question was whether she could trust him not to indulge in a *little* game of poker along the way.

It was one of the reasons she preferred to keep an eye on him, but now she just had to trust him.

"Okay, pack this shit and let's go, time's running out," the second man ordered.

With that, Edward obediently walked over to the table and began to stuff the cash into a bag. Stacy, on the other hand, went to the living room, sulking.

A few minutes later. The woman was sitting on the couch, nervously flipping through the TV channels with the remote control.

Then the men began to leave her apartment. First, two newcomers came out, followed by Edward.

But before he left, he approached her to say his goodbye before leaving.

"Relax, I'll be back before you notice," he said and kissed her forehead.

After which he turned on his heel, only to disappear behind the door a moment later.

Stacy was angry.

She put the remote on the table in front of her and leaned to the left to reach into the small cabinet next to the couch, then opened the top drawer and pulled out aluminium foil, a roll of paper, and a lighter.

She put the roll in her mouth and tilted her head over the foil, under which she kept the lit lighter.

The black streak of brown powder residue turned into a slowly dripping drop, from which black smoke rose.

Stacy inhaled the smoke greedily through the pipe, and it went straight into her lungs, sending a euphoric feeling through her brain.

The woman placed the foil next to her and leaned back.

It didn't matter to her now whether she went to Mexico, stayed home, or anywhere else.

Then she would be happy in all circumstances.

Edward joined his companions at the back of the house, where his car was parked.

The men had managed to open the trunk by then and began unscrewing the casing at the back of the vehicle to make enough room to hide the money and several weapons.

They had to hide it all well in order to cross the border with Mexico without any problems and avoid arrest for smuggling.

But they had done this job many times and were professionals in their field.

They knew exactly how and where to place the smuggled goods, and at the same time, they were aware that the success of such an undertaking was associated with high costs.

If they got busted, they would undoubtedly be arrested and would be in danger not only from the Brotherhood but also from the Mexican cartel.

There was no room for mistakes in this business. So, the gangsters did their job efficiently and then put everything together so that there was no trace of anyone tampering.

Edward and Stacy had joined the Brotherhood a year ago.

For him, it was an easy and quick way to make money, and Stacy liked the fact that she had constant access to heroin.

While Edward was performing various tasks for the gang, sometimes smaller or larger, Stacy was distributing the drug.

They both risked their own safety for the good of the society, but the reward was worth the risk many times over, so they had no intention of backing out of a profitable share.

Stacy, however, had to be especially careful. Because, as a person taking the narcotic she was selling, she knew that she was acting against the principles of the Brotherhood.

Edward, on the other hand, felt very comfortable among his new brothers.

He shaved his head, leaving only a neat beard, and tattooed a clover with the initials AB on his wrist.

For a time, the man was willing to do almost anything for the gang.

He was not afraid of the consequences, knowing that he had a strong and ruthless group of people behind him.

This made Edward feel almost completely devoted, wrongly thinking that this situation in his life would last forever.

At that moment, he had no reason to suspect that the same people he called brothers at the time would be responsible for his death, in the agony that awaited him.

9

Personality imbalance.

"I have sought unity with all my strength and will continue to do so until the end."

2:35 p.m., January 29, 1982.

Yesterday I had another nightmare. It was the same dream that had been recurring almost every night since my release from captivity for two weeks.

I was 18 years old at the time. I was starved, beaten, mentally tortured and spent almost 14 days in total darkness, tied to a chair, fed once a day, and dressed only in a t shirt and jeans. That was when Gary was born in my head.

It was exactly what my dream looked like. I was in that horrible place again, feeling scared and helpless.

This nightmare kept recurring in my dreams until I started taking sedatives. Then, everything calmed down.

However, under the current circumstances, I was forced to stop taking them, so it was no surprise when the memories came back.

The new environment had a very negative effect on me from the beginning.

I was nervous and felt like I was constantly walking on the edge.

My consciousness fluctuated between me and Gary, and there was no way to prevent it.

This chapter in my life forced me to forget everything I used to do when I was free, including controlling a dangerous personality.

It put me in a situation where I was myself, locked in a cell, and outside it was Gary who took control.

However, it was not such a bad solution, especially since after the last incident in the cafeteria, I gained a lot of respect from the members of the Brotherhood.

I found out about it after I was released from solitary confinement, where I spent 48 hours.

At that time, I did not know what had happened. But I could guess because my front teeth were hurting, which indicated that I had gotten into a fight with someone.

Another clue was, of course, the fact that he was placed in solitary confinement, which is not something you end up in accidentally.

When I was taken back to my cell after serving my sentence, the first person to tell me what had happened two days earlier was the prisoner on the left side of the block.

I learned that I had allegedly saved the life of an important Brotherhood commander by blacklisting myself from a Latino gang.

This occurred because Gary nearly inflicted a fatal injury on an assailant whose objective was to eliminate the second in command of the Brotherhood.

Fortunately, the prisoner survived, which meant that I was not given an additional accusation of murder.

It was not something that was easy to accept.

On the one hand, I was glad that I had saved someone's life, even if I had not intended to, but on the other hand, I was terrified to discover that I had made mortal enemies from the very beginning of my stay in prison.

The only consolation in this situation was the knowledge that I would most likely be able to count on the protection of the Brotherhood, who were grateful for my quick reaction and for defeating the attacker.

However, that remains to be determined.

It was almost 3:00 p.m.

"Johnson, get up…" I suddenly heard the guard's voice. "…you have a visitor."

After these words, I jumped out of my bed.

I didn't expect anyone to visit me, although I secretly hoped that Ed would come to visit me soon.

"Who came?" I asked.

"You'll find out soon enough," the guard replied reluctantly.

"Yeah, thanks for the explanation."

I went to the bars so he could put handcuffs on me, then together we went to the visiting room.

"HEY YOU!! PUTO!! YOU ARE DEAD!! YOU'RE FUCKING DEAD!! DO YOU HEAR ME?!?! YOU'RE FUCKING DEAD ALREADY PUTO!!"

I suddenly heard from the depths of the room. Immediately, I felt my heart start to accelerate.

I couldn't see the person who was threatening me, but it was easy to tell that it was someone from the Latino gang.

Luckily, everyone was locked in their cells, which saved me from panicking so much that Gary had to show himself.

I took a deep breath and closed my eyes for a moment, still walking forward.

"Stop." I heard and looked ahead.

The guard was just approaching the gate to open it.

"YOU'RE FUCKING DEAD YOU HEAR!?!?!"

A scream rang out behind me.

Shivers ran through my body, and then the metal door opened with a squeak.

"Get in."

I obediently moved forward.

After a while, we walked down a long and gloomy corridor to the very end, where there was a room for visitors. As I walked further, the echo of footsteps began to resonate in my head.

...*TUP... TUP... TUP...*

The guard's heavy boots touched the surface, causing a loud sound that bounced off the walls in the empty space.

It was very quiet and peaceful here.

Even the air seemed cleaner, less polluted by the smells emitted by human bodies and their excrement.

I took a deep and relaxing breath. I thought then that maybe it was Ed who had come to see me.

Or maybe it was my lawyer, who should also be here soon.

Besides these two, no one else came to mind. So, I was very surprised when I saw the detective there who put me behind bars.

"Third chair," the guard announced when we arrived.

The long, spacious room was divided in half by thick glass. There was a total of ten seats on either side.

Each space was separated by walls to ensure privacy. Improvised telephones were installed so that individuals could communicate with each other securely, without concern of eavesdropping.

I walked over to the designated spot where Michael Williams was already waiting for me. Before sitting down, I looked around.

There were only two other people besides me and the detective, and I was happy with that state of affairs.

I pulled out the chair to sit in it, keeping my eyes on the officer.

What could he possibly want from me...? I wondered. *...I guess everything has already been said.*

My surprise turned into curiosity.

Michael looked straight into my eyes, and then I realised something was on his mind.

His look gave it away, and it was different from before.

During the interrogation and subsequent meetings, I saw him look at me with a spark of inquisitiveness and even anger.

But now I registered none of those emotions. Instead, there was something I could describe as pity. It was hard to tell exactly what had caused this change, but I could definitely see that he was peaceful.

So, I took a seat and a moment later picked up the receiver. Michael did the same.

"Detective," I said.

"Hello, Steward, how are you?"

"I've had better days."

"I don't doubt it."

"To what do I owe this visit?" I asked.

"I'm here to talk to you about your conflicts."

I frowned, surprised.

About my conflicts? I thought.

"I don't know what I should understand by that," I answered truthfully.

"How many enemies do you have outside?"

"You don't want me to start listing them, you'd have to write something like a telephone book," I replied.

Michael smiled to himself.

"So many?"

"Yeah, because you see, I'm not the type of person who avoids alcohol, and where there's alcohol, there are also problems...."

I answered, leaning my elbows on the counter.

"...it's not exactly like I made enemies myself, only somewhat, most of them appeared after Gary's antics," I added.

"I understand, but I mean someone who would really want to ruin your life, even to the point of murder."

After these words, I stared at him more intently. At this point, I was completely thrown out of the flow.

To commit murder? I quoted his words in my mind, and then the faces of men I had dealt with in the past began to appear before my eyes.

"This is not a question he could answer right away, and I would need time to think about it."

"Absolutely, think about it..." Michael replied. "...it would be good if you could write down some names and surnames," he added.

"Yes, I think I can do that."

"Excellent, so I'll be back in a few days."

"But what is it about?" I asked, confused.

"I'll tell you honestly, Steward, I just don't want you to get any false hopes, because it's a long shot..." the detective began.

"...I think you might have been framed." he confessed suddenly.

15 minutes later, I was back in my cell.

All sorts of thoughts were running through my head, all thanks to the conversation with the detective.

I wondered what the person who had recently been gathering evidence of my guilt in the crime for which I had ultimately received the highest sentence, the death penalty, was getting at.

Could it be that he has changed his mind...? I thought. *...if so, is there a chance that I will be acquitted?*

It was difficult for me to understand what I should deduce from such a confession.

"...I think you could have been framed," the policeman's words came to mind.

"If that's what he thinks, then he probably has a good reason for it..." I talked to myself, walking around my personal space.

"...he wouldn't make such statements without evidence, so he must already have something." I decided.

Such an unexpected turn of events took me completely by surprise.

At that time, the only normal reaction on my part was to question everything that had happened up to that point. The lack of conviction in my innocence turned into serious doubts then.

The sense of a deserved punishment was replaced by a taste of injustice, and the remorse over taking the lives of innocent people turned into a desire for revenge.

It also became obvious that from that moment on, I had to make every effort to help the detective get to the bottom of this case as best I could.

However, the lack of any memories from that fateful evening effectively hindered my options.

I also couldn't forget, even for a moment, where I was currently.

The constraints of incarceration significantly restricted my options, necessitating the initial step of compiling a list of prospective suspects.

But before I could focus on that, I had to give my full attention to my safety first, because it was almost 5 p.m., which meant I could spend another 90 minutes outside, which I wanted to take advantage of.

I found myself outside a few minutes after 5 p.m. The frosty weather was already making itself felt in the place where I picked up my jacket, but only after opening the metal door did the cold air enter my nostrils, settling unpleasantly inside.

I winced a bit from the sensation.

The temperature that day was below zero, the frosty air blew over the open space of the exercise yard and the people there.

The hard and frozen ground, on which there were puddles from the recent rainfall, was only suitable for walking.

The basketball courts and metal exercise equipment were useless, most of which had frozen to each other.

Therefore, the prisoners mostly sat in their own groups or walked around the square, the size of a football pitch, surrounded by high, grey walls with four watchtowers placed in each corner.

I walked in line between a several metre high metal fence secured with barbed wire at the top. When I first arrived at the area designated for physical exercise for inmates, my attention was immediately drawn to the guards, who were walking along the walls with shotguns in their hands.

The next thing I wanted to establish right away was the division of the gang territory.

For my own safety, I wanted to stay away from everyone and just spend my time outdoors in peace.

However, it soon became clear that the hostile prisoners had completely different plans.

I walked a few steps to the right, where there were wooden benches to sit on.

I didn't want to stay there, though, and I just wanted to stop in one place for a moment before moving on.

In the distance, near the basketball court, I noticed a group of light brown men taking up most of the area, and I realised that this must be the area of the Latino gang.

Not far from them stood another group, Blacks, while the Whites, Aryans, were near the area with the exercise equipment. In addition to them, there were many people hanging around, also divided by race.

I stood safely by the fence and watched the area. Behind me stood a guard station.

Looking at the different men, I got the impression that each one was bigger than the other, and together they looked extremely menacing.

This worried me, but fortunately not enough to lose control of myself.

I waited a few minutes and found a moment when I could calmly join the others, so that the distance in front of me was as satisfactory as the one behind me.

Only then was I sure that I was far enough from the others. I put my hands in the pockets of my orange jacket and moved forward.

After a moment, I realised that I was attracting a lot of attention.

The group that drew the most attention to me was the Latino gang, for reasons I already knew, but in addition to them, I noticed a few Blacks who were also looking at me.

These were not friendly looks.

I quickly realised that after the incident in the cafeteria a few days ago, I had made a lot of enemies, and not only from one group.

I glanced at the Aryans furtively and noticed that only from them was no one looking at me.

I didn't know what to make of this.

On the one hand, I hoped that after almost inadvertently saving one of their commanders, I would receive recognition.

But then again, I had no idea what the fraternity recruitment process was like.

At this point, it was best not to think about it and just stay alert for the next hour until our time outside was over.

A moment later, I was a dozen or so metres from where the Latinos were standing.

That's when I noticed a few of them, not taking their eyes off me, talking to each other, and then two of them stood up and started walking towards me.

Oh, shit. I thought.

My heart was racing with each passing second.

"Calm down..." I said to myself under my breath. "...maybe it's just a coincidence."

...CRUNCH... CRUNCH... CRUNCH...

I focused on the sound coming from under my feet as I stepped on the frozen ground.

...CRUNCH... CRUNCH... CRUNCH...

I listened to my surroundings and breathed deeply, trying to stay calm. I looked towards the two men who were getting closer.

...CRUNCH... CRUNCH... CRUNCH...

They're coming for me. I thought.

The moment I realised I was in trouble, I suddenly heard loud footsteps right behind me.

...CRUNCH!! CRUNCH!! CRUNCH...!!

That's when I got a hard blow to the back of my head. That was the last thing I remembered because then Gary showed up.

The muscular black inmate punched Steward in the back of the head so hard that he almost immediately fell face down on the ground.

At that signal, two Latinos ran to jump at the fallen man and finish the job, which immediately caught the attention of the guards.

Steward's consciousness was taken over by Gary, who, despite the powerful blow, quickly turned his back to the ground and kicked the attacker in the left shin with his right foot.

The kick, delivered with incredible speed and precision, caused the attacker's leg to jump back.

He then stood on his left leg for a second, surprised by the retaliation, which could not support the weight of his body, so he staggered and fell on Gary, who was still lying on the ground.

However, Gary, thinking quickly, had foreseen such a turn of events, so before the huge man fell on him, he skilfully rolled away so as not to be crushed.

The painful injury to the attacker's leg effectively eliminated him from the fight, at least for the next few minutes. That was enough.

Gary stood up, and at that moment, one of the Latinos threw himself at him, causing him to land on the ground again.

The man sat on him and punched him square in the jaw, then tried to punch him a second time, but Gary dodged the blow at the last second, and his fist hit the frozen ground.

The attack, at a frantic pace and under the influence of adrenaline, caused the prisoner, having no control over his strength, to hit the hard ground with all his strength and feel it painfully.

Gary took the opportunity to grab him by the jacket with both hands and yank him to the right with all his might, causing him to fall on his side like a rag doll.

TUUUUUU…!!! The alarm was triggered.

"GET DOWN ON THE GROUND!! EVERYONE GET DOWN ON THE GROUND!!

Someone shouted through a megaphone.

Gary briefly observed the fence wall before rising to his feet. There, next to the guardhouse, he noticed a guard who was just aiming a shotgun at him.

Then he turned towards the last opponent who was still ready to attack him, and moved towards him. He took a few steps, then quickly crouched down, and at that moment, a shot rang out.

The guard aiming at his back missed, because his target suddenly disappeared from sight.

Instead, he hit the person Gary was standing in front of. The gang member was shot in the right shoulder with a rubber bullet.

"AAAA!!" he screamed in pain.

The force of the impact caused him to almost completely rotate around his own axis, after which he fell to the ground.

Gary was already lying on his stomach, calmly waiting for the workers who would arrive at any moment to restore order.

Three hours later.

I woke up lying on my bunk and didn't remember what had happened. Although experiencing some facial discomfort, I felt a peculiar sense of gratification.

I then heard distinct footsteps outside my cell.

I thought that in a moment, I would probably hear the characteristic sound of a lock being unlocked and someone telling me to get up, as it usually happens in such circumstances.

To my surprise, the footsteps suddenly stopped and then started again. I frowned in surprise and stood up to see what was going on.

I went to the bar and noticed a small note in the lower right corner. I picked her up and returned to my seat to sit down.

I then began to unfold a piece of paper that had been folded several times, the text of which read:

"Test passed, you may join the brotherhood."

10

Mission accomplished, part 1.

"I believe that the more you love, the more you do, because love, which is nothing more than a feeling, I couldn't even call it love."

Three days later, February 1, 1982.

It was approaching 10:00 p.m., as Edward slowly walked toward the border crossing into America from Mexico.

He was bloodied and beaten, without a vehicle or companions.

The only thing the cartel members allowed him to keep was his passport and a $100 bill so he could somehow get home.

He was approaching the city of Juarez in the state of Chihuahua. There, he planned to stay in a cheap hotel and get himself ready before continuing his journey to cross the border.

He had to walk nine miles to get to Miles' house, and unless someone took pity on him and picked him up off the street, he would be forced to walk that distance. But at that moment, he had no chance of convincing the stranger that he was not a threat, because he looked terrible.

His clothes were stained with the blood of the two colleagues whose bodies he had had to carry with his own hands less than an hour ago.

Exhausted, he could barely drag his feet along the ground.

He had a black eye, and blood was seeping from his right ear from being hit in the temple with a gun.

There was no way anyone would take him to a car in this condition, let alone be allowed to cross the border without any problems.

So, the only thing he could think about was stopping somewhere for the night, resting up, and figuring out exactly what he was going to tell his boss about the disastrous journey he had survived out of the three person crew of the brotherhood.

Finally, after more than an hour of walking, he reached the first buildings on the outskirts of the city.

From a distance, he noticed that the city was bustling with life.

The colourfully decorated buildings, loud music, and the sounds of people laughing indicated that some kind of festival was taking place, which he had no idea about, but he didn't care much.

Exhausted, he continued towards the city centre. A few minutes later, he passed a beautifully lit, historic church with two towers.

Not far from there, he noticed a building with a large sign saying *Hotel* and headed there.

A moment later, he entered, and his eyes met the spacious and neatly furnished hotel lobby.

The place was empty, the guests were clearly either out on the town or hiding in their rooms; either way, Ed was happy with such a situation.

He slipped through town and still didn't want anyone to see him.

Inside, a young man sat behind the reception desk on the left side of the entrance.

When Ed approached him, he immediately stood up from his seat to greet the new guest.

But the smile on his face, clearly developed over the years specifically for talking to strangers, disappeared and was replaced by a look of confusion.

"Buenas noches, ¿hablas inglés?" Ed asked.

"Yes sir." The young man with the name tag Jose pinned to his white shirt replied, maintaining complete professionalism.

"Great, I need a room for tonight."

"Of course, we have rooms available. Would you like a single or a double?"

"Single."

"Absolutely, that'll be 800 pesos."

Edward placed a hundred-dollar bill on the counter and held it up to the receptionist.

"Here..." he spoke. "...you'll change it tomorrow morning."

"I can change it for you right here. We do it for our guests." The man replied suddenly.

"Okay, that's even better, change me 50 dollars, do you have a phone here?"

"Of course, it's right here next to the reception desk."

The receptionist pointed to the phone hanging on the wall.

"Okay, I need to make a call. In the meantime, you get the money ready for me," Edward replied.

"Here's some change for you for the machine." Jose held out his hand to Ed to give him the money.

He picked it up and, without a word, went to the pay telephone.

The receptionist watched him go and discreetly shook his head in disapproval. As a long-time hotel employee, Jose had seen all sorts of scenes involving American vacationers.

Although his first impression upon seeing Ed was one of concern about his appearance, he remained calm.

Since this was not the first and probably not the last time a beaten and dirty American had sought refuge there.

Meanwhile, Ed walked over to the phone, picked up the receiver, and inserted a few coins into the machine to activate the machine.

When he heard the long beep, he knew he could start dialling the number.

A moment later, he connected.

"Hello?" a female voice answered.

"Hi Stacy, it's me, we made it, we are in business," Ed said.

12 hours earlier.

For the first time since Steward had been in prison, his older brother Edward was planning to visit him.

The man had wanted to do it earlier, but something always came up and he couldn't find the time, until now.

Although he had been ordered to go to Mexico that day, the planned departure wasn't until late afternoon, so he figured he had enough time to meet up with his brother.

It was after 10:00 a.m. when Ed left Stacy's apartment and went to the back of a local bar to pick up a bag of money that he would need later in the trip.

While this was standard procedure, it was different every time.

To avoid suspicion, the funds were always picked up from different locations. Sometimes it was a bar, sometimes even a hair salon.

Basically, it could be any place that belonged to the Aryan Brotherhood.

The cash was then transported to a safe location, in this case Stacy's apartment, where it was sprayed with a special substance that smelled like homemade pepper spray to deter the tracking dogs at the border.

Then it was additionally wrapped in black duct tape.

The money was always packed in stacks of $10,000 each, with only the total amount varying.

The smallest was one hundred thousand, the largest was half a million, because it was impossible to fit more into the interior of the car.

Ed returned to his girlfriend's apartment a few minutes after 12 with a black duffel bag filled with money.

Immediately after entering, he went to the kitchen and put it on the table. At that time, the woman was preparing the things she needed to complete the next part of the task.

Stacy Brook was a 36 year old former chemistry student.

Extremely intelligent, with an excellent understanding of chemical compounds, she once had a bright future.

Unfortunately, fate would have it that she found herself among the wrong people, who effectively distracted her from her studies and did not allow her to further develop her career.

The woman eventually dropped out of college, allowing her life to sink into the world of drugs, addictions and lawlessness.

However, some of the knowledge she once acquired has remained with her to this day, which is why she was able to easily create, for example, a product whose ingredients resembled pepper spray.

"Take it and get to work, I'm going to Steward's." Ed said.

"What are you going to tell him?"

"Nothing, I won't say anything that he won't ask," Ed replied.

"Fine, it's better if he doesn't know anything."

"I think so too, I basically want to see how he's doing there, if Gary hasn't already gotten him murdered."

"It's quite possible, or at least that he'll get into some serious trouble," Stacy admitted.

"I'll tell you how it looks when I get back, start packing, you've got about three hours."

"No problem, how much is in it?"

"300,000."

"Okay, it'll be ready by the time you get back. What time will the company show up?" Stacy asked.

"Planned at four, but they can be earlier, so hurry up, the sooner you finish, the better."

"Okay, go already." The woman said and walked up to Ed to kiss him.

The man grabbed her by the waist and pulled her closer to him, then kissed her passionately.

"From today, everything will change, you'll see." He said.

"I know, as long as they let you go."

"They'll let me go and they'll thank me." Ed replied.

"We'll see." Stacy replied and slipped out of his embrace.

"I'm going, see you."

Edward replied, and a moment later, he disappeared behind the door. Stacy feared the worst.

The woman knew perfectly well that they were playing a very dangerous game.

The risks were lurking on all sides. If something went wrong, Ed might not return home after his upcoming trip to Mexico.

At the same time, there was a possibility that the brotherhood would find out about their intrigue, and then they would both be in mortal danger from them.

The risk was great, but the reward was even greater.

It was almost 2:00 p.m. when Ed parked his car in the parking lot and headed toward the entrance to the Allan B. Polunsky Unit, where Steward was currently housed. The large, brown brick building made the man uneasy.

He had never been locked in there himself, but he knew people who were either currently inside or had been there before and had told him about the place.

Adding to his concerns was the fact that Ed was not entirely law-abiding and had mixed feelings about the building he might one day end up in, which was swarming with law enforcement officers.

Still, he knew Steward was waiting for him, and he couldn't let him down, so he took a deep, relaxing breath and walked confidently toward the entrance.

As the man entered the plant, he was approached by two tall employees.

"What is the purpose of your arrival?" one of them asked.

"Visiting." Ed replied.

"Who are you visiting?" the second added.

"My brother, Steward Johnson."

"Of course, please come with me to the side." The first employee pointed to the customs office on the left.

The three men moved further away from the entrance.

"Please empty your pockets." Ed heard and obediently began to take out everything he had on him: wallet, lighter, pack of cigarettes and car keys.

"Is that all?"

"Yes, I have nothing else," Ed replied truthfully.

"Okay, please stand facing the wall."

Edward walked to the indicated place and carried out the order.

"Hands high on the wall and spread your legs."

After taking this position, he felt the security guard pat his body from legs to torso.

"Now, turn around."

Ed found himself face to face with a tall man who checked his jacket and pants pockets before glancing around his belt.

"Okay," he confirmed after making sure.

"Now you can go to that window," the employee pointed out, another checkpoint he had to go through before he was allowed to enter.

After collecting his belongings, Ed continued on his way, still feeling like two security guards were watching him closely.

"Hello, sir, can I see your ID, please?" the Black woman said as he approached her.

"Here you are," he said, handing her a plastic card with his information.

"Who are you visiting today?"

"My brother, Steward Johnson."

"Of course, visiting hours end at 4 p.m.," the woman said while typing on her computer keyboard the data from Ed's ID. "...you can stay until then; all conversations take place in the presence of guards."

"Alright."

"I'm glad. Here's your pass, this guard will escort you further, you can collect your ID at the exit, are there any questions?" saying this, he called out to the employees who had been watching them from the corridor gate.

"No, thank you."

"Please follow me," he suddenly heard a male voice from behind him.

Ed turned around, and a moment later, he was walking past the guard down the long corridor to the visiting room, with a badge with the word *Visitor* pinned to his chest.

11

New Allies.

"Man cannot live without love. Man remains an incomprehensible being for himself, his life is meaningless unless love is revealed to him, if he does not encounter love, if he does not touch it and make it his own in some way, if he does not find living participation in it."

Two days earlier, January 27, 1982.

I was woken by the guards at six in the morning, and this was to become my routine.

Due to the incidents in the cafeteria and the exercise yard, I had been classified as a high-risk prisoner.

The authorities decided to put me first in line of people who took their meds each day.

To put it simply, I was picked up an hour early to avoid confrontation with other men.

Personally, it didn't matter to me because, firstly, I woke up at that time myself, and secondly, I was not taking medication, as was generally believed, so I felt that I could count on Gary's help at any time.

However, that day I had reason to believe that this day would be completely different from the previous ones, and all because of a note that had been left in my cell the day before.

This made me curious about what might happen.

After visiting the nurse and waiting 10 minutes in the waiting room for the pills I had in my hand to take effect, I was ready to go back to my cell, where I would stay until breakfast.

Before I left, the guards signalled that they were ready to bring in another patient.

Thanks to that, on my way upstairs, I noticed a huge Latino man, who had been number one on the list until now, coming out of one of the cells on the ground floor.

I found out from Tony, a Black inmate from the next cell with whom I sometimes talked, that the guy's name was Luis Ramirez and that he was the leader of a gang of his compatriots here.

This fact did not surprise me at all; on the contrary, I would have been disappointed if he had performed any other function than management.

Luis noticed me from a distance and gave me a blood-curdling look.

Just as I thought, they're not done with me yet. I thought to myself.

I had no doubt that I had seriously offended a significant portion of the prison population, but fortunately, my position would soon change, and I would be able to breathe a sigh of relief. But not yet.

I looked away from Luis so as not to provoke him and thus not to lose control of myself.

I didn't suspect that the gang leader would want to take revenge on me personally; it was different with his subordinates.

I expected that they would attack at any moment if they had the opportunity.

The time spent in the cafeteria was the worst because I had already witnessed what they were capable of, and I saw no obstacles to preventing them from doing the same thing again.

Therefore, I decided that I must contact the Brotherhood as soon as possible, additionally motivated by the invitation.

At eight o'clock, I left my cell as usual to line up with the others on the balcony, and then we all headed to the diner.

"What a show you put on yesterday..." Tony said, following me. "...I've never seen anything like that in my life, for a moment I thought you were going to get killed there," he added enthusiastically.

"Yeah, sure, I wish I could remember anything from it," I replied reluctantly.

"You don't remember anything? The adrenaline must have really fucked you up, hehe...."

"It's not as easy as it seems. Maybe I'll explain it to you later," I replied.

"You know you'll have to watch your ass now; the Latinos will definitely want to get you."

"I'm aware of that, " I added.

My acquaintance with Tony began the day he warned me about the brawl that was going to happen during the morning meal.

Since then, I've talked to him occasionally.

Tony was a 25 year old Black boy raised in Brooklyn, New York.

Tall and thin, eloquent and cunning, the type of man who could find his way in any situation and come to an understanding with anyone.

I liked him, but I remembered that when I joined the Brotherhood, I would have to break off all relations with him because of the colour of his skin.

These were the rules, and although I did not create them or necessarily agree with them, adherence was necessary to ensure my safety.

I got to the canteen and grabbed my food, then looked around to find a seat, when I heard a loud whistle that immediately caught my attention. It turned out that it came from the side designated for members of the brotherhood, and the one who made it was calling me to join them.

Hesitantly but determinedly, I moved in that direction.

It was then that I met John for the first time, the head of the Aryan Brotherhood on the prison side, and I immediately felt respect for him.

He was bald, well muscled, with an elegantly groomed black beard and moustache.

However, what distinguished him most was his glasses, round and sunglasses.

He resembled Charles Bronson, a famous criminal of British origin.

It was undoubtedly not something generally available to inmates, but as it later turned out, John had greater access to contraband due to his arrangements with the prison guards.

"Hey, new guy…" John greeted me with a voice full of confidence. "…Sit with us."

I sat down next to him, feeling the eyes of all the fraternity members on me.

I didn't feel comfortable, but I knew I had to keep a straight face if I wanted to survive.

The conversations revolved mostly around everyday prison matters and future plans.

John seemed to be well informed about what was happening both inside and outside the prison walls.

"I heard you're having some problems with Tony," John said out of the blue.

I was surprised by the question, but I tried to stay calm.

"No, no problems," I replied shortly.

John looked at me carefully for a moment, as if assessing whether I was telling the truth.

Then he nodded and went back to talking to the other members of the fraternity.

My mind was racing with thoughts. I knew I had to be careful not to betray any feelings or insecurities. Every word could be used against me.

The time spent at the table dragged on forever. Although the fraternity's conversations were full of suggestions and half words, I understood that my place in the group depended on how well I could adapt to their reality.

Even though I still had doubts deep down, I knew that for my own safety, I had to play by their rules.

I quickly realised that the eyes of the Brotherhood were everywhere; if they already knew about my conversations with Tony, they knew everything I could do when I thought no one was watching me.

The comprehensive surveillance was justified in my opinion, and asking about the Black neighbour in the cell next door was just a sly move to see what kind of relationship we had.

I dodged the bullet successfully, but as a non-member of the fraternity, I remained on the sidelines and could drop out at any moment.

"I'll meet you in the exercise yard..." John turned to me again. "...we'll have more time to talk there."

"Sure," I replied.

My thoughts began to circle around the upcoming meeting in the exercise yard. I knew it would be a key moment that could decide my future in the fraternity.

The exercise yard was a place where anything could happen, both good and bad. I looked around the room and realised how many people were staring at me.

On one side were Luis and his soldiers, on the other, Jayson, the leader of the black population of the prison, to which Tony belonged.

I knew that nothing good would come of me attracting so much attention, although Tony would have warned me if there was any danger coming from them, but as for the Latinos, I had no idea.

Fortunately, John was willing to meet with me that afternoon, which could mean that I would be drawn into the brotherhood structure and gain much-needed protection.

Later that day.

I went out into the yard with the others from my sector. It was 5:00 p.m., and the cold January weather was not giving up.

Once outside, Tony immediately headed towards his men, and I looked around for John and his team.

Against the background of a large space, there was a large group of White men, who at that time were still a minority of the prison population and disappeared quite easily among the others, so I noticed them after a while.

Although the *Aryans* were a much smaller group, they had the most influence both inside and outside the facility, making them the most respected organisation by both the prisoners and the people working there.

Just a few minutes later, as I approached John, I felt the sharp gazes of the other prisoners pierce through me.

The tension was almost palpable. I knew I had to keep my cool and not let my fears show.

John, standing at the head of his team, motioned for me to come closer.

"We've been waiting for you..." he said in a calm but determined tone. "...are you ready for what's going to happen today?"

I nodded, trying not to show any emotion. I knew this would be a crucial moment that would determine my future.

John turned and pointed to the circle of men standing around him.

My fate was in their hands.

"I've had you under surveillance since you almost killed that Latino in the canteen," he confessed suddenly.

"Oh, yeah?"

"Yes, I know that you saved my brother's life then, I like you, you are similar to us, you have principles and certain values, you would be a valuable asset," he replied.

I wondered why John decided to pull this card now.

Was this supposed to be a test of my loyalty, an attempt to establish my place in the hierarchy?

Subconsciously, I straightened up, preparing myself for what was to come.

"This is Jack..." John nodded towards him. "...he is our brains of the operation."

Jack, a tall white man with blond hair and blue eyes, with a large swastika tattooed on his neck, emerged from behind him.

Although he wasn't as heavily muscled as the others.

I immediately noticed a glint of extraordinary intelligence in his eyes.

His gaze was sharp and penetrating, and I felt as if he was reading me like an open book.

But I still had one surprise in store that he hadn't expected, and which I would reveal soon.

The biggest problem in all of this was that John had Gary on his mind the entire time.

The fact was, he had actually saved Jack, and it was he who deserved the gratitude of the brotherhood, not me.

Despite this, I continued in my role without revealing my emotions, aware that I would soon need to disclose the truth.

"The second confrontation in the yard was partly arranged by us," John added.

"Partly?" that intrigued me.

"Yeah, you were supposed to get a beating from that black guy, and the guard was ordered to intervene the moment the situation got out of control..." Jack joined the conversation.

"...we didn't expect the Latinos to attack at that particular time, but you did a great job anyway," he added.

"I understand." I replied uncertainly.

"The truth is that we rule here, in one way or another, everyone knows it, from the janitor to the warden, the blacks listen to us and the latinos too, it's only recently that they've started having problems, but you'll find out about that later. Are you ready to join the brotherhood?" John asked.

"Yes, but there's something you need to know about me first," I replied.

"What is it?"

"That person you saw in the cafeteria and later here during the fight wasn't me."

John frowned in surprise; I noticed the same expression on Jack's face.

The other people who had surrounded us until now also seemed confused as to what I meant.

"What are you saying?" John asked, staring at me in disbelief.

"It was Gary, my second personality, who takes control of me when I sense danger." I confessed.

John looked at Jack, as if looking for confirmation of the truth of my words, then fixed me with a watchful gaze.

"Really? Show me," he said after a moment.

"Excuse me?" I asked in disbelief.

"Show me, I want to see him," he added and made a gesture with his head.

At this signal, two of his men grabbed my arms, twisting them painfully behind my back.

"AAAA!!" I screamed in pain. "...what ... what the fuck are you doing?!"

"BULLSHIT?! Do you think I'm an idiot?"

John got angry, and those were the last words I remembered before Gary appeared.

Jack and John watched in disbelief as Steward's face changed.

At that moment, the man's scared and confused expression changed to one of satisfaction and excitement, and a sinister smile appeared on his lips.

The two fraternity members were still holding Gary's hands high on his back, and he leaned back even further, raised his right leg high and landed it with all his force just above one of their feet, hitting the exact spot called the anterior talofibular ligament and consequently breaking it right there.

"FUUUCK!!" the man screamed and let go of his hand.

Gary took advantage of this, swinging hard and hitting the other attacker in the stomach, causing him to drop his hand, freeing him.

Just when he was about to attack John, John stood confidently in front of him and said:

"Hello Gary, welcome to the brotherhood."

12

Mission accomplished, part 2.

*"There is in the human body the ability to express love, this love
in which man becomes a gift."*

Edward entered the visiting room with the guard.

He disliked this place more and more by the minute. Even though this part of the building was only directly connected to the prison a few dozen metres away, Ed thought that the smell of death was almost palpable, and he was instantly struck by the atmosphere of the place. Feelings of ruined lives and lost hopes.

"Wait by number three, your brother will come to you soon." The guard declared.

He walked further, past the rough walls, and a guard stood in the corner of the room, closely watching every move.

Besides him, there were six others present: two uniformed officers on either side of the glass wall and two women visiting their loved ones. Ed happened to be the only white person in the room, which annoyed him even more.

He took seat number three, and after a few minutes, he heard the metal door to his right open, accompanied by the sound of chains clanging against each other, of the person bound in them. A man with a sad face and tired eyes, dressed in standard prison garb, entered the room. His gaze met Ed's, and something like recognition appeared in his look. The guard showed him to a seat on the other side of the glass partition.

"Hello, brother," the man said, sitting down across from Ed and placing his hands on the table.

His voice was quiet and resigned, but at the same time, it exuded a certain calm that eased the tension in the air a little. Ed studied his interlocutor for a moment, trying to find in his face any traces of the old life the man might have led.

"Good to see you, Stew, how are you holding up?" Ed asked into the receiver, although he knew that in this place, the question made little sense.

The man on the other side of the glass held the black receiver to his ear with his handcuffed hands and smiled sadly.

"How am I holding up...?" He repeated. "...it depends on the day, sometimes I feel like I'm already dead, and sometimes... sometimes I think that maybe one day I'll be free again."

Ed nodded, not knowing what to say.

The room was silent, broken only by the occasional sound of conversation from other visitors. Ed knew that this moment, however brief, was the only connection the man on the other side of the glass had with the outside world.

"Sorry I didn't come earlier, I really wanted to, but something always came up." He confessed after a moment.

"Okay, you have your own life to lead and I, well, I'm not going anywhere," Steward replied, a slight smile appearing on his face.

"Yes, you know what it's like, living in a constant rush, but tell me, how are you coping? Gary's not causing any problems?"

"Contrary to appearances, I'm coping quite well. I started taking the pills again, but I think the most important thing is that I was invited to the Aryan Brotherhood, for now they're giving me a year's trial period." Steward said unexpectedly.

This made Edward take his hands off the table and tuck them under it to hide the clover tattooed on his wrist with the capital letters AB inside.

Even though he had been a member of the association for a long time, he didn't expect his brother to join them as well.

He didn't want Steward to know about it, because his past might come to light, and he wanted to appear as someone who had gotten over his gambling addiction and was living a normal, honest life.

"Are you sure this is what you want? They are ruthless. If you join, they will never let you go, you know that?" He finally asked.

"I know, but I have no other choice if I want to live to see my sentence. I'm a dead man walking; I have nothing to lose." Steward replied.

"Do you really think so?"

"Yes, the Mexican Mafia has me in their sights, but the BGF might as well get to me first. I'm a completely defenceless white man in a coloured prison, people like me won't last long here unless I have backup."

"I understand, I suspect you know what you're talking about, so I won't tell you what you should do since I have no idea what the realities are there," Ed replied.

"That's right, but there's something else..." Steward changed the subject. "...remember that cop who put me here?"

Edward frowned thoughtfully.

"Yes, I remember him, Michael something."

"Yeah, he came a few days ago to talk to me."

At this news, Ed's eyes widened, and his face showed a mixture of surprise and concern.

"What else could he possibly have to talk about with you? I guess he's done his job, what else could he want from you?" He asked in disbelief.

"It's just that he has doubts about the incident; he thinks I might have been set up." The Steward replied with a spark of hope in his eye.

Seeing this, Ed concluded that his brother was expecting a miracle. In his opinion, there was not even the slightest chance that he would be granted a pardon. That's why he decided to bring him down to earth immediately.

"Dude, listen..." He began. "...I'll tell you straight, because you don't deserve to have someone deceive you with false hopes. I was there with you at home, you went completely nuts then, you started screaming that Thomas had cheated you, when you were playing poker earlier..." Ed paused to catch his breath. "...you took father's gun and said that thieves should be killed. I didn't say that in my testimony because I didn't want to incriminate you even more, but you... you shot at me, man, twice, that's why I took off and left you alone."

Steward froze, looking at his brother with disbelief and pain in his eyes. The memories of that terrible night when everything went wrong came flooding back to him.

"I can't believe I did all that..." he whispered, trembling. "...I'm sorry, Ed, I'm sorry..."

Seeing the tears in his brother's eyes, Ed felt an internal conflict. His hard heart wanted to believe that there was no hope for Steward, but deep down, he understood that what he saw in his eyes was true remorse and pain.

"Listen, man..." He said more gently. "...you may have done some stupid shit, but that doesn't change the fact that you're my brother and I'll do everything in my power to help you through this difficult time."

Steward looked up, full of new hope, grateful for the support that flowed from Ed despite everything that had happened. At that moment, he knew he wasn't alone and that his brother would support him.

"Thanks, I really appreciate it," Steward replied.

That afternoon, I returned to my cell with very mixed feelings. On the one hand, I was grateful to my brother for his devotion and support, even though I knew there was little he could do for me from behind the wall. But considering what he had told me during our meeting, I was terrified of my behaviour that night, especially the fact that I could have shot my own brother, the only person I had left in this world.

With all this information in mind, I began to think that I was exactly where I should be - behind bars.

Edward left the prison facility and returned to his car. He straightened up in the driver's seat and closed his eyes, taking a deep breath.

"Shit! God damn it!" he cursed under his breath.

He was not pleased with the fact that Steward might soon be in the ranks of the Aryan Brotherhood, and it was because they knew too much about him.

Moreover, he knew that if his plan succeeded, a gang war would break out and Steward would be caught in the middle of it.

He wasn't going to give up, though; he had a job to do, and he was determined to do it, even if it meant putting his brother in danger. A lot depended on it, especially his future and Stacy's.

The clock showed 3:15 p.m.

Ed started the car and headed to Stacy's apartment, hoping she had finished her job.

There was little time left before the brothers' show-up arrived; they were supposed to arrive around 4:00 p.m. The drive to Stacy's apartment seemed longer than usual.

Ed couldn't stop thinking about the upcoming events. His mind was racing, analysing potential threats and possible scenarios. He knew he would have to be ready for anything.

When he got there, he parked the car and quickly entered the apartment.

Stacy sat at the table, focused on her notes. She looked at him and smiled slightly, though there was concern in her eyes.

"How did it go?" she asked, putting down her pen.

"Fine..." he replied, although his tone suggested otherwise. "...I'll tell you later, what about you?"

Stacy nodded.

"Everything is ready, now we just have to wait."

Ed sat down next to her, taking her hand. He felt that every minute was precious. They had to be ready for the arrival of the brothers and for what would come next. Time was running out, and the future was more uncertain than ever.

3 hours later, 18:57 p.m.

The estate of Frank Perez, one of the main bosses of the Mafia organization in this part of Mexico, was located a mile from the city of Juárez. A huge, luxurious villa surrounded by high walls guarded by private security, an impregnable place. Only selected guests appeared there, and those who should not have been there never left the area.

It was to this place that Edward and two members of the brotherhood were heading. It was not their first visit to Frank Perez, because they came there regularly on John's orders.

The brotherhood's cooperation with the Mexican Mafia had been ongoing since the mid 1970s. It was at this time that Barry Mills, the original founder of the brotherhood, decided that it was detrimental to their mutual interests to kill each other and ordered the brothers to find an alliance with the neighbouring organisation.

Similar steps were taken in the Latin Mafia's board of directors, although there were splinter groups from that side, such as the unexpected assassination of Jack recently in the Polunsky Unit prison.

Such situations led to a shake up in the structures of both groups and caused members to question the wisdom of continuing their activities.

However, that evening, all doubts would be dispelled once and for all by Edward, who would finally bring an end to the fragile cooperation.

Three hours later, 18:57 p.m.

The man felt the weight of responsibility resting on his shoulders. He knew that the approaching time of the meeting with Frank Perez would be decisive. Every move, every word could decide his existence.

As they approached the villa, his heartbeat sped up, and his thoughts revolved around the strategy he was to implement.

The Brotherhood could not afford another betrayal or lose the alliance that had been built for many years. Ed saw this as a huge opportunity for himself and knew that if he managed to become the main ally on the American side, he would be assured of prosperity for the rest of his life.

As they entered the gates of the estate, Edward looked first at his companions, then turned his gaze upwards to the wall of the fence to the right, where one of the guards stood, his gun clearly attached to his belt. This was it, the point of no return.

It's all or nothing. He thought.

The car made a roundabout and drove around a small garden with flowers and a fountain set in the very centre of the grounds in front of the house. Then Frank emerged from inside, followed by two security guards.

The man was wearing summer shorts and a Hawaiian shirt, which contrasted with the elegant atmosphere of the villa.

His casual attire could be misleading, but Edward knew that it was just a facade. Franko Perez was famous for not looking like a typical mafia boss, but his influence was far-reaching.

The sun was high in the cloudless sky, and the temperature was rising to 22°C, which could justify the man's good mood. Ed and his companions left the vehicle and headed towards the beautiful villa.

From that moment on, the car was to be taken to the garage by Frank's mechanics, then disassembled from the trunk side, where the money was hidden, and then reassembled back into a usable condition.

The time to complete such a task usually did not exceed 30 minutes, but this day was supposed to be different.

Frank, noticing the approaching guests, smiled widely and raised his hand in greeting. His bodyguards, like shadows, followed close behind him, ready for their boss's every command.

"Amigos! Welcome…" Franko called, stepping closer. "…It is an honour to welcome you to my humble residence."

"Thank you, we are honoured." One of the brothers replied.

"Come with me, you're welcome! I have prepared something special for you."

Edward and his companions followed Franko into the interior of the villa, passing a spacious hall decorated with marble and precious works of art.

The atmosphere was tense, but Ed knew that this was his big chance. A future full of possibilities stretched out before him – he just had to play his cards carefully and thoughtfully.

While Franko and Ed's two companions moved further to the front, he stayed back, placing himself between the gangsters' bodyguards.

He then pulled a small note from his pocket and handed it to one of them, saying quietly:

"Read it and give it to Frank."

The bodyguard looked at him suspiciously but took the note and put it in his pocket.

Edward felt his heart beating faster. He knew he was taking a risk, but the plan had to be carried out precisely.

When they reached the back of the house, where there was a spacious swimming pool, Franko turned to them with a smile and Edward tried to remain calm. He knew that everything would become clear soon.

"Sit down, friends! I've prepared a bottle of luxury Whiskey from the 26th for your arrival!" He announced enthusiastically. "...don't ask me how much I paid for it, but what don't you do for your friends?!"

Then suddenly, a security guard approached him and whispered something in his ear, then quickly left. Edward watched the incident carefully, but his companions seemed indifferent.

From their point of view, there was no reason to worry; they had done such tasks dozens of times, and no complications had ever arisen.

Everything was predetermined and arranged by the managers on both sides, and they were merely the liaisons. However, Edward saw something that the others did not see, a slight frown on Frank's brow, a shadow of concern in his eyes. This was the moment he had been waiting for.

He clenched his fists slightly, trying to hide the rising adrenaline. He knew that his chance would soon come, the moment when he would be able to outsmart his opponents.

The boss poured the drink into four crystal glasses and made a gesture with his hand.

"Help yourselves." He spoke.

At these words, Ed and the brothers approached him. Franko raised his glass, his voice resonating decisively:

"To our health and future business!" He exclaimed, raising the glass in a toast.

Everyone raised their glasses in silence, but Edward did not take his eyes off Franko, analysing his every move, every word.

"Ah! Delicious, isn't it?" he asked, savouring the drink.

"Indeed." One of the brothers replied.

"Come, I want to show you something." He replied and started walking along the property, heading to the further part of the garden.

The three newcomers obediently walked forward, not suspecting anything. Finally, they reached the edge of the house, where on the right side, in the previously invisible part, they saw a gloomy, medium-sized, wooden barn.

The view was strange to say the least, on the one hand a beautiful and modern villa and on the other a barn that looked like it came straight from the Middle Ages. The men looked at each other in surprise.

"Calm down, my friends, there is no reason to worry...!" Frank suddenly spoke up. "...I just want to show you my new acquisition, come on, it's inside." He added and confidently walked forward.

The men, having no other choice, followed his lead. Frank opened the wooden door and went inside first; the rest joined him after a moment.

"Oh! There it is!" he shouted, pointing with his finger.

As his companions looked in the direction he was pointing, huge pigs appeared in their field of vision. Considering the difficulty of counting moving animals, it looked like there could be as many as twenty of them. The brothers took a few steps closer, squinting to see the new acquisition that Franko had spoken of.

"Bang!"

A loud shot rang out from behind them, and the remains of one of the brothers' heads landed far in front of them before his body fell to the ground.

"What the fuck?!?" The second man shouted as Frank's bodyguards grabbed him by the arms overwhelmingly. "...what the fuck are you doing?! We had an agreement!!"

"HIJO DE PUTA! Fuck you and your agreement, if this is how you do business..." Franko replied calmly, approaching him. "...You!! Come here!!" He called Edward.

"Take it." He added when he was close enough.

Ed reached out and took the knife from Franko, which he pulled out from his belt.

"Prove which side you're on." He said clearly, making him understand what he expected of him.

The man had no other choice, but he also strove for such a turn of events, knowing that this is how it could end. He approached his companion, whom he had known for many years, and made the first stab of the knife into his stomach.

"TICK"

After that, another and another.

"TICK... TICK... TICK"

The sound of the knife cutting the skin echoed in Ed's ears. At the same time, he saw panic and terror in his friend's eyes until he took his last breath and fell limply to the ground.

"Good, throw them in the pigs, they'll take care of the rest, and I'll talk to you when you're done." He turned to Ed once more and immediately left.

A few minutes later, Ed also left the barn, covered in more blood than before. Franco's bodyguards didn't help him much in moving the bodies, so he had to do almost all the work himself.

Evening was approaching when he found himself in front of Perez's huge villa again. The night lights installed around the grounds began to illuminate it nicely, but the owner was nowhere to be seen.

Ed looked around worriedly, and he didn't know if the ruthless boss of the Latin mafia had prepared some deadly surprise for him as well.

Given the circumstances, anything was possible. Despite the warning note given to the bodyguard, he understood that he could have been killed, which would not alter Perez's current situation. The war had already begun, and there would soon be many more victims anyway.

"By the pool." He suddenly heard the security guard's voice.

The man glanced at him, then set off on a familiar path.

When he was a few metres from his destination, he saw Franko sitting on one of the folding loungers by the pool and drinking his exquisite Whiskey. The darkness of night was beginning to fall on the villa, and Ed felt the tension growing inside him.

Approaching Franko, he wondered what new challenges might await him. When he stood in front of the boss, he looked up and smiled slightly.

"I see you don't hesitate..." Franko nodded, showing him a place on the deckchair opposite. "...sit down, we need to discuss a few things."

Ed hesitantly followed his instructions and sat down, prepared for anything. This was to be the conversation he had been waiting for, the opportunity he wanted now stood before him.

Realizing what slippery ground he was treading on, any wrong word, any wrong gesture could mean inevitable death, yet he was exactly where he had wanted to be for a long time. It was either everything or nothing.

"Can you tell me, because I am very curious, why you decided to betray the brotherhood?" Franko asked, simultaneously fixing him with a focused gaze.

"The same reason you decided to eliminate them..." Ed moved his head towards the barn. "...I did not like the way they did business."

"Oh yes, but doesn't that mean you have issued a death sentence to yourself?"

A cold shiver ran across Edward's skin, and he wasn't entirely sure who Perez was referring to.

Common sense told him that he was referring to the way the Brotherhood dealt with traitors, but at the same time he knew that people like him only ended up in any organization one way, according to the code of honour, so there was a chance that Franco had already decided to send him to the next world.

"It probably could be, but not necessarily." He replied after a moment.

"Not necessarily, you say," Perez repeated after him.

"Yes, because I have a proposition for you, I want to join your organisation."

"HIJO DE PUTA! HAHAHA…!!" Franco burst out laughing. "…you have some balls; I can give you that! Where did you get the idea that I might want to do business with a person like you?! You've proven how easily you can betray your brothers; you better give me one reason why I shouldn't order you to be thrown into the pigs too." He added with a serious face.

"You'll need me on the other side, the brothers will want to take revenge for what happened here today, I can be your source of information, I'll inform you of their every move," Ed replied.

Franko remained silent, scenarios of the upcoming and inevitable gang war running through his head.

"Besides, we can continue the business as usual, I'm ready to buy the product from you for two hundred thousand, my people will take care of distribution and I will stay in the shadows, then I will deliver the cash to you and you can calmly focus on your actions against the Brotherhood…" Edward could see that Perez was considering accepting his offer, so he had to give him as many reasons as possible why he would do it. "...and of course, you keep what we brought today."

"I would have done it anyway..." Franko replied coldly. "...I can give you two weeks of trial, if you do well, I'll let you join us.

There it is! I did it! Edward thought.

"But if you fail or I find out that you're playing both sides, your death will be slow and painful." He added, pulling the man to the ground.

"Understood."

"If you understand that, then you probably know that I can't let you out of here unharmed? What would the brothers think if the only survivor came back safe and sound?"

Ed frowned, hearing those words. He looked at Franco carefully, through which he saw that the man tore his gaze away from him and directed it to something behind him, then made a commanding gesture with his head.

Seeing this, Edward turned in the direction the mafioso was looking and was hit in the face with a pistol by the bodyguard standing right behind him.

After that, the man threw him to the ground and hit him a few more times until Franco ordered him to stop.

"Get him out of here t of here and leave him outside the city, give him some money so he can go back to the US." He said.

The security guard grabbed Ed by the collar as he lay on the ground, spitting blood, and began dragging him toward the parked cars.

"Where's that note? I want to see it."

The second man immediately reached into his pants pocket, pulled out a note, and handed it to his boss. He opened it and read it in his mind:

"For every ten thousand, one bill is counterfeit."

A hundred-dollar bill for ten thousand might not seem like a big difference. But it wasn't just about the money; for Franko, it was an insult he couldn't bear. The missing cash out of ten thousand was only one hundred dollars, but out of one hundred thousand it was already worth one thousand dollars in missing money.

Edward and his companions were transporting three hundred thousand that day, three thousand of which were counterfeit bills. This meant a death sentence for carriers if such fraud was discovered.

That was exactly what Ed had to do if he wanted to eliminate the brotherhood from the game. Earlier that day, Stacy had opened each bundle of money, mixed in the counterfeit bill, and then repacked it all. Ed's job was to inform Perez, wait to see what would happen, but most importantly, not get killed. Thanks to a carefully planned plot, the plan worked, and Edward was relieved to consider the mission over.

13

Mission accomplished, part 3

"We are richer the more unnecessary things we can throw away."

February 2, 1982.

The next morning, Edward woke up at eight in the morning in his hotel room. The bruises on his body were still bothering him, especially the cut on his left eyebrow, but he was fully satisfied with the way the task was performed. Last night, he managed to get his appearance back into working order.

He had taken a long, relaxing shower, washing off all the dirt, including the dried blood and the stench of the pigsty that had soaked into his clothes.

Luckily for him, the hotel he was staying at offered its guests tacky Mexican souvenirs in a tourist shop located on the ground floor. The shop was already closed by the time he got there, but he decided to take advantage of it before he finally made his way back to the U.S.

So, he went down the stairs and found the least embarrassing T-shirt he could find, then asked the salesperson for a disposable bag and went back to his room.

He rolled up the bloody clothes and stuffed them into a bag to throw away later, put on a red T-shirt with the words *I love Mexico* written in small yellow letters, took his passport from the bedside table, the rest of the money, and left the room, closing the door behind him.

On the ground floor, he gave the key to the receptionist, said a quick *Gracias*, and left the building. Despite the early hour of the day, the sun was fully visible in the almost cloudless sky, and the temperature exceeded 20 degrees Celsius.

It matched Ed's new clothes perfectly, and he now looked like a tourist returning from vacation. The man found a trash can in front of the hotel, left his dirty clothes there and was free to go towards the border, looking for a ride. After fifteen minutes of walking, luck smiled at him again.

Then he saw a group of cheerful teenagers, who were packing into two cars at one of the shops. He heard an American accent over the loud conversations and had no doubt that the young people in a party mood would be heading in the same direction as he.

So, he went over to them to ask for help. The four teenagers were loading their backpacks into the trunk while their three friends were leaving the store. They were getting ready to take off.

"Hey!" Ed called out from a few steps away.

The young women stopped to see who was talking to them.

"Hey." One of them replied.

"Sorry to interrupt, but could you do me a favour?" he asked.

At that moment, the three companions approached the cars.

"Sure, man! What's going on?" one shouted.

"I need a ride to El Paso. I had a fight with my friends yesterday, and they left me here. I woke up today and they were gone."

"Oh, that sucks bro." The second man added, noticing the bruises on Edward's face.

"Not a problem, we have one seat free, get in!"

"We'll be passing through El Paso, so that's all good." Another woman added.

"Great, thanks, I really appreciate it," Ed replied.

"Okay, it's not a big deal." The man replied, and everyone went back to what they were doing.

Ten minutes later, they were all on their way to the American border.

Young people were joking all the way, laughing loudly and drinking alcohol. This atmosphere also affected Edward, who, without hesitation, took up the offer of a tequila drink. A long line of cars formed in front of them when they reached the main street leading to the border.

This was a completely normal occurrence in this place because no matter the time of day or night, you always had to wait your turn at the gates.

People used this time in different ways. Some got out of their cars to stretch their legs on the street, others stayed inside to listen to music, and some even took a few minutes to nap.

Ed's companions were drinking tequila at this point, clearly not finished partying from the previous day. Edward didn't like this situation because he knew the border guards would soon start watching them.

A group of drunk teenagers would undoubtedly attract the special attention of uniformed customs officers, and Edward knew it.

But it was too late to ditch the vehicle and try to join the other strangers. All he could do was wait patiently to see what would happen. The important thing was that the drivers kept their cool and stayed sober.

"Hello, I would like to see your passports, driving license, registration number and vehicle insurance." The officer said in a serious tone to the driver of the first car.

The second one said the same to the driver of the car Ed was in. Both men obediently handed over the documents they had prepared earlier.

While two uniformed officers were looking through them, the other two slowly walked around the cars, carefully examining them and the people inside. After checking the legality of the vehicle's documents, it's time to compare the faces in the photos with those of the passengers. All the while, the previously loud women remained calm and serious at the customs checkpoint, much to Ed's pleasant surprise.

Then his turn came. The officer walked over to the back seat where he was sitting, passport in hand, and lifted it higher in the air, intending to place the two images side by side as Edward looked at her. Serious-looking, bruised, with a split eyebrow and an "I Love Mexico" T-shirt, thirty-six-year-old Ed fit into the company of barely legal age people like a third wheel on a wagon.

A faint smile spread across the woman's face at the sight.

"Okay..." she said, giving him back the passport. "...let them through!" she called out to her colleagues at the front, letting them know that the inspection had just ended. Then the gates were raised high, and both vehicles were allowed to continue their journey to American soil. On this side of the border, the journey passed quickly, and Ed felt both relief and nervous.

On the one hand, he was glad that he had managed to successfully complete the dangerous undertaking, but now another problem appeared on the horizon. Namely, he had to report on the expedition to the brotherhood soon, and he was not sure what the reaction would be. It was not hard to guess that the brotherhood would be furious, and Edward could not predict how it would directly affect him.

Twenty minutes later, the temporary company left Ed not far from Stacy's apartment. He heard an amused "ADIOS!" from the car driving away, and then he headed towards the house where his girlfriend lived. It was past eleven when the man entered the house. Stacy was sitting in the living room, and when she heard the door open, she immediately jumped up from the couch.

"There you are." She said when he entered the room.

Her voice sounded flat to Ed, devoid of surprise or joy at his return. The man knew this tone of voice in a woman, which is why he immediately thought she was on drugs.

"How did it go? I didn't think you'd be back so soon." She added, looking at him with an absent gaze.

"We'll talk about it later, when you sober up. I have to call." He replied and turned his back on her, then went to the kitchen, where the phone was.

"Okay." Stacy said shortly and slumped back on the couch, completely unconcerned that Ed was going through a difficult time.

The man picked up the phone and dialled the number, after a few rings a male voice answered.

"It's me..." "Ed said. *"...We need to talk; things have gotten complicated."*

14

Anxious awareness.

"Learn to love what is good, true and beautiful."

February 3, 1982.

Michael was off work, but as someone without children and a wife, he liked to spend that time reviewing materials related to ongoing investigations, and that was what he did that day.

The detective planned to meet with Steward that afternoon and continue the conversation they had recently had.

He expected to receive from the man a list of people who might have had something to do with the murder at the gas station.

The circumstances were extremely complicated, and Michael was officially conducting several investigations and could not focus solely on the case he was working on unofficially. Regardless, the policeman set himself the task of clearing up any inconsistencies and obtaining a final answer as to Steward's guilt.

The man thought that perhaps it was a waste of time, but he could not rest in peace until he found out.

It was 1 p.m. when the detective left his apartment. The gloomy weather was not encouraging; the rain was constantly falling from the cloudy sky, and there was no sign that it would stop anytime soon.

However, the detective could no longer stay within these four walls; since morning, he had a strange feeling that something terrible was going to happen.

It was one of those days when you feel that something sinister is hanging in the air, you don't know where such thoughts come from, but they are there, and you can't get rid of them.

These were the emotions that had been tormenting him since he woke up in the morning.

There was still an hour before visiting the state prison began, so he decided to stop at the American Dinner nearby for coffee and wait there until the time was right.

1:55 p.m. Polunsky Unit.

Since Ed's visit, I have started having new dreams. There were nights when memories of torture from my youth regularly haunted me. But now they were replaced by new, more realistic dreams in which I found myself in a gas station with a gun in my hand.

I heard screams, pleas for mercy, shots and saw blood spurting everywhere. Sometimes I shot at Ed, and sometimes at Thomas and Katy.

The most terrifying thing was that I could see every detail, the faces, the clothes, the details of the circumstances, and even the heavy rain hitting the windows.

All this made me not sure if it was just a figment of my imagination or real memories. Either way, I couldn't ignore it because there was no doubt that there had to be a reason why my subconscious had created such a vision. The afternoon passed very peacefully, and most of the prisoners were unusually calm.

I thought that maybe it was the weather outside that was affecting them. I had not yet realised that this was just the calm before the coming storm.

…Thump…Thump…Thump…

I heard footsteps on the metal balcony.

"Johnson, you have a visitor." The guard said suddenly, standing in front of my cell. I slowly slid off the bunk and looked in his direction.

"My brother?" I asked.

"No, some cop." He replied.

Michael. I thought.

It made sense, I should have expected it, even though some time had passed since his last visit. He said he would be back.

I got up and went to the table where my notebook was lying. I opened it to the page where I had written down the list of people the detective asked me for and stopped in my tracks.

Just a few days ago, I thought there was a chance, but now I wasn't so sure. All because of the belief that was growing more and more in my head, saying that I was responsible for the tragedy that happened.

In such a situation, I felt it would be unfair to avoid due punishment or to subject the detective to charges against people who most likely had nothing to do with the case.

Regardless, I tore the page out and put it in my pocket, knowing that this was the reason for the policeman's visit.

When I arrived at the guard escorted visiting room, Michael was already waiting for me. I walked in and he immediately noticed my presence, giving me a small smile.

I wasn't entirely sure why he was doing all this.

On the one hand, I might have suspected that he simply wanted to know the truth, but on the other hand, he was someone who, until recently, was determined to put me here, which created an unclear picture of his true intentions.

However, in this situation, I was absolutely sure of one thing: I shouldn't talk to him if I wanted the brotherhood to accept me, because it would be against the rules.

I sat down, picked up the receiver and put it to my ear. Michael did the same.

"Hello, Steward," he spoke.

"Detective," I replied.

"It's been a while since we last spoke." He stated.

"Yes, that's right," I admitted.

"How's life behind bars treating you? I heard you had some trouble."

"Nothing I couldn't handle," I replied.

"Yeah, I heard that too, I hope you don't have to do that anymore." He spoke.

I sensed empathy in his voice, which made me inclined to believe that he was truly speaking with compassion. However, after a few minutes of conversation, his compassion was about to be greatly shaken by what I was about to tell him.

"I assume you know why I came to you today?" He asked after a moment.

"Yes, but I don't know if it makes sense." I replied.

The detective frowned, clearly surprised.

"What do you mean?"

"I prepared this list earlier, only now I think it won't be needed for anything." I replied.

"Why?" Michael didn't give up, but he was surprised by such a change of attitude.

During his first conversation with Steward, he had seen enthusiasm in him, a spark of hope in his eyes at the news that he might be innocent of the murders he was accused of. But now that spark was gone, and the cop saw nothing but hopelessness and the desire to give up. The man raised a sad look at Michael and said:

"I'm almost completely certain that I did it."

"What do you mean, almost completely..." he repeated after him, not hiding his surprise. "...you previously claimed that you didn't remember anything from that night, so now your memories have returned?"

"Sort of, I started having dreams about this incident." He confessed.

The policeman listened to him carefully, at the same time noting every word in his mind.

The matter was serious because if Steward started remembering the events, it would mean that he was guilty, and Michael should immediately stop further activities.

On the other hand, however, he knew about the existing inconsistencies that could clearly indicate the involvement of third parties, which also left a serious gap in the theory about whether Steward or Gary killed that night.

The detective leaned closer to me, looking deeply into my eyes.

"Dreams...?" he asked quietly, trying to hide his growing interest. "...tell me about them."

I thought for a moment, trying to recall the images in my memory.

"These are fragments, flashbacks... I see blood on my hands, I smell metal and gunpowder, I hear screams..."

Michael was silent, giving me time to continue.

"But there are also moments when I see myself standing over a body... With a gun in my hand... and then I'm sure... I killed."

"So, you think these dreams are memories?" - The detective tried to understand.

"I don't know..." I answered truthfully. "...I'm not sure what's real and what's not, and this uncertainty is eating me up."

Michael took a deep breath.

"We must find out what really happened that night."

"I wrote down the people who hate me so much that they will gladly watch me die." I said and reached into my pocket for a piece of paper.

This immediately caught the attention of the guard, who looked at me suspiciously. Michael, seeing this, shook his head gently, giving him a sign that everything was fine.

"Even if these people are my enemies and I have or had personal scores to settle with each of them, I don't want innocent people to suffer because of me. It wouldn't be fair; enough people have already suffered because of my actions." I confessed and slid the folded note under the glass. Michael took it from his side.

"If more memories come back to you, you will tell me about them next time, and then we will consider further cooperation." He replied, at the same time putting the note into the inside pocket of his jacket.

I didn't like this idea.

Even during this visit, I had serious doubts whether I should talk to him at all; I was afraid of what the Brotherhood might do to me if the news spread that I was talking to the police.

"I don't think it's a good idea." I spoke.

"Steward, listen to me..." He began. "...if you are guilty, then you have already been punished, it won't hurt anyone, if I dispel all doubts for my own peace of mind, it can only help you."

"You don't understand what I'm saying, it's not just about whether I'm guilty or not, I can't bring suspicion on myself that I'm a snitch," I replied.

The detective nodded, a sign of understanding.

The circumstances I was in were extremely dangerous, and Michael knew it. All it took was one admission that I was an informer, and that meant imminent death at the hands of fellow prisoners. The centre housed mainly murderers, rapists, gangsters, thieves and other people from the underworld who lived outside the law and were governed by their own rules.

"I understand..." He spoke. "...I will arrange the next meeting so that only three people know about it."

"Three people?" I repeated after him.

"Yes, you, me and my trusted colleague who works here..." he explained. "...I will let you know about the next visit through him, for now, try to organise your thoughts, remember as much as you can and don't get into trouble." He added.

I nodded in agreement as he stood up from the chair.

"I'll see what I can do for you." He said as he left and headed towards the exit.

I watched him disappear behind the metal door for a moment, then a guard came over to escort me to my cell.

A gust of rain began as Michael left the building. The man pulled out his car keys, covered his head with his jacket, and quickly headed for the parking lot. A few seconds later, he was behind the wheel of his vehicle. He then decided to look at the note he had received from Steward.

"Oh wow." He said quietly.

It was a reaction to the names he saw. He didn't recognise all of them, but the ones he knew belonged to very dangerous people. They were hardened criminals who had had numerous run-ins with law enforcement officers.

At the time, the detective didn't remember exactly what crimes these people might have been involved in, but he knew it would be foolish to mess with even one of them. Steward maintained a comprehensive list, consisting of ten individuals, with at least seven possessing the capability to commit homicide.

This doesn't look good. He thought.

In other circumstances, he probably would have gone home and spent the rest of the day resting, but in this situation, he decided to go to the police station. Not wanting to waste time, he wanted to immediately review the files to be able to match faces with names and check for what crimes these people were entered into the police database. The man turned the key in the ignition and the car engines purred, and the windshield wipers began to work rhythmically, fighting the heavy raindrops.

Michael turned on the lights, which reflected in the wet road. It was almost 3:00 p.m. and despite the early hour, the road ahead of him was empty and dark, with only the streetlights casting a faint light on the road.

The pitch-black clouds made it seem like the middle of the night when the stubborn detective drove out onto the street and headed towards the police station.

A few minutes later, the man parked his car in front of the building where all the documents he needed were kept. When he entered the office, the busy officers did not even notice his arrival. The detective went straight to the room, where all the files were kept. He had ten names to find, which was a time-consuming task.

Each drawer contained the details of previously registered individuals, arranged in alphabetical order, so he had to check each one himself. Fortunately, he knew some of these people, so he knew exactly where to start. He decided to check out the most outstanding men first and return to the rest if he had time.

"So, it is true." He suddenly heard a familiar voice.

"Hi Paul." He said to his partner, who unexpectedly appeared in the room.

"I thought they were joking when they said you were here..." Paul came closer. "...but you really can't keep your ass away of this place, even on your day off." He joked.

"As it happened, I went to talk to the Steward."

"Oh yeah, and what are you looking for here...? Paul glanced over Michael's shoulder. "...what is wrong with you? You want to single-handedly take down the biggest scumbags in this city?" he added, seeing the files Michael was looking at.

"Not exactly, I just want to take a closer look at the suspects Steward pointed out."

"What do you mean, pointed out? In what sense?" the partner asked.

"In the sense that these gentlemen here have an unsettled score with him." The detective tapped the photos on the table with his finger.

Paul froze, and his face became serious.

"Uuuu... if they had a bone to pick with him, I'm surprised this guy hasn't bitten the dust yet..." He stated. "... like this one here, Henry Martinez, arrested for burglary and armed robbery, or this one..." he pointed to another photo. "...Eric Wilson, member of the guerrilla family gang suspected of murder, remember? We were investigating, dismissed for lack of evidence."

"I remember." Michael nodded reluctantly.

"I don't want to be pessimistic, my friend, let me tell you honestly, you're dealing with a group of really fucked up people here."

"Yeah, no shit, tell me something I don't know."

"What are you going to do about it?"

"Officially nothing, unofficially I'll try to track down these guys and find out which one of them had the greatest motive and opportunity to pull off this gas station stunt."

Paul shook his head, unconvinced.

"I guess I don't have to tell you that your theory is as inflated as a balloon; one scratch and it'll shatter into a million fucking pieces." He stated.

"I understand that, but I can't shake off the feeling that things aren't as they seem here..." the detective replied thoughtfully. "...although Steward himself claims that memories of that night are coming back to him now."

Paul's eyes widened considerably, indicating his complete interest.

"Are you kidding me? Did he tell you what the memories were?" he asked.

"Not so much memories as dreams, he claims that he started seeing himself during the incident, gunshots, blood, screams and things like that," Michael explained.

"So that's it, he's guilty, end of investigation, case closed, what else are you looking for?"

"I won't be so sure, he's extremely mentally unstable, he has two personalities, which means two individuals with their own memories and character..." Michael turned to face his partner. "...I think their consciousnesses can sometimes get tangled up and what Steward dreams about could actually be Gary's memory."

"So what? So, it turns out Gary killed, same shit. They had to put the person in prison, not the personality. Steward took the blame, but that's how it had to end." Paul replied.

"I agree, but there's one more catch..." Michael's face was focused. "...namely, I read a report from April 1966, when a young Steward, or rather Gary, managed to free himself at some point during a kidnapping and shoot one of his captors, I have a feeling that what he is dreaming about now may be a result of this event."

"Sometimes I don't know if you're a genius or a complete moron, but it doesn't matter, I'll help you however I can," Paul replied.

"Yeah, I love you too, brother." Michael smiled.

"Okay, I'll leave you now so you can look at the photos in peace. Let me know if you need anything."

"Will do."

Paul left the room, and Michael went back to studying the files.

Little did he know at the time that this would be the last evening he would be able to fully focus on the Steward Johnson case that troubled him, because soon the streets of El Paso would run red with blood and the investigators, including Detective Michael Williams, would have their hands full.

15

Gang warfare.

"No one can kill in the name of God, no one can accept the taking of the lives of brothers."

4 February 1982.

The news of the execution of two Brotherhood members on Mexican soil on the orders of Franco Perez reached John the very next day. Edward gave a statement about the incident, which was then encrypted and forwarded to the boss. The man, of course, omitted his involvement in the circumstances of the event, presenting himself as the *sole survivor.*

According to his version, Perez was to give the order to kill the two men, and Ed was to deliver a brutal message to the brotherhood, which was the only reason he was released with minor injuries.

John found it hard to believe such unexpected behaviour by one of the bosses of the Mexican mafia.

The men had known each other for years and had done business together, never having had any disagreements, until now.

John's personal feelings on the matter were irrelevant at the time, as he knew that the organisation's rules clearly stated that retaliation was the only appropriate response in such cases, and there was nothing he could do to stem the tide of anger that would rise if his comrades were informed.

The commander of the Aryan Brotherhood was in a dilemma. On the one hand, he knew he had to tell his brothers, but on the other, he feared uncontrolled violence that could ultimately end the cooperation between the two groups.

Adding fuel to the fire in a situation that had already been tense since the assassination attempt on his second-in-command, Jack, could have disastrous consequences.

John knew that this was an isolated and unintentional incident, as he later cleared it up with Luis Ramirez, who punished his subordinate and assured him that it would never happen again.

Despite this, the brothers behind prison walls became especially vigilant, and a gang war was inevitable.

Polunsky Unit, 11:45 PM.

I had the impression that something very bad was coming. It was impossible to tell what it could be, but I had a feeling that things would soon change.

I had been observing John since yesterday, and he looked as if he had some burden inside him that was eating him from the inside.

I didn't know him before, but I was able to recognise strange behaviour in people.

For instance, John was usually very chatty and liked to be the centre of attention, but now he avoided conversations and kept to himself, and the only person who kept him company was Jack. They talked quietly together and watched their surroundings carefully, as if expecting an attack that could come at any moment.

Tension hung in the air, and every move seemed to be controlled by an invisible hand of fear.

Even the staff at Polunsky Unit observed a noticeable change in the prisoners' behaviour, though they were unable to identify the exact cause of this shift.

At night, when the prison walls seemed to whisper stories of hidden violence, John and Jack would talk quietly, trying to strategise for the coming days.

Eventually, Jack helped make the decision that would start all hell.

"We must act now..." he said, looking John straight in the eye. "...we can't wait for them to strike first, if you keep this a secret any longer, you yourself will be considered a traitor." He added seriously.

John nodded, agreeing with his friend. He knew Jack was right. There was no room for hesitation at this point. They were ready for whatever the coming days would bring. The Brotherhood was strong, constantly recruiting new members.

John looked at Jack, his eyes shining with resolve and determination. The man had no doubts that they would survive this turbulent time, but he feared for the lives of his brothers, who would suffer greatly in this clash.

Despite everything, he knew what he had to do.

"Okay, gather everyone in the yard tomorrow, and we'll have a talk," John ordered.

Jack nodded in agreement. His mind began to replay scenes of violence that would soon become a daily occurrence in prison.

5:45 p.m. the next day.

Michael sat at his desk, sorting through paperwork. Everywhere you could hear ringing telephones, people talking, the clicking of typewriter keys, a few computers and the typical sounds associated with work in an office.

At this time, nothing was happening that required immediate attention, so he could work on outstanding matters.

"Mike, you have a visitor." He heard suddenly above his head.

When he looked up, he saw that it was an officer who had come to inform him about the person who had asked about him at the duty station.

"Who is it?" Michael asked reluctantly and went back to work.

"Edward, Edward Johnson, he said you would know who he is."

The detective narrowed his eyes slightly and stared back at the officer on duty.

"Move, he's waiting for you there." The man added and turned back in the direction he had come from.

"I'll be damned." Thought Michael.

Brother Steward's unexpected visit took the detective completely by surprise, as he thought Edward was the last person he expected to see at the police station, and certainly not of his own accord.

Michael rose from his chair, intrigued by the reason for the unexpected guest's arrival. When he got there, he saw Edward standing with his hands in his pockets, as if he was waiting for something more than just a meeting. His face was serious, with obvious tension in his eyes.

"Hello Ed…" the policeman greeted him upon arrival. "…you wanted to see me?"

"Yes, can we talk somewhere privately?" Ed replied.

"Of course, please follow me."

Michael headed towards the hallway, and Edward followed him. A moment later, they reached one of the interrogation rooms, where they could talk privately. Ed entered and looked around, and he did not like what he saw.

"Is there no better place?" he asked.

The detective smiled slightly under his breath.

"What`s the matter? Bad memories?"

"No, never mind."

"Sit down if you want." The policeman pointed to the chair behind the table.

"No thanks, I won't be here long."

"So, how can I help you?" Michael crossed his arms over his chest and sat down on the table.

"I talked to Steward." Ed began.

"Oh yes, I'm not surprised, he's your brother after all."

"That's right, he's my brother and I want the best for him."

"That's understandable." Michael agreed.

"I cared for him for many years, especially after the death of our parents. What Gary did shouldn't happen."

The detective listened carefully and started to get an idea of what his interlocutor was getting at.

"I agree, it shouldn't have, but it did. " He replied, not wanting to reveal his true opinion on the subject."

"I know you visit him too..." Ed suddenly confessed. "...I don't want you to do this anymore."

"You don't want me to help your brother?"

"That's not the point, you don't understand anything..." Ed was outraged. "...You think you know something, but in reality, you have no idea."

"Where do you draw such conclusions?"

"Because you weren't there, and you didn't know what Gary was capable of."

"Honestly, I had the opportunity to see him in action, and I know how he can behave." Michael replied."

"Exactly, so if you saw it, you know he's a psychopath, capable of anything..." Ed said, and paused for a moment. "...look, I didn't say this at the hearing because I didn't want to incriminate Steward any further..." He added thoughtfully. "...I wasn't asked about it, so I didn't say anything, but the night Gary took over, he wanted to kill me too, so I ran away and left him alone."

Michael listened to the man intently, following every movement of his body language as he revealed something he had clearly been hiding for a long time. From these observations, it seemed that Edward was either an excellent actor or was actually telling the truth.

"What do you mean by saying, he wanted to kill you too?" he finally asked.

"He pulled out our late father's revolver and started swinging it, he went completely nuts, he was like a wild animal, he was screaming that Thomas had robbed him of his money..." Edward was giving an account that no one had ever heard before. "...I wanted to calm him down, stop him from doing something stupid, and I failed; he shot at me twice, but somehow, I managed to dodge the bullet that hit the sofa I was sitting on..." Ed stopped to take a breath. "...I was afraid for my life." He added.

"Do you think Gary murdered Thomas and Katy?"

"Yes, I'm one hundred per cent sure of that; it couldn't have been anyone else."

The policeman had extremely mixed feelings at this point.

Could I have been so wrong? He wondered.

Thoughts ran through his head about bits and pieces of things that he had previously considered supposed evidence, but they were slowly being replaced by hard facts that proved the opposite. In addition, Edward's testimony appeared, which will undoubtedly be remembered by the detective for a long time.

"Alright, I'll take it all into account," Michael replied, keeping a straight face.

"Don't get me wrong, I don't mean to leave my brother in this shit, I just don't want him to get false hopes, and I know that's how it is when you talk to him."

"I see, thank you for talking to me, Mr. Johnson, I have to get back to my duties..." the detective wanted to end the conversation.

"...come on, you know the way out." he added, opening the door to the room.

"Of course, thank you." Ed replied and headed towards the on-call office and then to the exit of the building.

Shit. Michael thought as he walked between the desks.

Just as he was about to return to his seat, a premonition came over him, and he instead walked to the window overlooking the parking lot.

The man looked outside and observed the square for a moment. Then he saw Edward come around the corner and walk quickly towards his car. When he finally reached it, the detective squinted to get a closer look. He wanted to see the license plate number and generally see what kind of vehicle he drove.

Then, to his surprise, he discovered that Ed wasn't alone and that someone was waiting for him in the car. Unfortunately, from this position, he couldn't see exactly who it was, and it wasn't until the car started moving and then pulled closer to the building that the detective recognised the passenger.

"Well, who do we have here?" he said quietly to himself as he identified him as one of the prime suspects on Steward's list.

Polunsky Unit, 6:14 p.m.

Jack sent word to all the brothers about an emergency meeting in the yard that afternoon. Although I was not a full member, I was included, too.

Assuming back then, that John would want to tell everyone what had been on his mind lately and what had affected his wellbeing so much.

I didn't know what it could be at the time, but my instincts told me it was not good, and I wasn't wrong.

At 6:15 p.m., the men gathered at the agreed place, and John took the main seat in the middle, where everyone could hear him clearly.

The pleasant weather that day had a positive effect on some of the men, who came out wearing white short-sleeved shirts, revealing all their tattoos.

At one point I noticed that I was surrounded by Nazi symbols, such as swastikas, SS initials, skulls, the number 666, and clovers with capital letters AB. Although I was standing at the edge of the circle, I felt overwhelmed. Then John began to speak.

"The commission of the brotherhood has decided to issue a death sentence to Franco Perez..." he said, "...he is guilty of murdering two brothers." He added.

After these words, the men became restless and began to whisper quietly to each other, not wanting to offend the boss who had just started talking to them.

"A few days ago, three of our brothers went to Perez's estate, but only one returned, who later told about the execution of his comrades..." John stopped while looking at Jack, the man's face was stony and determined.

John did what he had to do, knowing that he had the full support of his deputy.

"...therefore, Barry Mills and other members of the commission have decided to end the alliance with the Mexicans, I will not tell you what to do, but from now on the ban on entering into conflict with them is lifted, and a generous reward awaits whoever reaches Perez, go in peace, brothers." He added in conclusion.

The gathered men began to disperse, visibly excited. Many of them were just waiting for the opportunity to beat up people belonging to the coexisting gang, and they got what they were waiting for, not hiding their satisfaction.

I did not yet know what effect the new orders would have on me personally. Although I had not yet achieved official membership in the brotherhood and was in a transitional phase, my uncertainty regarding this status would soon be resolved.

Jack approached John after the meeting ended.

"What are your plans?" he asked.

"Our boys will deal with them outside..." John replied. "...they are tasked with locating and eliminating cooking spots. Barry wants to wipe them out on this side of America."

"I expected this, he wants to take complete control of the market." Jack replied.

"Yeah, plan B is already in motion, and I will find Perez myself as soon as I get out of this shithole."

"Well, let the show begin." Jack added happily.

16

Investigation.

"Let's not harden our hearts when we hear the cry of the poor. Let's try to hear this cry. Let's try to act and live in such a way that no one in our homeland lacks a roof over their heads and bread on the table, so that no one feels lonely, left without care."

February 6, 1982.

Michael decided to do some snooping around the area where Stacy lived. Remembering Edward's words that he was in her apartment during the gas station murder, Ed admitted that he left the Johnson house around 12 p.m., right after an angry and stunned Gary tried to shoot him.

According to the detective's calculations, he must have returned to this place several dozen minutes after midnight, and he was curious if anyone would confirm this version.

Armed with a photo of Ed's car, a red Ford Escort, he went for a walk around the neighbourhood to ask if any neighbours remembered the car parked outside the house on the night of the tragedy.

The woman was renting the ground floor apartment that she currently shared with Edward. In addition to them, a single elderly woman lived in the single family home in the Horizon City neighbourhoods, who rarely left her first-floor apartment.

This is where the policeman wanted to start his investigation. She was seventy-four-year-old Edith Smith, who, despite her age, was known for her excellent memory and observation skills.

Michael hoped that the elderly lady might have noticed something that night that could help solve the case.

Especially since he knew that people like her were often underestimated in terms of the knowledge they had about their neighbours and what was going on in the neighbourhood, and from his own experience, he knew that they could be an excellent source of valuable information.

Michael parked his car on Darrington Road at 5:30 p.m., not far from the house he was heading to.

"Really, you should do it in your free time..." Paul said unfavourably. "...I don't feel comfortable that we spend time on private matters during our service."

"It's not a private matter..." Michael replied. "...besides, you know how few days off we have from work, if I only wanted to do it then, I would never finish it." He added.

"Yes, I know."

"Then stop complaining, we won't be here long, thirty minutes at most."

"Okay, go, I'll stay in the car, in case something comes over the radio." Paul agreed.

Michael nodded, got out of the vehicle and headed towards the house, trying to be as discreet as possible.

He crossed the gate and approached the front door, feeling a slight tension in the air. When he reached the first floor, a brown door appeared in front of him. He knocked gently but firmly, hoping that the old lady was home. After a moment, the door opened and a short, grey-haired woman with a sharp gaze stood on the threshold.

"Good day, ma'am, my name is Michael Williams, and I am a detective." He introduced himself politely and showed his badge to confirm his words.

Edith Smith invited him inside, indicating a small, cosy living room filled with memorabilia from the past. The man reluctantly entered.

"Excuse me for disturbing you at this hour, Mrs. Smith..." Michael began, sitting down in the offered chair. "...I would like to ask you a few questions about the night of January 8, 1982, when there was a murder at a gas station."

Edith nodded, settling comfortably on the couch.

"Oh yes, I remember that night very well... she replied calmly. "...the news spread very quickly; it was truly a terrible tragedy." She added.

"I agree, because you see, I am investigating the case," Michael replied.

The older woman frowned in surprise.

"But the verdict has already been passed, isn't it, young Johnson, who is the perpetrator?" she asked.

"Excuse me, but I cannot give details of my investigation, but yes, Mr. Johnson is currently in prison." The policeman replied.

Edith's face brightened after these words.

"Ma'am, have you seen this car on the street here?" Michael got to the point, showing her the photo.

The woman took the photo in her hand, then reached for the nightstand where her reading glasses were lying. She put them on her face and leaned closer to the photo.

"Oh yes, it belongs to the boyfriend of the girl who lives below me." She confirmed.

"That's right, can you recall the car parked somewhere around here that night? After midnight, to be precise." Michael pricked up his ears, waiting for an answer.

"Oh, unfortunately not." She replied after a moment.

"Do you remember if it was anywhere on the street?" He probed.

"I can't answer this question, I was already asleep at this time, I felt bad all day." She replied.

"I understand..." Michael was inconsolable. "...regardless, thank you for talking to me." He added, getting up from the armchair.

"I'm sorry I couldn't help." He heard a woman's voice as he walked to the door.

"No problem, Mrs. Smith, please don't worry." He replied, turning to her for a moment.

"Of course, but you know what, try talking to the neighbour in the house across the street..." She said suddenly, with excitement in her voice. "...there lives a black man who walks his dog every night, his name is Theodore Davis, if anyone knows, it will be him." She added.

"Fantastic, thank you very much," Michael replied enthusiastically, which brought a smile to the older woman's face.

The detective left the building and was about to head to the other location when he saw Paul walking towards him at a fast pace.

"Let's go!" he shouted while still quite a distance away from him.

"What's up?" Michael stopped in his tracks.

"We got to go...!" Paul repeated. "...we've got a shooting! Three dead!"

"Shit!" the detective cursed under his breath, then ran to the vehicle, forgetting everything.

A few seconds later, he quickly sat down in the driver's seat and immediately started the engine.

"What's going on?" he asked.

"Headquarters reports a triple murder at the end of Horizon Boulevard, police officers on site report a shooting, three young Mexicans are dead," Paul explained.

"Horizon Boulevard? It's a few minutes from here." Michael stated.

"That's right."

"Gang fights?" Michael wondered as he manoeuvred the vehicle at the signal after exceeding the speed limit.

"I wouldn't be so sure about that..." his partner replied. "...We haven't had a gang fight here in years."

"Well, there is nothing left to do but to check it out." Michael added.

The two officers found themselves on a long street called Horizon Boulevard, which they had to travel to get to the place from which the call had come.

Michael was forced to postpone his visit to Theodore Davis, but that didn't mean he wouldn't come back to it.

A moment later, detectives arrived at the address, and the place was already swarming with police and emergency services.

By this time, four police cars and two ambulances had arrived, and the police had managed to cordon off the area with yellow security tape. As is usually the case in such situations, the circumstances also attracted dozens of curious civilians.

The time on the clock was 6:15 p.m. when Michael and Paul exited the vehicle.

"What a circus." Paul said as he buttoned his coat.

"No wonder, such events always attract onlookers," Michael replied.

The men approached the police tape where the officer was standing.

"Hey Steve, what are the initial findings?" Michael asked the officer.

"Three male bodies, young Mexicans in their twenties, look like they had a cleverly set up kitchen in the basement here." Reported the policeman, while pointing at a nondescript apartment block.

The term *kitchen* was police parlance for a small laboratory where methamphetamine, crack cocaine, and even, in many cases, heroin were produced.

"All shot? Did the neighbours see anything?" Paul spoke up.

"Yeah, someone made a bloodbath down there..." he began to answer the question. "...as for the residents, well, they claim they don't know anything, but we think they're afraid to testify, all Latino, the call came from a passing civilian who heard the shots and then saw two hooded men quickly exiting the building." He added.

"Okay, have you taken a statement from that person yet?" Michael said.

"We're working on it, he's in the patrol car, he's agreed to testify."

"Okay, take his personal information and with his permission, we'll get back to you." Michael added.

"Of course." The officer said, then raised the tape high so the detectives could get under it.

"Kitchen, Mexicans, bloodbath." Paul repeated the key points of the conversation.

"Yeah, it doesn't look good." Michael agreed.

On the way to the building, they passed two more uniformed officers, and only at the entrance did the third one show them the direction they should go.

"This way, gentlemen, down the stairs." He said.

Heading towards his destination via a dimly lit staircase, Michael's mind was filled with an image of what he might see next. The sight of blood, corpses and drug production sites was not unfamiliar to him, as he had encountered them many times. However, what he saw after reaching the site exceeded his wildest expectations.

The medium-sized underground room was furnished very professionally, and it was obvious that it had been operating here for years. The necessary equipment for distilling liquids, chemicals, burners and everything needed for production and carrying out the final phase, so that the drug could be portioned, packaged and prepared for sale.

"Son of a bitch." Paul was impressed; he too expected a dingy room with old, used bottles, basic equipment, raw materials of dubious quality and origin, as is usually the case with a home *kitchen*.

The only detail that did not fit the scenery, which looked as if it had been taken straight from an advertisement for a painkiller, was the walls stained with blood and brain fragments of the people working there.

"Thoughts?" Michael asked, looking around.

"Yeah, I think, I don`t even know where to start," Paul replied in shock.

Three headless bodies lay next to each other in an almost perfect row in the middle of the room, each of them had their hands tied behind their backs with a black cable. The men were kneeling before their deaths, which clearly meant a ruthless execution.

"Gentlemen, can you leave us a room for one minute?" Michael turned to the two officers in the room.

"Yes, sir." One of them replied, and they both began to climb the stairs.

Michael approached the bodies, carefully scanning every inch of the space. Blood, pieces of skull and brain were literally everywhere, from the ceiling to every corner; it was difficult to take a step without stepping on one of them.

"That had to be a shotgun. " He stated after a moment.

"Yeah, that would explain why a random passerby was able to hear the shots," Paul replied without moving from his seat.

"I wondered about that at first too, this place is almost completely soundproof in the basement, only shots from such a large calibre would be able to cause such great damage, additionally carrying the noise far from here." Michael summed up.

"It's even hard to tell that they are Mexicans, if it weren't for the tattoos, I wouldn't be able to tell."

"But these aren't just any tattoos..." Michael replied suddenly. "...see?"

Paul crouched down to get a better view.

"Oh fuck." He said that when he saw what his partner was trying to show him.

"Exactly, those three men without heads are members of the Mexican mafia," Michael replied, looking at the letter *M* tattooed on the front of the dead men's arms.

"Okay, I see two possibilities here, first, someone attacked them to steal the product and money, not knowing who they were messing with..." Paul thought aloud. "...But the second possibility is that they were killed on purpose, then we would have a much bigger problem." He added.

"That's right, let's hope it was an isolated incident, otherwise we could be dealing with a gang war." Michael replied, straightening up on his feet.

"So, let the technicians in and go downtown?"

"That would be the best solution. I doubt they'll find any useful information for us here. We'll try asking around town, maybe Henry will know something about it." Michael agreed.

A short time later, detectives left the crime scene. Their next goal was to find the informant, Henry, a local drunkard and member of the Aryan Brotherhood, who was facing charges that occasionally served as a hook for the detectives when they needed to find out what was going on in the criminal underworld. The men knew exactly where to find him.

To do this, all they had to do was drive to the Five Points area, where most bars were, and simply check out a few of them. Once they arrived, the officers began looking for the least crowded places at that time of day, knowing that Henry avoided those. 20 minutes later, they got lucky when they found the informant in one of the establishments, drinking a beer by himself at the bar.

"Fuck my life." Henry said quietly when he saw them.

The detectives approached the older man and stood on either side of him.

"Hi Henry, a soul of the party as always, I see." Paul joked.

"What the hell do you want?" Henry asked.

"To talk, we haven't seen each other for a long time," Michael replied.

"Are you guys nuts? You know I can't be seen with you; do you want me to get wacked?" The man was indignant.

"No one wants you dead, even if you have a lot on your conscience," Paul said.

"Speaking of death, there were three new visitors of Mexican descent on the mortuary register today, do you know anything about that?" Michael echoed his partner.

"How the fuck should I know? I haven't moved from here all day!"

"Yeah, I can smell you've been here all day." Paul replied, who had the dubious pleasure of feeling the breath of his interlocutor.

"But we're not just interested in the whole incident, we want to know why it happened." Michael added.

"Who the hell do you think I am, a fortune teller? Do you think I carry a crystal ball in my pocket or what?" Henry was nervous.

"Crystal ball maybe not, but you've definitely heard something from your colleagues." Paul continued.

Michael glanced at his partner, who also looked in his direction. Over the years of working together, they sometimes managed to understand each other without words, and this was no different. Paul's facial expression clearly said - the guy's hiding something.

"Be honest with us, Henry, we need to know if there's going to be more dead bodies." Michael tried again.

"People die all the time, and I don't know what you expect from me," Henry replied evasively, then took a sip of his beer.

"Okay, Michael, clearly, he doesn't know anything," Paul said suddenly.

Henry's eyes lit up with hope that the police would soon leave him alone.

"Yes, we still have to reopen the investigation into that robbery at the jeweller's from four months ago, new evidence has come to light," Michael replied, and they both pretended to leave.

Henry knew exactly what kind of robbery the detectives were talking about because he had been involved in one himself, so he had no choice but to fall for this primitive ruse.

"All right, then! Come over here!" He called after them.

The policemen returned to their seats, satisfied.

"There's a rumour that the Mexicans wacked two brothers recently," he said quietly.

After these words, Paul's eyes immediately focused on Michael, and the man felt fear pierce him. If what Henry said was true, it meant that the worst-case scenario had just been confirmed.

"Where did they kill them? Here?" Michael asked.

"No..." Henry replied and took a long sip of beer. "...in Mexico."

"So, the Aryans are taking revenge," Paul stated.

"The board has issued a death sentence for Franco Perez, and I don't know how they plan to get him. I only know that they want him dead." The informant added.

"Well, this is going to be quite a slaughterhouse," Michael added.

"I don't know anything more, now, get lost, before someone sees you."

The police had no reason to press the informant any longer, and they had already got what they wanted to know.

Although the news was not what they wanted to hear, it was information that allowed them to prepare for the upcoming events.

Events that were to claim many lives in a short time and usher in a new chapter in the history of gangster wars.

17

An eye for an eye.

"Tell me what your love is, and I'll tell you who you are."

It had been a week since Edward had last returned from Mexico. According to the agreement he had made with Franco Perez, he was now to return to his estate and report to him on the events in El Paso.

One of the main commanders of the Mexican Mafia realised that revenge from the brotherhood for the death of two members was inevitable. That is why he ordered Ed to observe the situation on the spot and report on the planned steps of the opponent.

However, Edward, not being a higher-ranking person in the hierarchy, had no access to decisions made at the top, he could only rely on rumours or what was passed on by brothers occupying the same level as him, which is why he was unable to obtain the latest information or quickly pass it on to the head of the opposing organization.

Because of this, he couldn't warn him about the upcoming attack on one of the gangsters' drug production facilities, which he learned about after the fact.

The matter was also complicated by the fact that the fraternity members had been given the green light to attack a rival gang, and some of the attacks were simply spontaneous.

Edward realised that in this chaos, his information was too unreliable and impossible for Perez to use. In this situation, Edward had to act carefully, so as not to be caught in a trap by both sides of the conflict. But on this day, he felt confident because he had important information that Perez needed and that he would not learn anywhere else.

It was 4:00 p.m., and Edward got into his red Ford Escort, ready to go. Not wanting to arouse suspicion, he casually informed his colleagues that he would not be in town that day.

Ed was not considered a serious player, so his colleagues were not interested in what he did in his free time, which worked to his advantage.

Because no one suspected him, he was able to move around the organisation like a shadow, pursuing his personal agenda without drawing attention to himself. It was like that this time too.

The back of his car was stuffed with $200,000 in carefully concealed cash, which he intended to give to Perez in exchange for some pure cocaine ready to sell.

"I hope you know what you're doing," Stacy said as she walked him to his car.

"Don't worry about a thing, I have a deal with him," he replied.

"You better be, because if you lose that money, I'll personally kill you."

"It's all set, nothing's going to happen, I'm sure of it," Ed replied.

"Okay, let's get going, it's getting late."

"I'll be back tomorrow with the product, make sure the customers know that," he added and started the engine.

As he set off, his thoughts revolved around the risks he was taking.

He was travelling alone and knew his mission was dangerous, but the adrenaline and the prospect of a big payoff kept him going.

By not taking any backup with him, he wanted to show his unconditional trust and loyalty.

Perez, who was not only a ruthless criminal but also an ambitious drug trafficker, needed access to cash to expand his operations, and Edward realised that this meeting could determine his future.

The drive was long, and Edward spent the entire route analysing the details of his exchange, wondering if Perez would be pleased. He also wondered if Stacy was up to the task.

The man assumed that he would soon come into possession of a large amount of the drug and intended to sell it as quickly as possible without attracting unwanted attention from the brotherhood.

All it would take was for one person to notice that Ed was dealing, and the risky game would be over.

There would undoubtedly be questions about where he got the substance from, and Ed would be in a lot of trouble, so he couldn't let that happen.

The city had become an extremely dangerous place by then, so he needed wealthy outsiders who would be willing to buy large quantities of the drug from him at once, rather than single doses. That was Stacy's job, to get people involved who weren't connected to El Paso.

Crossing the border from the American side went remarkably smoothly, and in less than an hour, he was already driving through the city of Juárez. As he approached Perez's estate, he began to feel unpleasant cramps in his stomach, his nerves making themselves known.

Even though the man had been to this place many times before, he still felt alien there, and every step he took on this land aroused anxiety in him. Fears that had been buried deep in his mind but were now crawling to the surface like unwanted demons.

He could not afford to make a mistake, and he knew that in this game, there was no room for weakness or a moment of hesitation. Every decision, every move had its consequences, and in this world, it was a matter of life or death.

The world Ed lived in was ruled by money, power, and violence, and people used one to gain the other without hesitation.

Power was gained by force and used to gather the money needed to maintain it, and the whole process was almost always achieved by violence, making the three inseparable.

In any case, human life was as important as last year's snow, and each new person was very easily replaced by another, and Edward knew it perfectly well.

Edward looked up at the imposing walls of Perez's mansion, taking in every detail as if his life depended on it, because it did.

The tension grew as he wondered what the next hour would bring.

If he had disappeared that day, only a few people would have wondered for a moment what happened to him? After which, the memory of him would fade away.

While a Mexican mafioso could, with a smile on his face, order his dead body to be thrown into the pigs to be devoured.

Security guards positioned high on the walls, as well as those on the ground, closely watched his car as it passed through the huge metal gates that guaranteed safety.

As customary, he navigated around the fountain situated in front of the house and halted his vehicle near the garage, where it would be promptly taken.

Then he left the keys in the ignition and got out of the car. Franco Perez was already waiting for him. He was standing between two muscular and armed private security guards.

As Ed got close enough to see his boss's face, he noticed that he wasn't smiling like he used to. Instead, his expression was serious and thoughtful, as if he was very nervous about something.

A red light went off in Edward's mind. *I don't like this; something is definitely wrong.* He thought.

At the same time.

Michael found an opportunity to visit the home of Theodore Davis, Stacy's neighbour across the street. According to Edith Smith, the woman who lived downstairs in Stacy's house, the man was seen walking his dog every night and there was a strong possibility that he remembered whether the red Ford Escort (Edward's car) was parked in front of the house after midnight on the night of the gas station murder.

The detective considered this detail to be very significant because it was not mentioned anywhere in the testimony of Steward's brother, who only said that he left the family home after midnight, leaving the man there alone.

If this were true, he must have appeared in this district late at night, logically. However, if this didn't happen, it could mean that Edward was hiding something else.

The time on the watch showed 5:34 p.m. when the officer parked his car in front of Theodore Davis's house. The area was pleasantly quiet, with the sun breaking through the few clouds in the sky. Michael opened the metal gate of the fence and had to pass through a small garden before reaching the porch of the property.

Before he could knock on the door, he heard the sound of birds chirping carried by the cool wind from a nearby tree.

This made the policeman stop for a moment to enjoy the peace, which contrasted with the tension of the investigation.

When he finally raised his hand to knock, the door suddenly opened, and Theodore Davis stood in the doorway, surprised by the unexpected visit. A black man in his 50s looked at him with a surprised look.

"Can I help you with something?" he asked after a moment.

"Yes, I'm sorry..." Michael was slightly embarrassed. "...I'm a detective, my name is Michael Williams, I'd like to ask you a few questions." He added quickly and showed his badge.

"Oh, hell no! I already told you; I have nothing to do with him!" Theodore replied suddenly.

"Excuse me?"

"Yes! You're here to ask about my nephew, I don't know what's going on with him and I don't care! Just like I told your colleagues, I have nothing to do with him!" The man explained.

"Excuse me, but there's been a misunderstanding. I'm not here to talk about your nephew." Michael replied.

"Oh yes, so what do you want?"

"A few days ago, I spoke to Edith Smith, an elderly woman who lives in this house." The detective pointed to the house across the street.

"Yes, I know Edith, a very handsome woman, did she send you after me?" The man's voice changed from indignation to suspicion.

"No, sir, I'm trying to determine if this car was parked somewhere here on Sunday night, January 8th-9th, after midnight...?" Michael handed the photo to Theodore. "... Edith told me that you walk your dog every evening and you might have seen him."

"Yes, the damn mutt. My wife harassed me for months to get a dog for our daughter, and when I finally gave in and did, she stopped taking care of him after two weeks. And you know, who has to walk that bastard every night?! Yes, you're fucking right, me!" Theodore got angry, completely forgetting about the photo and Michael's question.

"I can imagine how frustrating this must be..." The detective nodded, gaining the man's favour. "...do you recognise this vehicle?"

Theodore calmed down and looked at the photograph.

"Of course..." He answered after a moment. "...He comes here almost every night, usually parks in this spot..." He pointed to a spot under a tree on the road. "...I know, because the mutt likes to piss there, every night at twelve-thirty, as if he waits until that exact hour to piss me off." He added, clearly irritating himself.

"Okay, do you remember walking the dog on Sunday night from January 8th to 9th?"

"Let me think..." the man fell silent for a moment. "...it's certain that I left the house, because that little bastard always waits by the door at this time, as if he fucking knew the clock..." he started to get irritated again, thinking about the dog. *"...but I don't think that car was here then."* He added.

"But are you sure about that?" The detective wanted to make sure.

"Yes, I think I'm sure, because you see, that little prick always goes there to pee." The elderly man kept repeating himself.

For Michael, this was a good sign, indicating that there might be a hidden meaning to Edward's story. If that were the case, he would now have a reason to continue investigating.

Of course, this was not proof, and Stacy's neighbours' memory could be unreliable, but it was a plus and motivation to continue digging into the subject.

"Can you think of anyone else who can confirm this?"

"Sure...!" Theodore replied enthusiastically. "...just like the guy who lives next to me. The guy is paranoid, he doesn't leave the house and checks everyone who comes here, I don't know if he's afraid of someone, he's on drugs or something else, but there are even rumours that he records his neighbours with a camera."

This was music to the detective's ears; words such as "camera" and "recording" took on special meaning in those days and were always received with great enthusiasm, especially in the profession of a policeman.

"Great, thanks for your cooperation, what's this man's name?"

"James Campbell, I just doubt he'll open the door; the guy's crazy, he probably already knows there's a stranger hanging around here," Theodore added.

"I'll try anyway." The detective said, walking away to the exit of the property. Theodore just shrugged and went back to his apartment.

A moment later, Michael was standing in front of James' house, and at first glance it was obvious that a mentally ill person lived there. You could tell by the fact that all the windows were tightly covered with various materials. In some of them, it was just ordinary curtains, but in others, there were even blankets and newspapers. All this was undoubtedly intended to effectively block the view of what was inside.

The detective thought the place looked like a typical drug addict's home, but with Theodore's words in mind, he didn't assume that and braced himself for someone who simply wasn't completely sane. Michael moved towards the door, and as he passed under the house, he noticed one of the window curtains move slightly.

"Well, that's right, he's not leaving the house." He said to himself.

...BOOM... BOOM... BOOM... He knocked on the door.

"Mr. James Campbell! Please open up! I'm with the police!" he called, moving his head closer to the crack in the door and then taking three steps back.

There was silence for a moment, and Michael felt impatient.

...*BOOM... BOOM... BOOM...* he knocked again.

"Mr. Campbell, I know you're in there! Open up! I just want to ask you a few questions!" he said and moved back again.

Finally, he heard gentle footsteps from inside the house.

"Show me your badge." He suddenly heard a quiet voice. The detective obediently took out his ID and, stretching his hand at head level, presented it to the peephole in the door.

Then the door opened slowly, and behind it appeared a man in his thirties with an unhealthy appearance. Slim and dirty with red eyes and a clearly tired face. James Campbell looked at Michael distrustfully.

"What do you want?" he asked quietly, almost in a whisper.

"Mr. Campbell, I need to talk to you, please don't be afraid, I'm not here because of you," Michael replied calmly, trying to ease the atmosphere as much as possible.

James nodded and opened the door wider, inviting the detective inside. Michael was hit by the smell of damp and forgetfulness that emanated from the house.

"Please sit down." He gestured to an old armchair, covered in dust and stains.

Michael reluctantly sat down, looking up at his host, knowing he had to tread carefully to gain James' trust and learn more about his situation. The detective discreetly looked around the apartment, searching for the recording equipment Theodore had mentioned, but found nothing. Instead, he found himself among piles of garbage in the form of old and dirty clothes, shoes, empty pizza boxes and Coke bottles, as well as the general mess that was the result of not cleaning the apartment for months.

Jesus, doesn't he have any family? Or anyone who could help him? He thought.

However, he kept this thought to himself, not wanting to offend his interlocutor.

"James..." He began to speak calmly. "...Relax, you're not in trouble, I'm here because I think you can help me with something."

"Me?" The young man was surprised.

"Yes, Theodore told me that you know the neighbourhood well and keep an eye on the people hanging around here." Michael replied.

James nervously looked from him to the door, to the floor, and then back to him. It looked like he was expecting someone to enter the apartment or emerge unexpectedly from underground at any moment.

"If his behaviour is not caused by psychoactive substances, then he probably suffers from persecutory paranoia." The detective thought to himself.

"Theodore said that?"

"Luckily, he recognises his neighbour." He added to himself in his thoughts.

"That's right..." He replied after a moment. "...He also said that you are like a local guardian angel who looks after everyone." He lied in good faith.

Seeing James' state and the way he was acting, Michael decided to talk to him differently. In his opinion, the best way to reach the slightly mentally disabled man would be to talk to him like he were a child. Slowly and friendly, using terms of endearment that best described in his mind what the policeman was trying to get out of him.

The young man looked at him with large, surprised eyes and a modest smile on his lips. Then he quickly lowered his head, embarrassed.

"I don't like strangers coming here..." he replied after a moment, not taking his eyes off the floor. "...strangers always bring problems." He added.

"I think so too..." Michael noticed James smiling again, even though he still kept his face turned towards the floor. "...did you hear what happened at the gas station a few weeks ago? A bad man hurt innocent people." He finally got to the point, not having the whole day to hunt, his time was limited.

James slowly raised his head and looked into the detective's eyes with an absent gaze. The slight smile disappeared, replaced by a look of confusion.

"James, I need to know, did you see this car here on January 9th after 12 o'clock at night?" the policeman handed him a photo.

James suddenly jumped up from his seat, and instead of accepting the photo handed to him, he quickly walked over to the closet standing against the wall on his right. Surprised by this reaction, Michael frowned and watched the man's actions with interest.

Then James opened the closet door and everything became obvious. Inside were dozens of VHS tapes stacked vertically, one on top of the other. The man leaned down and began checking the notes on the covers. After a moment, he pulled out one of them and, holding it in both hands, wordlessly crossed the room and went to the TV at the other end - all under the detective's watchful eye. A few seconds later, the sound of an old mechanism echoed through the room, which began to eat away at the plastic casing inside with all its force.

Michael stood up from his seat and walked over to James, who was kneeling on his knees in front of the TV. Then, horizontal white stripes began to scroll across the screen before the actual image appeared.

The detective looked at the lower left corner, where the date and time of the recording were displayed – 08.01.1982/23:26:11.

At first, the chaotic movements of the camera, directed just outside the apartment window, between the frame and the curtain, made no sense and nothing could be seen on them, apart from sudden jumps from the floor to the window and so on. The recording took a moment to stabilise.

Michael realised that James was trying to record two Latinos standing in front of his house, and when the men left, the recording cut off.

The camera then restarted, showing the same jerky movements on the screen, combined with the indecisiveness and inexperience of the operator.

The only difference between this and the earlier shot was the date – 09.01.1982/00:19:57. A few seconds passed, and finally the camera image stabilised, showing the street lit by streetlights.

The car that caught James's attention was parked under a tree that Michael recognised as the "toilet" of Mr. Theodore's pet.

The car's headlights were on, and whoever it was must have recently been standing there, because he hadn't even gotten out of the vehicle yet before he became the target of James's anxious curiosity.

"Is this the car you're talking about?" James asked.

The detective wasn't sure yet. He did see a car in the distance, but the poor quality of the recording prevented him from even recognising the colour at that moment. So, he ignored the man's question and continued to watch carefully.

Only after a moment did James casually use the *zoom in* option in the camera functions, thanks to which the detective felt that the details of the vehicle he was looking for were coming to light. The brand and colour were the same, which wasn't good news.

"Oh, damn it!" the policeman said, not hiding his dissatisfaction.

His disappointment was even greater because, after talking to Theodore, the man had a glimmer of hope that the vehicle had not been there on the night of the murder. But now it was becoming clear that the neighbour had been mistaken.

As the minutes passed, Michael noticed the car door slowly opening and the silhouette of a man emerging from inside. The person looked around cautiously, as if afraid that someone was watching him.

"Stop the tape." He ordered suddenly, and James obediently pressed the stop button on the player. The detective squinted, trying to make out more details, but the darkness and the flickering light of the streetlights made it difficult to make out the face, especially since it was covered by a baseball cap.

At that point, he had no choice but to rely on his memory. As an experienced investigator, he was skilled at absorbing details related to the characteristics of the physical appearance of people he had previously interviewed. Therefore, in his mind's eye, he recalled the figure of Edward, both his posture and the clothes he was wearing, when he visited him in the morning on January 9, 1982. Taking stock of all the details, he sadly realised that he was most likely watching Ed return to Stacy's apartment, as he had said earlier.

Fuck! This is a dead end. He thought.

The young man turned the recording back on as Michael was getting ready to leave.

"Thank you for your help, James. I really appreciate it."

"I'm glad I could be useful." The man replied and then pressed the "play" button.

Michael followed the figure on the screen with his eyes, who disappeared in the darkness after a moment, and in its place appeared another person in a blue bathrobe with a dog on a leash.

"At least he wasn't mistaken about one thing." Michael stated, looking at Theodore for a moment before the recording ended.

"There is one more thing, James, in a few days you will be visited by a nice lady who will help you sort out your affairs, do you agree to that?" The detective asked, slowly walking to the door.

The young man flinched slightly at these words, and Michael noticed it.

"Don't be afraid, she's my good friend, we just want to help you." He hurried to explain.

"Okay, I'm here every day." James nodded shyly.

"Okay, see you in a few days then." The policeman added and left the apartment.

At that point, he began to have serious doubts about whether it would be possible to prove Steward's innocence.

The detective began to think that perhaps it really didn't make sense, and he should accept the fact that the man was rightly convicted.

Given the circumstances, he felt that in the meantime he could at least help James, who clearly needed support, so he decided to talk to a friend who worked in social services to find out what options were available to people like him, and he planned to return to the Steward case later, or not at all.

7:24 p.m., Franco Perez's residence.

Edward spoke to Franco as he sat by his pool.

"...They'll be bringing in materials from Colombia..." Ed spoke. "...I don't know where or when yet, but there will be new production sites." Franco greedily absorbed information obtained through the double agent.

Although he was initially negative, especially since he had lost one *kitchen* and several people in the city, and Edward had not warned him of the coming threat, he put that thought aside because Edward's report had proven surprisingly useful. Now every detail counted and could decide in favour of one of the parties in taking over the domination in the criminal underworld.

What mattered was strategy and planning the next moves so that the opponent could not predict them. Franco, although unknowingly started this deadly game, was in a better position at the time, having an ace up his sleeve: Ed.

"...I can't tell you in detail about all their plans, because I simply don't have access to them..." Ed said, pulling Franco out of his thoughts. "...there will be casualties and attacks, it can't be avoided, but you are probably aware of that?"

The gangster looked at him with an icy gaze.

"You will be given a contact in the city, if you hear of an upcoming attack, you will call..." He replied harshly. "...my men are like brothers to me, for everyone killed two Aryans will die, and your task is to make sure that any information intercepted immediately ends up in my hands, in return, I will provide you with the best product on the market, on which you will make a fortune."

A greedy smile appeared on Edward's face; this was exactly what he had been aiming for. Now he had what he wanted.

By informing Franco about his limited access to the brotherhood's intentions, he also ensured that he could avoid being accused of negligence in the event of the death of additional Mexican Mafia members, and at the same time, he guaranteed himself an endless source of the most popular intoxicant among drug addicts.

Reading between the lines, the man understood that Franco, in his own way, simply intended to move him a rung higher in the hierarchy of the criminal organisation.

Franco, seeing the reaction of his associate, wondered how far Edward would go to achieve his goals. He knew there was no room for scruples in this game and that both of them would have to act ruthlessly to maintain their position.

"Just remember..." he said suddenly. "...even if there's a suspicion that you're playing both sides, you won't make it out alive."

Edward gulped and nodded, his smile disappearing as quickly as it had appeared. Then Franco's employee emerged from behind the house, and the gangster saw him immediately.

"Your car is ready for the road, you can go." He announced.

18

An eye for an eye.

"Tell me what your love is and I'll tell you who you are."

Three days later.

Polunsky Unit Texas, 5:55 p.m.

It was almost time to get out for some fresh air. Ever since John had announced at a fraternity meeting that the commission had lifted the ban on engaging in direct conflict with Latino prisoners, the facility had been in a state of lawlessness. Incidents occurred daily, almost always ending in a full-blown brawl.

Disorder prevailed.

The situation had become so dangerous that prison officials had decided to increase the number of staff.

However, this did not discourage people who had previously identified their target, and then the task became to reach it, regardless of the forces and equipment that the guards had at their disposal.

The attack could occur anywhere and at any time, which is why it was a wise move to grow a third eye on the back of the head. At this point, I decided to go off the sedatives again, because I had no intention of becoming anyone's punching bag. Brotherhood members acted both together and separately.

They talked openly among themselves about who their next target would be, and no one objected.

John, in particular, with only a week left on his sentence before he was to be released, clearly had no intention of doing anything to jeopardise it.

Since one of the fraternity's board members suggested that I join the organisation, many new white men have appeared in prison who also wanted to follow in my footsteps.

Each of them tried to prove themselves to the brotherhood in such a way as to be accepted into the organisation.

The idea was to show who among them was the most ruthless and tough, and in such circumstances, nothing showed this better than massacring a person of a different skin colour. Brutality and violence had become a daily part of prison life.

As the pressure and uncertainty mounted, each day brought a new wave of tension. Survival depended on the ability to quickly adapt to changing conditions and, above all, on the ability to defend oneself.

The members of the brotherhood that caught my attention were relentless in their pursuit of dominance, clearly defining boundaries and ruling through fear. With each passing day, their methods became more sophisticated and deliberate.

In prison, there was no room for weakness or sentiment. However, deep down, I knew that I had to find a way to survive without submitting to their brutal rules. In this world where force was the only law, moral principles were becoming a relic of the past.

My thoughts revolved around one idea: how to retain my humanity in a place where every step could mean a fight for life.

Over time, I began to notice clear divisions between the groups of prisoners that were driven by the Brotherhood. Alliances were formed to protect their members and intimidate their opponents.

I felt like I was walking a fine line between conforming to their rules and maintaining my own beliefs. Although every day was full of challenges, I was not going to give in to the omnipresent terror.

I knew I had to be stronger than ever before to maintain control of my destiny and not lose the hope for the future that might still await me outside the walls of this place.

Then I began to wait for the detective's next visit, my thoughts would return to his words every now and then, which helped me maintain a positive attitude, believing that there might still be a chance to free myself from this horrible environment.

However, I couldn't rely on it and succumb to my own illusions; the reality was here and now, making itself painfully felt from time to time. This was not the time to let down my guard and forget where I was, quite the opposite.

So, I stopped taking the pills, let Gary off the leash and allowed him to tame any naive person who thought he could attack me with impunity.

At the same time, I had in the back of my mind that one day, Michael Williams would show up here with good news.

Montana Avenue, State Road No. 62, same time.

"ALL EAST CITY UNITS!! REPORT OF A SHOOTING ON KURLER STREET IN THE BUTTERFIELD AREA!! SPECIAL PRECAUTIONS REQUIRED...!!" the woman from the headquarters transmitted the report over the radio, periodically adding some new facts about the event. Michael and Paul were already on their way, sirens blaring down Route 62. This was the second such incident in a week, and the detectives had no doubt that they would find several more bodies at the scene.

"The party continues," Paul said with his heart in his throat, watching his partner deftly manoeuvre the car, avoiding other road users.

"No doubt, and I'm afraid we'll get many more reports like that," Michael replied.

"Do you think it's worth visiting Henry again later and seeing if he knows anything?"

"I don't think he'll tell us anything we don't already know. In my opinion, the Aryans are eliminating the Mexicans and vice versa."

"The drug war?"

"Exactly, they're fighting for territory, and it'll calm down only when one side gives in," Michael summed up.

"It may take some time, but at least they're only killing each other and not civilians," Paul stated.

"Not yet. But it looks bad for our department, like we can't keep the peace in the city," Michael replied, slowly slowing down the car.

The detective turned onto *Commercial Dr* from where there were only a few hundred metres left to the destination.

The men fell silent in concentration, preparing themselves for what might await them in a moment.

A moment later, their vehicle pulled up on Kurler Street, where four police cars were already parked. The sun was slowly setting, and the lights of police refractors were illuminating the area, traditionally attracting the attention of those who were not welcome there at that time.

The detectives got out of the car and headed to the scene, which had apparently ended no more than twenty minutes ago. In the meantime, the officers managed to secure the area with police tape and began checking it. The circumstances were similar to the previous incident, again in a usually quiet area, with the difference that this time the target of the attack was a single-family home, which most likely contained another *kitchen*.

When Michael got close enough, from behind the police cars that had blocked his view until now, he saw four bodies covered in black oilcloth on the lawn in front of the house. His mind immediately began to analyse this fact.

"It looks like they didn't even make it to the house." He said.

"That's right, the shooting happened outside, like..." Paul replied, but Michael interrupted him.

"Like they were expected." He finished for his partner.

"Have you checked the house yet?" Michael asked the officer.

"We're waiting for the techs, but our boys are inside." The officer by the police car replied.

The detectives ducked to get under the yellow tape. Paul immediately started walking towards the building, but Michael first wanted to see who was hiding under the black oilcloth closest to him. So, he went to one of the bodies and uncovered his face, while Paul stopped in place, waiting for his partner, watching him carefully. Michael looked underneath the material and saw a white man in his 30s. His eyes were open, and his face was frozen in an expression of suffering and surprise in the last moments of his life.

The detective had never seen him before, but he easily recognised the stranger's origin. It was all because of the characteristic shaved head and the swastika tattooed on the right side of his neck.

"Aryans." Michael heard his partner's voice behind him.

"Yeah..." He answered, straightening up on his feet. "...and inside we will probably find some dead Latino." He added, turning to face Paul.

Both officers entered the building, passing another officer in the doorway. It was then that Michael realised how wrong he had been a moment ago. The place was spotlessly clean, and it looked as if someone had recently done a thorough cleaning. There was not even a trace appropriate to the dramatic scene that had taken place less than half an hour ago. The interior of the house resembled a typical establishment where drugs were sold discreetly. Aside from a few couches, a table, and electronics, the living room wasn't furnished in the way that a legitimate resident would normally.

The kitchen was also empty, except for an empty refrigerator and microwave, indicating that the occupants had been warming up meals bought in town.

"There are stairs to the basement to the left," the officer guarding the entrance said.

Michael slowly walked down the short hallway, mentally taking notes. First, he carefully looked around the living room, which was on the right. Then he looked at the front windows, tightly covered with curtains. There were no traces of glass shards on the floor, which in theory should have been there, since the gunmen had attacked the front of the house, but it remained untouched. Paul turned the corner and began to descend the stairs, Michael a few steps behind him.

"Four dead attackers and a drug den with no signs of a struggle..." he analysed the facts in his mind. "...they knew about the attack, no doubt."

"And what do you think?" Paul asked, standing at the bottom of the empty basement.

"I think it's a nice house, if only there were flowers in front of it instead of dead Aryans," Michael joked.

"Haha, very funny, look at this..." Paul pointed to the interior of the room. "...they tried really hard to clean this place perfectly, you can still smell the bleach in the air." He added.

"Yes, but that won't be enough to cover all the tracks, I'm sure we'll get a whole list of fingerprints that we'll have to check, we're definitely dealing with drug dealers here."

"Absolutely," Paul replied.

"Let's see what the neighbours' have to say, maybe we will learn something interesting."

"First, let's check the first floor, I have a feeling we'll find something interesting there," Paul replied.

Michael nodded and headed for the exit, Paul following him. As they emerged from the basement, they saw that several new rapid response units had arrived outside, as well as ambulances waiting for permission to remove the bodies.

"You can start working downstairs." Michael said to the officer at the door, while Paul, without waiting for his partner, began to climb the stairs.

"Roger that, what about the bodies, Detective?"

"Wait another five minutes and have them removed, we know what the cause of death was"

"Understood." The officer replied and whistled loudly to the team of technicians who were already waiting for their turn.

A moment later, Michael joined Paul upstairs. The other detective was already in the room above the front door of the house, looking through the window at the situation from the perspective of the shooter.

"Check this out..." he said when he saw Michael enter the room. "...a few shots."

Michael stepped closer, and Paul gave him the space where he was standing so he could see exactly what he meant.

"Yes, for someone with experience, it could be enough." He confirmed.

"It could and was enough, especially since the shooting was not done in a hurry or panic, look..." Paul extended his right hand and pretended to hold a gun in it.

"Bang... Bang... Bang... Bang... Four shots, four dead bodies, the fourth tried to escape, it is clear that he is further away from the others."

"The shooter must have been a professional, incredibly fast," Michael stated.

"Not necessarily, any experienced shooter is able to fire four accurate shots in two or three seconds, especially from such a short distance and calmly."

"I agree, they were surprised and didn't even have a chance to react." Michael admitted.

"That's exactly the point of an ambush."

"Indeed, but how did they know about the upcoming attack?"

"It looks to me like the Aryans have a rat among their ranks." Paul summed up.

"I think so too, let's go and ask the neighbours," Michael replied and turned towards the exit.

When they went outside, they noticed that interest in the event had waned, especially since the paramedics were already taking the dead to the ambulances.

There was still a small group of onlookers there, but the detectives didn't want to waste their time randomly searching for their nearest neighbours, so they decided to go to the house on the right. The first neighbour they knocked on was an older man who looked at them suspiciously from behind a closed door.

"Good evening, we're from the police, we'd like to ask you a few questions about your neighbours and what happened today," Paul began, showing his badge.

"I don't know anything..." The old man replied firmly. "...there's always something going on here, but I don't poke my nose into other people's business."

"Didn't you hear the shooting? Or have you noticed something disturbing in the last few days?" Michael asked, trying to be polite.

"I may have seen some suspicious cars parked on the street..." The old man muttered reluctantly. "...but you can check it out for yourselves."

"Thank you for your help, please remember that every little observation can be crucial," Paul smiled, trying to ease the mood.

They continued their search, but most of the neighbours were just as cautious and reserved. Only the young woman from across the street turned out to be more talkative.

"Yes, I heard shots, and when I looked out the window, I saw a black delivery truck screeching away, and it took me a moment to realise that there were bodies lying on the lawn..." She said, playing with the keys in her hands to calm her nerves. "...also, last night I noticed a group of men taking things out of the house. They looked stressed, and, in a hurry, they avoided eye contact, which seemed suspicious to me."

The cleaning crew. Michael thought.

"Could you describe these men in more detail?" He asked, pulling out a notebook.

"There were four of them, all dressed in dark clothes, maybe 30-40 years old," the woman frowned, trying to remember the details. "One of them had the number 13 tattooed on the back of his neck."

Paul looked at Michael, and understanding flashed in his eyes.

"Thank you for this information, it could be very helpful..." he said, handing the woman his business card. "...please contact us if you remember anything else."

Returning to the car, Paul and Michael exchanged glances.

"I think it's clear what happened here."

"Yes, the Aryans tried to eliminate the second hole, but the Mexicans were ready for them," Paul replied.

"Exactly, I'm afraid that will only lead to more carnage," Michael replied, concerned.

19

A dangerous game.

"Remembering the past means committing to the future."

"You did well, the boss told me to express his gratitude to you." A male voice spoke on the phone.

"I did what I had to do. I hope our agreement is still valid." Edward replied.

"Of course, the product will be waiting for you in three days." He heard in response.

"Perfect. I understand that the place and time remain the same?"

"That's right, and in the meantime, call me if you learn anything new."

"I will," Ed replied and hung up the phone.

Steward's brother was doing great. Not only did he quickly sell the drug he had previously smuggled from Mexico, as planned, diluting it with another substance to increase the quantity, but he also managed to overhear a conversation in a bar between the brothers, who were discussing the details of the upcoming operation.

Ed called the number Franco had given him and informed them of the approaching threat, which resulted in a quick evacuation of the premises and appropriate preparations for the arrival of uninvited guests.

So far, he had been doing exceptionally well in balancing between the two factions, and the dangerous game he was playing was bringing the expected results.

Thanks to the large amount that he had successfully invested in the product, his and Stacy's capital increased by 50%, which made him even more optimistic.

However, he had no intention of stopping there. The next step was to buy the drug again for the full amount, taking a huge risk once again, which, if successful, would bring 100% of the invested capital.

The extremely risky venture required not only cunning but also great mental resilience.

Ed, a naturally composed man, grew more confident with each success, but he understood any slip-up could cost him his life.

During another meeting with his partner, Franco, Edward wanted to discuss a new plan that aimed to increase profits.

Franco, who had much more experience in smuggling, had the knowledge the man wanted to gain.

Ed, in turn, knew how the brotherhood intended to break away from their former Mexican ally and start producing drugs on their own.

For this purpose, they intended to import the necessary substances from Colombia, and before finally taking over the market, they wanted to completely bleed out the competition, which Edward could not allow.

Having such a powerful business partner as Franco at the time, he was able to freely import cocaine into the country, where, over time, he planned to produce crack from it, a business worth millions.

However, if the entire business fell into the hands of the Aryans, Edward would have no choice but to abandon it.

In order to win the war for control of the drug market, it was necessary to obtain and pass on new information so that new ventures of the brotherhood could then be nipped in the bud.

These factors made the two men very dangerous allies, and their cooperation had been flawless so far. Ed hoped it would remain that way because there was a war going on, and to win it, they had to be exceptionally well organised.

The Aryan Brotherhood was not just any opponent.

It was an extremely deadly organization whose members were practically everywhere, from policemen to politicians, and its most effective bargaining chip was violence, ruthlessness and murder.

People who were willing to do anything to achieve their goals. Both Ed and Franco knew exactly how far the brothers would go to catch up with their enemies.

Therefore, Edward took all necessary security measures to remain in the shadows, while Franco Perez, who was in Mexico, thought that the tentacles of the Aryans would not reach him that far, but his belief in untouchability was soon to be questioned.

Meanwhile, Stacy, who had the right contacts and full confidence in Ed's skills, was involved in mass sales in their joint business, which allowed Ed to keep up appearances and avoid suspicion.

Her commitment and dedication were invaluable in this complicated undertaking. Ed knew that their success depended not only on their wits but also on perfect cooperation.

Every step had to be considered, and every move was carefully planned.

The future looked promising, but inherent uncertainty and risk were always lurking on the horizon.

Polunsky Unit, 2:57 p.m.

To pass the time, I talked to a friend from the next cell. Even though the brotherhood frowned upon correlation with other races, I found myself ignoring this rule.

Especially when time dragged on forever, and I didn't know what to do with myself.

That afternoon, I felt particularly nervous because I had received a message from a security guard who was a trusted friend of Michael's that a detective would be visiting me today.

The excitement and uncertainty of what he would tell me today made it difficult to control my emotions, and I eagerly awaited his arrival.

"I never thought I'd say this, but I'm glad I'm here and not outside," Tony said half-jokingly, half-seriously.

"Aren't you exaggerating a little? I don't think it's worse anywhere than here." I replied.

"Dude, you don't really know what's going on there, are you? Seven bodies have been found in just one week!"

"And where do you get this information from?" I asked.

"Jason keeps up with everything and tells us about interesting news." He confessed.

"And you think it's interesting?"

"Fuck yeah! And you don't?" he was surprised.

"Not really. From our side, the management neglects to provide the situation from behind the walls. Everyone is focused on what's happening inside." I confessed.

I was, of course, referring to the war with the Latinos. Since John had given his companions free rein, he stopped worrying about sharing news from the outside world.

This made it difficult to escape the impression that the conflict had also had a negative impact on the way the group was led.

"So far, four whites and three Latinos have fallen. Your war does not affect.

Black brothers." He added with satisfaction.

I had to agree with him here. It is no wonder that the *BGF,* as a neutral organization at that time, remained on the sidelines of the fierce conflict between the *Aryan Brotherhood* and the *Mexican Mafia,* maintaining itself in the most advantageous position.

While both sides were busy destroying each other, the *Black Guerrilla Family* could calmly strengthen their structures and, temporarily sidelined, focus on their own interests without drawing anyone's attention.

It was a time they had to make the most of because the group's management knew that this opportunity wouldn't last forever and that sooner or later, there would come a time when they would have to get back into the game.

There were also prospects of fundamental changes in the leadership of the brotherhood, as everyone knew that in a few days, the ten-year sentence John was serving would expire, and someone would have to replace him as leader.

Rumours and speculations left no doubt that Jack was the second person in command, and it was almost certain that he would become the new leader of the brotherhood in the *Polunsky Unit*.

The tension grew with each passing day, and the members of the brotherhood increasingly discussed the future of the organization.

Jack, although not yet officially named leader, has already begun to make changes to the structures, preparing to take full control.

He knew that his first decisions would be of key importance for the further fate of the *Aryan Brotherhood*.

In the meantime, Luis was in constant contact with Franco Perez's men and knew that the temporary advantage they had over their enemy would soon diminish if they did not take decisive action.

Their leaders were intensively planning their next moves, trying to anticipate every possible scenario.

In this atmosphere of uncertainty and constant danger, everyone eagerly awaited the day when John would leave the prison walls because he was the person who could make the necessary changes in the way the brotherhood was run outside the prison walls.

A skilled and ruthless strategist with vast experience in the criminal underworld, he could once and for all tip the scales of victory in the brotherhood's favour.

His return would be a turning point that would redefine the balance of power both outside and within the *Polunsky B. Unit*.

Jack, despite his self-confidence, knew that he would have to earn the respect and loyalty of all members to maintain his position as leader.

The long-awaited day was coming, and emotions were running high even before John joined his closest allies in freedom.

Everyone knew that from then on, nothing would be the same. Jack faced the biggest challenge of his career, and the *Aryan Brotherhood* had to prove that despite internal changes, it was still a force to be reckoned with.

…Thump…Thump…Thump…

I suddenly heard footsteps on a metal surface.

"A guard is coming," Tony announced and moved further into the cell.

"Johnson, visiting..." the man announced, standing by my cell. "...hands."

I turned my back to him and put my hands on my back, then moved closer to the bars so he could put handcuffs on me.

At that moment, I felt a slight contraction in my stomach caused by nervousness.

Could it be that the detective has good news for me? I thought.

On the one hand, it was good to have hope, but on the other hand, I knew it was slim.

Anyway, in this depressing environment, I had to hold on to positive thoughts.

A few minutes later, I was on my way through a familiar corridor.

The guard was walking right behind me, and I noticed with concern that I was getting used to the walls surrounding me, which could mean that deep down, I knew that I would not leave this place until the day I died.

When we reached the visiting room, the guard opened the door and gently pushed me inside. Michael, as usual, sat at the third window.

When I got there, I noticed that his expression was unreadable, which only increased my nerves. I sat down across from him, trying to stay calm even though my heart was beating like crazy.

"Hello, Steward," he said as I put the receiver to my ear.

"Detective."

"I have some information for you," he began slowly.

"Is this good information?" I asked, trying to camouflage my emotions.

"I'm afraid I wouldn't put it that way," he replied.

That was enough to know that I had to get rid of the last bit of hope.

Although, at this point in the conversation, I should have expected the worst, my mind seemed not to want to accept it yet. I kept a straight face, even though emotions were passing through my body caused by my rapid heartbeat.

"I see. Please tell me," I added after a moment.

"I managed to identify two men from your list. Unfortunately, both died in a shooting recently."

"I heard something about it," I said, recalling the conversation with Tony. It was easy to connect the two facts.

"If so, you probably also heard how many people lost their lives in total?" Michael asked.

"I know about seven dead," I answered truthfully.

"That's right, my department is bursting at the seams from the workload and under the circumstances, I am not able to devote time to your case."

So, it's over. I thought.

I could see on Michael's face the obvious regret at having to end his attempts to find out the inconsistencies related to the tragedy at the gas station.

At the same time, I knew that these were just his pains because I personally had doubts about the sense of this undertaking.

Yes, sometimes I liked to think that they would prove my innocence, but it was fleeting, like a dream that you forget as soon as you wake up.

It's good to think about a different life without losing touch with reality.

My new life was already behind prison bars, and no dream could change that. All that was left was to get used to it and adapt to the current circumstances.

"I also looked at the testimony of your brother Edward. I checked his alibi, which was confirmed. It was the last clue that landed in a dead end," he said suddenly.

"Ed...?" I was surprised. "...you don't think my own brother could have set me up for this, do you?"

"Honestly, I haven't ruled it out. You know his past, and you know well that he's not innocent. You've had huge problems because of him before."

Michael was referring to an incident that had happened eighteen years ago.

The fact was that my brother's recklessness and his gambling problem had led me to the thugs, who had created a selfpreservation system in my mind that would eventually take the name Gary and accompany me in all stressful situations.

But a lot of time had passed since that incident, and Edward had proven to me at every turn that he felt guilty about having led to such a disastrous situation for me.

This made me believe that he would change over time, and I wanted to think of him as a person who deserved a second chance.

"Yes, but Ed is a different person now. I'm not surprised that his statements were confirmed," I replied naively.

A slight smile appeared on Michael's face. The man lowered his head for a moment, then looked at me again, this time with a serious expression on his face.

"I think you underestimate him..." he said gruffly. "...but this is not my place to interfere with the family."

"So, this is where our collaboration ends?" I asked.

"For now, yes, but I will look around for any evidence related to the gas station case."

"Thanks. I understand the position you are in, and I really appreciate your help." I replied honestly.

"Hang in there, Steward and don't lose hope. If you are innocent, it will come out sooner or later." He added as a farewell.

The detective stood up from his chair and nodded politely at me in understanding before slowly walking towards the exit.

I sat in my seat for a moment, processing everything in my head. I didn't hold any grudge against the policeman for giving up his investigation into my case.

I understood his dedication and willingness to help while also knowing the differences in fate that had influenced the detective's final decision.

This was not the time or place for weakness and self-pity. I had to face the brutal reality of prison, and that was what I focused all my energy on.

20

People against people.

"The desire to live better is not a bad thing, but a lifestyle that places the pursuit of having above being, and wants to have more, not in order to be more, but to experience the greatest pleasure in life, is a mistake."

Three days later, 3:45 p.m.

"…John got out of prison yesterday…" Ed was talking into the phone. "…the Aryans are going to send their brothers to Mexico.

I don't know why…" he added and listened to the caller. "…sure, tell Franco I'll be at his place today like we agreed. See you later," he added and hung up the phone.

"Do you have any idea what John's planning? And how many brothers are going to Mexico?" Asked Stacy, who had been sitting at the kitchen table waiting for Edward to finish the call.

"I don't know how many, probably a few, they need people here on the spot…" Ed replied. "…the management board is planning something, but what it will be, I will only find out when it happens. You know that I have no access to the committee's plans, but John got to work hard. He called a meeting right after he left."

"There's something big coming; it would be good to know what it is so we don't get caught in the crossfire," Stacy replied.

"Tell me something I don't know, but don't worry about it now. We have a task to do today, you better focus on it."

"I'm ready. We have the means to grind and pack the product, and my people are waiting. You just need to deliver the goods." She replied with pride in her voice.

"Alright, I'm going to pack the money. I'll be back when I'm done."

"250 thousand?"

"As we agreed, we leave 50, just in case," Ed replied.

"This will be the best. You never know what might happen."

"You know my opinion on this." Ed got angry.

"To buy for everything and double the profit?"

"Exactly, you have to take advantage of it when you can!"

"You're an idiot. You never knew how to handle money." Stacy retorted.

"You talk like you know? At least I don't pay to smoke that shit!" Ed referred to heroin.

"No, you lose everything in the casino!"

"Shut up already. I'm going to the car. Time is running out," Ed replied, then grabbed a black duffel bag with money that was lying on the table next to Stacy and left the apartment.

"Moron." Stacy summed up the argument in one word.

Polunsky Unit, at the same time.

Before leaving prison, John announced that Jack would take his place from now on, which was not the slightest surprise.

The brothers did not question this decision, although it was more because each of them was more focused on surviving each day than seriously considering whether Jack was the right person for the job.

The Brotherhood made important decisions among a small group of high-ranking members, and it was rare for the dissenting opinions of lower-ranking members of the organization to be taken into account, even when the topdown decision was clearly contrary to the generally respected principles that prevailed among the brothers at the time.

In this way, there were even situations in which orders were given to eliminate one of the brothers due to suspicions of disloyalty before it was proven that such betrayal had actually taken place.

At the time, people spoke of the lack of logic in the commission's actions, but no one was stupid enough to oppose it and thus bring the death penalty upon themselves.

So, when Jack became the leader, I personally didn't think it would have any major impact on the mood of the brothers behind the prison walls.

In my opinion, it was more of a symbolic move than an actual introduction of a new person who had the potential to make major changes in the structure of the organization.

However, the situation that would arise outside when John joined the fight for territory was thought of completely differently.

His long-standing presence in the organization and his undeniable organizational experience made many believe in his skills and ability to rise to the challenges that awaited him outside the prison walls.

Some believed he could unite the scattered factions and restore the Brotherhood to its former glory, but others were convinced he could once and for all destroy the Mexican gangsters in the area and permanently establish the Aryan Brotherhood as the dominant organization.

The decision to put John in charge of the brothers living in and around El Paso had been made before his release, and those familiar with his reputation felt that this was the perfect time to bring him into the fight that was then raging in southwest Texas.

However, he still had personal scores to settle.

He promised himself that he would find Franco Perez and execute him.

The sense of betrayal by the Mexican boss who had ordered the murder of the two brothers remained in his mind, and he felt responsible for punishing him.

This was particularly deeply ingrained in his consciousness, especially since the two men had known each other for many years, and John had never expected Franco to turn on him in such a perfidious way.

The plan for revenge began to take shape the day he found out about everything, and when the gates of prison opened for him, and he took his first steps into the outside world, it was fully developed.

John not only wanted to kill Franco but to humiliate him and his men, and he knew exactly how to do it.

The first stage of his plan was to send the four brothers to Mexico. Their task was to hide discreetly somewhere near Perez's estate and, in turn, observe his villa day and night.

John wanted to know every detail about what was going on in this area 24 hours a day.

What time does the changing of the guard take place, which side is the least guarded, what are Franco's habits when he's home, and any other information that might be useful?

Perez's stronghold was the place where he felt safest, thinking that no one would be crazy enough to undertake such a dangerous mission as to attack him in his own home.

It made him feel untouchable there, but John wanted to prove to him that it was the exact opposite.

Although one of the main bosses of the Mexican Mafia already knew about the arrival of the Aryans in his territory, he had no idea where they were, what it meant for him, or what threat it could pose to him.

Which, after all, gave John an advantage over his opponent.

He quickly selected the people most suitable for the task and ordered them to go abroad.

The four brothers were highly trained and perfectly aware of the gravity of the situation.

They knew that the slightest mistake could cost them their lives, so they acted with the utmost caution and precision.

Each of them had a specific scope of responsibilities: one monitored changes in security, the second observed Perez's daily habits, the third checked the strong and weak points of security, and the fourth anticipated possible emergency situations.

John wanted to receive reports for analysis on a regular basis.

He knew that patience was the key to success, so he took his time with the implementation of his plan. Every detail had to be perfected.

The new boss's second order was to crack down on the means of transporting cocaine into Texas. John knew exactly what routes the Mexican smugglers took and what vehicles they used.

The idea was to deploy armed teams of Aryans along potential routes, who were to watch for cars and seize them from the rival gang at all costs; in this case, the members of the brotherhood were also given a free hand as to what they wanted to do with their crew.

While John was introducing new orders in the wild, I was called to talk to Jacek.

The new leader sent me a message out of the blue saying he wanted to talk to me while we were out in the yard.

Not knowing what he wanted from me at first because we had never talked for more than a few seconds before, I walked up to him as he lifted a barbell while lying on a weight bench, surrounded by his brothers.

"Jack," I said, standing next to him.

"Steward, it's good you're here." He replied, putting the weight back in its place.

The metal plates hit each other with a loud clang. Jack kicked his legs up and sat up straight.

"What is it about? Apparently, you want to tell me something." I got to the point.

Jack looked at me carefully.

"Yes, that's right, I'm going to need you…" he said, slightly out of breath. "…your reputation is well known among all."

"My reputation?" I asked, starting to dislike the direction he was heading.

"Exactly, everyone knows what a monster lies inside you."

"So, you're not talking about me but Gary?"

"You're one person, aren't you?"

"No, Gary is someone completely different," I answered truthfully.

"It doesn't matter either way. Few people would dare to approach you here, and I need someone like that by my side."

"You want me to be your bodyguard?" I was surprised.

"I don't need protection. I'm perfectly capable of defending myself…" Jack replied, lying down under the barbell again. "…I want you to be in my trusted circle." He added before he started lifting.

I couldn't refuse the boss's offer; he was in charge here now, and for my own good, I had to agree.

"Fine," I replied.

"Great." He said with effort, swinging the weight.

I waited a few seconds before he finished the series of ten repetitions.

"Great that we understand each other. You can leave now. I will call you when I need you."

After these words, I turned around and started walking. I had a bad feeling about what to expect soon, and it didn't take long to find out I was right.

21

One step too far.

"Only love can exclude the use of one person by another."

The next afternoon, 3:46 p.m.

Ed was driving back from Mexico in a car loaded with cocaine.

The conversation with Franco had gone well, and the gangster didn't think the Aryans' arrival in his territory posed any threat.

He felt confident in having a small private army at his disposal, but he appreciated his informant's loyalty and commitment.

The man was now on the American side of the border, and although he had once again successfully outwitted the customs officers, he was feeling stressed due to the apparent doubling of government workers.

"Fuck." He cursed under his breath, pressing the gas pedal harder.

Concerns about future smuggling operations entered his mind as he realised that they would become more difficult as time went on.

The shootings and the number of people killed also had an impact on city authorities, who were forced to call in more officers to prevent the wave of violence from spreading.

This time, he managed to do it, but he already knew that he would have to seriously consider further transport.

The disturbing situation on the US-Mexico border was also noticed by Franco's men, who were transporting goods unrelated to Ed's business that day.

The two Latino men were to pass through El Paso, where they planned to stop at two places to supply them with cocaine needed to produce crack.

These locations were unable to produce the drug without the main ingredient, cocaine, so the demand for the substance never diminished.

They beat Edward with several vehicles and eventually crossed the border first while he, unaware of anything, followed them.

When Ed was halfway down the road, he noticed two cars suddenly pulling out of a wild side road.

This would not be unusual, were it not for the fact that the fast and violently moving vehicles clearly targeted the truck in front of them.

They had apparently been following it as soon as they merged into traffic, regardless of the other road users who had to be particularly careful to avoid hitting them.

The whole situation was accompanied by loud honking of horns and flashing of lights by nervous drivers.

Ed watched from a distance as the road pirates managed to catch up with the targeted truck and then block the unsuspecting crew.

The last detail Edward remembered as he passed three cars on his right was that the first one was driving right in front of the van, clearly slowing it down, and the second was right next to it so that the car could not turn left and free itself from the trap.

What the fuck is going on here? he thought, surprised.

At the same time, the driver of the van tried to overtake the car in front of him, but the car in front was gradually preventing him from passing by, driving in a slalom.

Every now and then, the driver looked to the left, towards the second vehicle, where he saw a white man pointing a gun at him through an open window.

It was then that the two Mexicans realised that they had just fallen victim to the Aryan Brotherhood.

Cornered, defenceless, and completely taken by surprise, they had no choice but to pull over on the right side of the highway.

As they did so, they were immediately surrounded by four members of the brotherhood.

"Get the fuck out of the car!" one of them shouted, standing by the driver's door and pointing a gun at him.

The sun was pleasantly warm on their faces, and the wind caused by the speeding cars caused refreshing oxygen to flow into the nostrils of the men standing next to the stopped truck against the background of the forest landscape looming just behind them.

Hundreds of vehicles passed them on the busy highway, and none of the people inside had any idea that a real drama was about to unfold there in broad daylight.

After a few seconds, one of the attackers shouted again:

"FUCKING NOW!! OPEN THE DOOR!!"

Then, the Mexicans surrendered, realising the hopeless situation they were in.

The moment they unlocked the door, the Aryans threw it wide open and forcibly dragged them to the ground, then one of them jumped in, reversed the truck a few metres, and drove away quickly.

The task was half completed. All that remained was to get rid of the witnesses and leave the area before anything got in the way.

"MOVE! RÁPIDO!" One of the brothers ordered and pushed the prisoner towards the forest.

He began to walk forward uncertainly, and his companion did the same. The men held at gunpoint began to realise the seriousness of the situation.

"No por favor, please…" one whispered to the executioner. "…you don't have to do this; we'll disappear from here, and you'll never see us again." He added.

"Shut the fuck up! Keep going!" he heard in response.

The last thing before the end of the mission was to get rid of the witnesses, which, in the minds of the attackers, meant only one thing: death.

This was encoded in their consciousness, and no amount of request or persuasion could change it.

It was also important to do it as quickly as possible, but it's not easy to rush someone who knows they're about to be killed.

The third brother stayed by the cars, watching as his two companions disappeared between the trees, along with the prisoners.

"Come on, fucking move it." He said to himself impatiently.

Less than ten seconds later, he saw a police patrol stop next to him.

"SHIT!" He cursed in his mind.

"Hello, partner! Is there a problem?" one of the policemen asked after getting out of the police car.

"No, officer, everything's fine. My friend went to pee!" he said the last words louder, hoping they would reach his companions' ears.

However, it was impossible due to the noise made by the constantly moving cars.

"Are you travelling in two cars?" the officer asked, approaching.

During this time, his partner remained in the police car.

"As it happens, my friends and I are going to my brother's wedding."

"Oh, yeah?" the officer replied, noting the unusual positioning of the cars.

One was further ahead, and the other on the left side, closer to the road.

"So where is this friend of yours? I'd like to ask him a few questions."

"Fucking asshole, he won't back off." Thought the man.

The policeman's curiosity ultimately determined his fate, as it became obvious that he had no intention of letting go.

After a few seconds of an agonizing conversation with the official, the armed brotherhood member slowly began to reach for the gun he had hidden in the back of his pants when suddenly there was a bang from deep in the forest, followed by another.

BANG...!! BANG...!!

The policeman's eyes opened wide with fear. He took two steps back and grabbed the weapon, but the gangster was faster.

BANG...!!

The young officer was shot directly in the head and died before his body hit the ground. At this sight, his partner grabbed the radio to call for reinforcements, but before he could say a single word, the assailant, approaching the police car, fired two shots.

BANG...!! BANG!!

The first bullet hit his chest, the second his arm. The policeman was still alive when the gangster approached him from the side of the passenger seat where he was sitting and ended his life at close range with a third shot straight to the temple.

BANG!!

The whole incident lasted no more than ten seconds, but it was enough for the brothers to run out of the woods to see what had happened.

"Get in the car!" ordered the man standing by the police car.

"What the fuck have you…" another one said, but he wasn't allowed to finish his sentence.

"GET INTO YOUR FUCKING CAR!! NOW!!"

They did as they were told, and when a third member joined them, the three of them screeched away, leaving dust, blood, and death behind them.

Michael and Paul arrived there ten minutes after receiving the call.

Two police teams were already on the scene, and four officers were searching the area for clues that could lead them to the perpetrators.

The call came from a young man who was travelling on that route with his wife at the time of the shooting and reported to the police station.

 His wife, who had a better view of the incident from the right side of the passenger seat, testified that she noticed three men running towards the cars, two of them running from the direction of the forest and the third one quickly moving away from the police car.

Unfortunately, the time she had to look at the circumstances was too short to describe the appearance of the perpetrators.

All she could say was that they were white, and the sight was so drastic that she and her husband immediately decided to call the police.

"Jesus Christ," Paul said, looking at the gruesome sight.

"If officers begin to die, the situation is truly tragic," Michael added.

Indeed, incidents in which law enforcement officers lose their lives always have a great resonance within law enforcement structures, and the community that law enforcement officers create takes it extremely personally.

"It's hard to believe this happened," Paul replied, leaning slightly over the right door of the patrol car and peering inside.

The young policeman's body was slumped against the seat with his eyes open, pain and panic written all over his face, and everything around him was covered in blood, even the back seats.

"Sergeant Steven Murphy and Corporal Dave Hopkins," one of the officers introduced the victims, approaching the detectives.

"What do we have to start with?" Michael asked.

"We know that there were three perpetrators, all white males, and they drove away in two cars. Apart from the young woman, no other witnesses have come forward to give statements. We are waiting for news from headquarters."

"What are we looking for in the woods?" Paul added.

"We don't know yet. It could be anything: weapons, drugs or something else." The officer replied.

"Two ran out of the woods," Michael said. "This can't be a coincidence."

"HERE!!" Suddenly, a voice rang out from behind the trees.

Without hesitation, Michael, Paul, and the policeman accompanying them ran in the direction from which the shout was coming.

As they made their way through the undergrowth, the men began to imagine what might be hidden behind them.

Paul and the other officer were sure that the perpetrators had thrown away the weapons used in the shooting, but Michael suspected that they would find something much more gruesome.

And he was right.

After overcoming the last thick bushes, two more bodies came into view. Two men lying face down on the ground had been shot in an execution manner.

The perpetrators of this incident undoubtedly told them to kneel before the execution and await the approaching death.

"Latinos," Paul stated and looked at Michael suggestively.

"Yeah, I think we already know what happened here," Michael replied.

At that time, six policemen stood by the bodies of unknown men, and the air was filled with disbelief, anger, and despair.

None of them could fully understand how someone could do such a horrible thing to another person.

Forgetting for a moment that they had just found themselves in the middle of an ongoing war between two ruthless gangs, and what they had seen in the picturesque forest was just a small example of the consequences that a fight over territory brings.

"Aryans?" Paul turned to Michael.

"For sure." The detective replied shortly.

"Well, they're screwed, then…" one of the policemen suddenly said. "…if this gets out, every cop in the state will be keeping an eye on them." He added, referring to his dead colleagues.

"I don't think they care too much about it now…" Michael confessed. "…they have much bigger problems with the thirteens, and until one of the sides finally surrenders, many more people will die." The detective used slang when talking about the Mexican mafia because the number *13* was their trademark, and every gangster had it tattooed somewhere on his body.

22

Thin red line.

"The hands are the landscape of the heart."

Despite hearing the brothers' testimony that they had no choice but to take out the smugglers and officers, John knew it was a huge mistake that would likely haunt the organization and was not happy with the outcome of the drug seizure.

The unwritten and universal rule among gangsters was, *you don't kill policemen*. All repeat offenders and hardened criminals knew that this was one of the biggest mistakes that could be made in this underworld, the so-called *Thin Red Line*.

The officers and people associated with the law enforcement side were very close to each other, and even those who did not know each other personally perceived the death of *their own* as a slap in the face directly against them.

Therefore, John was convinced that as soon as it became known who was behind the policemen's murders, the others would redouble their efforts to pursue the entire organization from which the perpetrators came.

There was a lot going on in the affairs of the brotherhood at this time, and its forces needed to be evenly and appropriately divided.

The import of opium poppies from Colombia, intended for heroin production, began, new production sites for the drug were established, and units were created in the city and on the outskirts to control and combat the rival gang operating in the brotherhood.

All this made it difficult for John to control every aspect, especially when, in addition, the federals turned their forces against them. It was too early to take the last step against the Latino leader in this part of the country.

John did not have enough information to be sure that he could proceed with the final phase of the plan to eliminate Franco Perez.

Reports from the brothers in Mexico were coming slowly, and they had not yet managed to establish anything concrete.

As the days passed, the man became impatient. The situation was becoming increasingly difficult to control, and he had to make another decision that would undermine the morale of the Mexican Mafia.

By now, they had managed to seize a large amount of cocaine belonging to the gangsters, and despite the unsuccessful completion of the interception process, John could consider the whole thing a success.

This was a very costly and painful blow from the Brotherhood, which undoubtedly had a strong influence on Franco himself and his associates.

However, it was not enough to make the Mexican gangsters surrender and withdraw from the area. John needed to strike again where it hurt the most, and he knew exactly how to do it.

Contrary to appearances, most of the information and drugs were in prison, and it was from there that Luis, Perez's right-hand man, was in command, and he became the next target.

The head of the brotherhood knew that getting rid of Luis would seriously disrupt Franco's activities in this part of Texas, and he decided to contact Jack to order him to issue the order.

This task was exceptionally difficult to accomplish because getting to Luis required planning to bypass his numerous companions, who always accompanied the boss.

Moreover, the man was huge, almost two metres tall, with the mass and physique of a statue, and here another problem arose because it was difficult to choose a person who would be able not only to defeat such a powerful opponent but also to take his life.

Still, John had a potential candidate for the job in mind, and Jack also knew who to assign the job to.

February 18, 1982, Polunsky Unit.

Jack received an encrypted message from John. The text was short but left no doubt. The order was, *Get rid of Luis at all costs.*

The man was not surprised by this decision. He himself believed that it should have been done sooner or later.

The situation had calmed down a bit on the prison side, but Jack knew what was happening outside, so in his opinion the war was still far from over.

   "If you want to win the game, you must get rid of your opponent's strongest pieces," he stated.

Jack had been watching Luis for a while. He had seen how the gangster avoided crowded places and usually stayed somewhere in the distance among his men.

This clearly indicated that he was afraid of something; he suspected that an attack would happen, but he just didn't know when yet.

Additionally, he was seen talking to Jason, the leader of the BGF, which did not bode well for the brotherhood.

If the Mexican Mafia and the Black Guerrilla Family join forces and fight the Aryan Brotherhood together, they will not be left with the slightest chance.

It was necessary to act quickly, and only Luis' death could thwart the plans of the alliance of these two groups.

It didn't take long for Jack to remind me that I was at his service.

He called me out to the yard for another chat.

"You must do something for the brotherhood." He announced.

"I'm listening."

"I was informed about the need to take care of Luis." He added vaguely.

"Okay, but what do you expect from me?" I asked.

"I'm giving you this task for the good of the brotherhood. You have to eliminate him."

"And how am I supposed to do it alone? You know very well that he always has guards with him." I replied.

"We'll take care of it. Tomorrow, before breakfast, you will get a weapon, and after the meal, we will attack. Our boys will distract the rest, and, in the meantime, you will have the opportunity to get close to him." Jack explained.

"I understand that you want me to kill him."

"Those are your words, not mine. You will do what you have to and make sure you are ready. Another opportunity like this may not happen again." He replied with a serious expression on his face.

"And what if I fail?"

"This is not within your possibilities. Believe me, it will be better if you succeed. Am I making myself clear?" he replied, fixing me with an icy stare.

"Yes, I'll do what I can," I replied.

"Perfect. Get some sleep tonight and regain your strength. Tomorrow is an important day and remember, the brotherhood is counting on you. This assignment can bring you great recognition and respect, but it can also push you to the sidelines. It's only up to you that you will achieve with it."

"Sure," I replied.

Seeing clearly that Jack was done talking to me and was returning to his exercises, I walked away from him and the group of brothers who accompanied him.

A scenario of what the next day should look like started to take shape in my head. It was obvious that Gary would have to take care of this, so the first thing I had to do in the morning was to pretend to take my medication so that my second personality would be ready.

Gary was an incredibly strong person, much stronger than me, and from what I learned after the fact, he had proven more than once that he was able to defeat opponents much bigger than me.

In addition, since being incarcerated, I had started exercising regularly twice a day, morning and night, which improved my vitality and muscles and gave me a pretty good figure.

However, I was far from Luis, who was built like a locomotive and a head taller than me. The guy looked like a professional bodybuilder, and next to him, I looked like an amateur who had just started working out in the gym.

Although I was undoubtedly no match for this colossus, I had to accept the task from the brotherhood, remembering that to refuse it was tantamount to giving myself a death sentence.

You don't refuse the brotherhood if you value life. These words kept coming back to my mind.

It was then that it became clear to me that this fight would not be won by the stronger but by the more determined.

It was incredibly difficult to beat a man like Luis, but taking his life was almost impossible. A normal person fighting in a frenzy and panic for his life could demonstrate superhuman strength, and someone who was naturally strong could be capable of anything.

There was no longer any doubt in my mind.

Either him or me. I thought.

One of us would not survive tomorrow morning.

23

Revenge.

That same day, El Centro District, 11:38 p.m.

John and a group of his most trusted men met at a bar belonging to the Aryan Brotherhood.

The meeting was organised in secret so as not to attract unwanted attention from undesirable people.

One of the leaders of the brotherhood wanted to check how the activities were going in the different areas.

There were people involved in the import of goods from Colombia, those supervising drug production, those responsible for distribution, sales and collection of cash, as well as those who commanded Aryan militias fighting against Latino gangsters.

Generally speaking, everyone who counted in the organization and had something important to say was there.

As is usually the case at this type of meeting, immediately after the talks regarding the organization's interests, the party began, during which the gathered people, in the company of women, did not spare alcohol and drugs.

This location was situated away from the main street, where most people gathered, to ensure the security and confidentiality of the meetings held there.

The brotherhood had several such places that its members liked to visit to spend time together, often getting blackout drunk.

However, this was no ordinary meeting, and extra security guards were deployed outside to ensure security in the area.

The reports from each sector of the organization were positive, and John was fully satisfied with the good news. Everything indicated that business was going very well and nothing would disrupt the plans for the coming future.

After spending the next two hours in the bar, the men, heavily drunk and dazed by other stimulants, lost their instinct for vigilance.

Feeling too comfortable, they allowed themselves to let their guard down for a moment. It was their mistake.

When you were involved in an extremely important and unpredictable battle with an enemy like the Mexican Mafia, you could not afford to underestimate your opponent for even a minute because you were in a life-or-death situation.

While the party was in full swing, the well-informed and patient gangsters led by Franco Perez knew exactly where some of the brotherhood's most important men were and were waiting for their opportunity to strike.

That night, they were about to taste revenge because, in a few minutes, the entire elite of the rival group would be served to them on a silver platter, almost defenceless. Four motorcycles and a total of eight armed gangsters were waiting nearby for the green light from an observer who was discreetly watching the bar where the Aryans were hanging out.

It was almost 2 a.m. when a crackly voice came over the walkie-talkie: "NOW, NOW, NOW!!"

At this signal, the machines' engines were started, and action began.

During that time. John, accompanied by ten trusted brothers and five women, left the building amused. Everyone joked and laughed loudly as they left the premises.

There were four security guards waiting for them outside, and none of them had noticed anything suspicious beforehand, which meant the area was clear and safe for them to call it a night and head home.

The almost full moon shone beautifully in the cloudless sky, and the area was pleasantly quiet and peaceful, considering it was late at night. The sleepy atmosphere was broken by the loud laughter of people going outside, but there was no sign of approaching danger.

Then, in the distance, you could hear the irritating roar of dirt bike engines, growing louder by the second.

The intoxicated brothers didn't even notice at first that someone was clearly approaching in that direction at high speed.

Only the sober guards looked around wildly, trying to locate the approaching vehicles.

A few seconds later, the first source of ear-splitting noise emerged from around the corner, then another, and another, and another.

One by one, the motorcycles quickly found themselves in front of the group of people on the street.

At this point, John realised what was happening, but it was too late to react.

The security guards grabbed their weapons as bullets rained down on them.

BANG!!! BANG!!! BANG!!! BANG!!!

The attackers began firing indiscriminately at random people. Their mission was not to kill any specific person but as many as they could, preferably everyone.

The motorcycle drivers slowed down in front of the bar so that the passengers behind them could get a better shot, and they succeeded.

The women were screaming, and everyone was trying to hide somewhere in the chaos.

The entire incident lasted no longer than 20 seconds, and three security guards, four brothers, and two women were killed instantly before the attackers fled with a stunning noise, leaving devastation in their wake.

Of the nineteen people who were on the street outside the bar that night, only ten survived. The rest died on the spot or moments later in the ambulance or hospital.

Despite the unexpected ambush that should never have happened, John was one of the few who managed to survive.

Surprised and devastated by the event and high on adrenaline, he initially had difficulty understanding how it had happened.

However, the momentary daze did not last long, and the man immediately began to put the facts together.

In the end, in his opinion, there was no longer any doubt because everything pointed to someone from the brotherhood being behind the attack.

Polunsky Unit, next day, 05:03 am.

I woke up at the scheduled time so I could get some exercise in my cell before heading to the nurse's office.

I thought a lot about my life last night, which made it impossible for me to sleep. I feared what the next day would bring, which led to involuntary reflections on my existence.

Was I a good person? Will anyone miss me if I die today?

I couldn't clearly answer any of the questions that appeared in my head because most of my life related to Gary, who was a real mean guy. Where I am, there he is.

Personally, I liked to use alcohol and other drugs, which changed my personality, and I was not very friendly.

However, this was the result of a traumatic past that I had no control over. Either way, my thoughts, or rather self-pity, ended when I heard a knock on the metal grate just above my head.

At first, I thought it was Tony trying to wake me up, but then I realised that it was early in the morning, and he never got up at sunrise and always slept as late as he could.

BANG…BANG…

Since I had no intention of sleeping any longer and it was time for my morning exercises, I got up to see who was calling me.

I approached the bars as close as I could to get a better view of the outside. However, whoever it was had already left.

I frowned in surprise, and as I was about to turn around and go back to my place, my eyes landed on the left corner of the bars next to my bunk.

There was a white cloth lying there that I hadn't seen before.

When I picked it up, I realised that it wasn't as light as regular clothes should be and that there was something inside.

Then I remembered yesterday's conversation with Jacek when he said that I would receive a weapon before breakfast, and from that moment, I knew what was hidden under the mysterious fabric.

I sat down on the bunk and unrolled the material. It was exactly as I thought. There was a handmade knife inside.

This meant two things: first, the guards on shift one were affiliated with the Aryan Brotherhood and would allow bloodshed; two, there was no turning back.

An hour later.

Tony stood behind me when it was time to go down to the canteen.

Feeling unpleasantly nervous about the upcoming events, fuelled by the fact that there were no sedatives coursing through the digestive system that would give me a pleasant inner peace at this time of day, I decided it would be a good idea to warn my cellmate in the next cell while repaying the favour he had done me when I first found myself in the prison canteen where a fight had broken out.

Back then, Tony knew something I didn't and warned me even though he had no obligation to do so. Now I knew something he needed to know, too, to stay safe.

"Watch yourself after breakfast," I said quietly, turning my head slightly back.

"Something`s up?" he asked.

"Yeah, shit is about to go down," I replied shortly.

I didn't want to discuss this with him now, standing on the metal balcony. There were many men nearby who could have overheard our conversation and warned the Latinos of the planned fight if they heard anything specific that might give away such intentions.

Then the Aryans might have thought that I had knowingly revealed the plans and considered me a traitor, then I would not have had to wait long for my punishment, which would almost certainly have meant my death.

But now my conscience was clear because Tony already knew that something was coming. Although I doubted that the BGF would be involved in today's riots, my colleague had been informed that he was to stay away from whatever was about to happen.

We went downstairs and, as every day, entered the canteen at ten minutes after eight in the morning. Jack was already sitting at a table at the end of the room, surrounded by his men.

When he saw that I had arrived, he looked at me carefully. This sent shivers down my spine, and with every second, the whole situation became more and more real, and I knew exactly where this would lead.

The Brotherhood was ready, but I wasn't.

The homemade knife began to bother me more and more.

I could feel it on my back, hidden behind my pants and T-shirt. Even though it was small, it seemed to be getting heavier and heavier.

My mind was playing tricks on me.

It had been a long time since I had last been off my meds, and I had forgotten what it was like. Now, in my full sanity, the whole situation felt almost unreal. The canteen, the inmates, the security guards, and the kitchen staff.

Those eating, those talking, those working, and those just standing there doing nothing. Black, White, Latino.

Everything was a blur in my head as I waited my turn to receive my portion of concrete porridge.

Where the fuck am I? a question suddenly popped up in my head.

What the fuck is going on? followed by another question.

Before I could finally pull myself together, I heard:

"White or brown?"

I realised then that I was standing in front of the cook, who was asking me what kind of bread I wanted for my meal. I was brought back to earth and looked at the woman in the white apron with a hairnet.

"White," I replied.

The elderly woman threw two pieces of white bread on my tray, and I was able to continue on my way.

So, I slowly walked toward the brothers, discreetly looking around the canteen.

As usual, the Latinos were on my left, the blacks on my right, and the whites in the back of the room.

When I saw Luis, my stomach lurched. The guy looked even scarier than I remembered.

I didn't know if that was possible or if it was just my imagination. In any case, I felt real fear, which caused my second consciousness to start receiving impulses to activate.

"Not yet," I said quietly to myself under my breath. "It's not the time yet," I added to calm myself down.

A few seconds later, I reached my companions, who looked as if they couldn't wait for me to join them. Everyone looked at me intently, and some had a mocking smile on their faces.

That's right, a man of the hour. I thought.

All individuals were already aware of their responsibilities and my role in this endeavour.

"Why are you so pale? Didn't get enough sleep last night?" Jack asked as I sat up.

"I didn't take my pills," I replied shortly.

"You look like you're about to faint..." he replied. "...don't fucking die here, man. We need you today." He added jokingly, causing some of the brothers to laugh.

"You need Gary, not me. That's why I couldn't take the meds if you want him to show up."

"Whatever..." Jack replied. "...did you get the package?"

"Yeah, I have it on my back."

"Perfect, we'll strike before breakfast is finished. They'll be split into two groups, and each of us knows where to attack to disperse them…" he began to describe the details. "…when they're in a panic, Stan and I will distract Luis's bodyguards, then you'll have direct access to him."

"What about the guards?" I asked, although subconsciously, I knew the answer.

"They've been instructed not to intervene for the first two minutes of the fight…" he answered. "…that's more than enough for us to complete the task."

"They don't stand a chance. They're outnumbered." Stan added, who had been listening in silence with the others until now.

"That's right, we have twenty more boys. That should be the deciding factor in our success…" Jack confirmed. "…our brothers are dying outside. That's why we must end this. After today, they won't be as strong anymore." He added to raise morale before the fight.

At that moment, Jack had no idea what had happened the night before outside one of the Aryan bars. The information was too fresh to have reached the outpost in Polunsky B. Unit so quickly. If this had happened, the brothers would have been extremely motivated at this point, but there was no shortage of enthusiasm in their ranks, and each of them was 100% ready to give their all and show once and for all who was stronger in this fight. It was 8:30 a.m., and less than 30 minutes remained until the action began.

30 minutes was far too long for the bloodthirsty brotherhood members.

Time passed, and the atmosphere was becoming tense. The brothers looked more and more excited with each passing minute.

They joked, laughed, and warmed up for the attack, and Jack occasionally threw meaningful glances at his friendly guards.

As I looked around, I thought that every man present suspected that a fight was about to break out, though perhaps it was just my instincts kicking in at that moment. I also wondered if Tony had told Jason, the head of the BGF, anything about what I had mentioned to him half an hour earlier.

But even if he had, it wouldn't have changed the course of events since prisoners were not allowed to move freely around the room during breakfast, so even if Jason had wanted to warn Luis, he wouldn't have had the chance.

Footsteps echoed along the hallway, and additional guards arrived at the canteen hall.

Jack checked his watch. At 8:35 a.m., time was ticking away, and adrenaline was pumping.

The brothers began to exchange short, nervous comments, but despite the tension, each knew they had to stay calm and not reveal their intentions prematurely.

Jack turned to Stan, his right hand, whose face expressed concentration and determination.

"Are you ready?" he asked quietly.

Stan nodded, his eyes flashing.

"Everything is going according to plan," he replied with certainty, referring to the additional reinforcements that had just arrived.

Jack looked towards the door, where new guards were entering. He knew that something was about to begin that no one would be able to stop.

He still had the image of Jason and Luis in his head, the two leaders who could change the course of this fight if only they had the chance to communicate.

Even if that wasn't possible, Jack had one more ace up his sleeve that would ensure his victory.

Namely, not only were the guards not to intervene for the first two minutes, but they were also to ensure that neither Jason nor any member of the *Black Guerrilla Family* entered the fray.

The Brotherhood didn't need many subordinates among the prison authorities.

One person in a high position was enough to keep the rest under control, and that was exactly what happened here.

It was almost 8:45.

Jack took a deep breath, knowing there was no turning back now. The tension in the air was almost palpable at this point. Every man in the room was ready to plunge into the fray that would decide who was the strongest.

"Five minutes," Jack announced.

The final moment was approaching inexorably, and I felt my legs jump under the table with a surge of nerves. I had never knowingly attacked anyone before, always under the influence of some drug, and most of all, Gary.

So, I didn't know what it was like. Now, not only was I completely sober, but my life depended on how the next few minutes would unfold.

"Two minutes," Jack added.

Whatever will be, will be. I thought.

I really had nothing to lose; my life was over, and it shouldn't matter to me whether I died here or in the gas chamber.

So, I decided to just attack Luis and let fate decide how the fight would go. At the same time, I was aware that soon Gary would be at the controls, and either I would wake up or I wouldn't, and it would all be over.

"Let's go!" Jack said and stood up from the table. The rest of the brothers followed his example.

A prison like Polunsky B. Unit can hold over 2,900 prisoners at any one time.

At the time the Aryan Brotherhood attacked the Mexican Mafia, there were just over 1,500 people inside the facility, 600 of whom were Aryans.

Even though half the population could have been in the common area of the prison at the time, it was still the largest attack in the history of the place.

The brothers got up from the tables, and as if nothing had happened, they started walking towards the Latin minority.

This immediately caught the attention of both the BGF and the interested parties themselves.

It seemed that everyone reacted except for the guards, who stood rigidly in their seats and simply watched the situation.

After a moment, the Aryans split into two huge groups, and the Latino gangsters realised what was happening.

They jumped up from their seats, ready to fight back. Jack, Stan and I stayed back to spot Luis' position.

Then I turned around for a moment to see Tony and Jason watching our every move. In a split second, the brothers rushed at their opponents, trying to pick off the strongest of them so they could be eliminated from the fight immediately.

A terrible noise filled the room, with screams, curses and objects flying around the room.

"There is," Jack said, pointing to Luis, who was trying to retreat, surrounded by several of his men.

My heart sped up, further aided by adrenaline, and I felt that it was only a matter of time before I lost consciousness and found out how this was going to end.

"Let's go," he added and was the first to push through the fighting men. Not even 20 seconds had passed, and the air was already filled with the smell of blood.

Some fell to the ground, knocked out, while others punched their enemies as hard as they could. Then, the screams and shouts were drowned out by a loud alarm siren activated by one of the guards.

The alarm honked, but the guards did not respond. They were to stand there for another 90 seconds.

Before we reached our destination, Jack and Stan, who were walking ahead of me, helped to defeat several of the gangsters the brothers were fighting.

Luis, who was standing against the wall, noticed us when we were already a few metres away, and I saw fear in his eyes.

I then realised that even a giant like him was afraid of the brotherhood's wrath and knew that he could become the next victim at any moment if the committee decided so. That was exactly the case here.

Stan and Jack charged with fists, ready to fight Luis's four bodyguards, who were looking around wildly, stunned by the chaos. The men spread out in two directions, trying to fend off the brothers' attacks, but they hit mercilessly and consistently.

Thanks to this, their boss stayed behind, so that I stood face to-face with him. Luis looked at me with a gaze full of aggression, then moved towards me with a force. This was the moment. From now on, I lost touch with reality, and Gary took my place.

The gangster looked from Steward to his men fighting nearby. It became clear in his mind that the man standing before him was the one he would have to face.

From his perspective, Steward did not seem like a person he would be afraid of in other circumstances.

This was not an ordinary situation, however, and the reputation of an inconspicuous man had even reached him.

Luis pushed himself away from the wall and took the first steps towards Steward, then noticed that something strange was happening to his appearance.

The man, a head shorter and nearly 20 kilograms lighter, adopted a different stance. He had been standing straight up until now, and the expression on his face clearly showed fear, but now he looked at him aggressively from under his scowl, and a sinister smile appeared on his lips.

When he looked Luis straight in the eyes, the gang leader unexpectedly felt fear because the man's eyes showed the indifference of a person ready for anything.

But this was someone he had to defeat, and he had no intention of showing him mercy.

That's why he jumped up from his place, running to be the first to deliver a surprising blow.

Seeing this, Gary knew how to react. Luis was not the first person in this building he had to fight.

That's why when he was only a few steps away from him, he leaned even closer and jumped on him, grabbing him by the waist.

Gary tried to throw Luis on his back, but he was too heavy to do it so easily.

Instead, he jammed himself, holding his thighs, while Luis beat him painfully on the back.

After a few seconds, Gary realised that such a tactic was pointless, so he pushed him away with his hands, trying to create a small distance between them.

As he did so, Luis struck him in the face with a right hook, splitting his lip. Despite the powerful and effective blow, Gary paid no attention to it and continued the attack.

Ignoring the pain and blood running down his chin, he lunged at Luis with renewed strength and determination.

With each passing second, the fight became fiercer, with both opponents fighting at the limits of their abilities.

Gary decided to change tactics, and instead of trying to take Luis down, he focused on delivering a series of quick and precise blows, aiming for his ribs and stomach.

Luis, despite his superior strength, was starting to feel tired. His blows were losing their precision, and Gary was gaining more and more advantage.

Finally, with one powerful blow, he managed to bend Luis in half.

Taking advantage of this moment, Gary grabbed Luis by the neck and pulled his head towards his knee, striking with all his strength.

Luis fell to his knees, and Gary stood over him, breathing heavily but with a sense of victory written all over his face.

Under the influence of emotion and adrenaline, the man did not even realise that he had the knife with him the whole time. The object was still behind the belt on his back, where Steward had hidden it.

Exhausted and bloody, Luis had no strength to stand on his own feet. Then he looked at Gary, his eyes showing both surprise and the awareness of defeat.

But that was exactly what Gary was counting on, knowing that with Luis' height and weight, he wouldn't be able to fight intensely for long and that a few accurate blows would be enough for him to finally tire out and have no strength left to fight any longer.

"ON THE GROUND!!! EVERYONE ON THE GROUND!!! NOW!!!"

The sounds of the emergency siren were now joined by a male voice shouting through a megaphone. The two minutes were up.

Gary felt a touch on his back, and as he was about to turn around, ready to attack, he saw Jack take a knife from his belt that he hadn't used yet.

The man walked up to Luis, who was breathing heavily and unevenly, looked him in the bloody face and plunged the blade straight into his throat.

A stream of blood flowed down the gangster's arm, and he fell limply to the ground.

"ON THE GROUND!!! EVERYONE!!! ON THE GROUND!!!"

The prison guards were thundering through a megaphone.

"Lie down," Jack ordered Gary, then lay on his stomach on the floor. Gary obeyed as armed guards rushed into the room, restoring order.

The fight is over.

24

Fireworks.

"You can spot people by closing your eyes."

Seven days after the incident at the Polunsky B. Unit prison, John finally received useful information from his brothers in Mexico.

He was indeed happy to hear that the brothers had managed to defeat the Latino gangsters, sending many of them to the hospital with serious injuries and finally getting rid of Luis, who did not survive the incident.

But John needed something more because, in his eyes, the rivalry was not over yet, especially after the attack on him and his elite.

He believed that the forces were still evenly matched.

However, the scales of victory were increasingly tilted in the brotherhood's favour, as they managed to take control of the prison, and now facts were coming to light that would pave the way to reach Franco Perez himself.

Before this happened, however, John wanted to punish the arrogant gangsters who thought they could attack him and the Aryan Brotherhood with impunity and avoid the consequences.

Even though he didn't know exactly who fired the shots that night, it didn't stop him from planning to strike at the heart of the Latino community in a way the organization had never done before.

"We're ready," he suddenly heard the voice of one of his companions.

"Alright, I'll join you in a moment," he replied.

The Aryan nodded and turned to leave. John stood in a dingy room on the ground floor, waiting for the prisoner to be delivered.

Apart from him, there were only two other people in the building, but when the chosen young man was brought there, there were already five of them.

They were all in an old house outside the city, a place specially chosen by John, who wanted to make sure that there would not be a repeat of the situation from last week when someone had clearly betrayed the brotherhood.

The boss had this in mind all the time. Even if he hadn't figured out who it was yet, he was going to find this person and send him to the other world personally, but until then, he had to be especially careful.

There were three brothers in the basement, and among them sat a tied man with a cloth bag over his head. The room was lit by a single bare bulb that was barely able to illuminate anything around it, leaving most of the room in darkness.

The captured man was breathing heavily with fear, and his white shirt was stained with blood. Apparently, he wasn't going to let himself be captured without a fight and had to be taken away by force.

THUMP… THUMP… THUMP…

Loud footsteps of a heavy person descending the wooden stairs were heard.

…THUMP… THUMP… THUMP…

Accompanied by the creaking of old boards, John reached the room where his companions were waiting for him.

"Take this off him." He ordered.

After these words, one of the brothers standing closest to the prisoner grabbed the fabric on his head and, with a quick movement, uncovered his face.

The dark-skinned man looked around the room in panic, squinting his eyes, which had been covered for a long time and needed time to get used to the brightness. Finally, his gaze stopped on the figure standing in front of him.

John approached with a calm step, slowly emerging from the all-encompassing darkness. Then he stood right in front of him and silently stretched his hand behind his back.

At this sight, the prisoner shuddered nervously at the same time, quickening his breathing through his nose and the adhesive tape that covered his mouth. From his perspective, it looked like John was reaching for a gun and was about to execute him.

He also knew who he was dealing with and tried to be prepared for anything. In his state of panic, he didn't consider that if the brotherhood wanted this, he would already be dead.

He was there because they had completely different plans for him. John slowly pulled a rectangular piece of cardboard out of his back pocket and suddenly said:

"Release his hands."

One of the brothers immediately cut the rubber cable that bound his hands with a knife, while the other brother put a gun to his head in case he had any stupid ideas.

The young man started massaging his wrists where red welts appeared on the skin. Then John pulled out the photograph he was holding in his hand.

The prisoner took it from him, revealing the *13* tattoo he once proudly displayed. But when he looked at what was in the picture, his pupils dilated in fear. He looked at the photo for a few seconds, then raised his eyes and looked at John.

"I hope I don't have to tell you what will happen to them if you don't do what I want?" John said coldly.

"No, I understand. I'll do anything. Just please don't hurt them." The Latino barely managed to choke out.

"Good boy…" John replied. "…you will get a package to put in Casa Mexicana tomorrow evening. Further instructions will be given by my people."

"But sir, there are a lot of security guards there. Someone will catch me with this." The man replied with tears in his eyes.

"It's not my concern anymore. Make sure you don't get caught. And remember, I also know where your wife and daughter are. Let that motivate you to think creatively."

There was a moment of silence in the room as the brothers stood around the young gangster and waited for his answer.

"I want to see this on the morning news after tomorrow," John said in conclusion, and without waiting any longer, he headed for the stairs.

In his opinion, he had told the prisoner everything he had to say, and he should know what to do.

The leader of the brotherhood was not joking; he knew where his wife and daughter lived, and the photo he showed him had been taken recently from a close distance in front of his family home in Mexico and showed his ageing parents doing their daily chores.

The next day, 10:07 p.m.

Michael had already been relieved of his duties, but he was still sitting at his desk, going through documents.

There were so many cases piling up in the criminal investigation department that the detective could barely find any respite.

In the past few weeks alone, 16 people have been shot dead, an absolutely devastating record in the history of this city in terms of murders in the organised crime underworld.

Expectations exceeded all suspicions of the detective, who knew that a war between gangs had begun.

However, although the death toll was already drastically overwhelming, meaning that all security services were put on high alert, and fear and chaos were becoming increasingly visible within their structures and among the public, there were to be more victims, and there was no indication that the conflict would end anytime soon.

What Michael was to find out in just a few minutes

It was 10:10 p.m., and the officers had their hands full in the crowded office. The mostly quiet night shift until then had turned into a real mess.

The extra staff were everywhere, making calls, talking on the phone, interviewing witnesses, and typing on typewriters and computer keyboards, and nothing resembled the circumstances that should accompany late hours at the police station.

Even Michael was someone who shouldn't have been there at that time.

Busy with his own business, sipping another cup of coffee from the machine, the detective managed to distract himself from the noise around him.

His mind didn't register what was happening around him until the awful sound of dozens of phones ringing at the same time rang throughout the office.

This caused the man to snap out of his thoughts in a split second and start frantically looking around the room, trying to understand what was going on.

Police officers responding to calls spoke quickly, chaotically and one over another.

So, for the first few seconds, he was unable to make out anything from what they were saying. But then he heard phrases like "explosion" and "club," and his subconscious began to put together a coherent picture.

Bomb attack? He thought in surprise.

Something like this had never happened before, and at first, Michael could not imagine that it could be real.

It was only when he saw the policemen quickly get up from their seats and run out of the office that he realised that he was definitely dealing with reality now.

"Ninth district!! Everyone available at Casa Mexicana!!" someone shouted from under the door.

The detective quickly got up from his desk, grabbed his jacket hanging on the back of a chair and joined the people heading to the scene. He had to see it with his own eyes

8:40 p.m., 90 minutes until explosion.

A man with a backpack was heading to a wellknown club for the Mexican community, *Casa Mexicana*. The place was popular with gangsters who liked to go there on Friday and Saturday nights.

In the company of club regulars, young women and men, they spent their money wastefully and competed to see which of them looked the most spectacular.

This was where the young gangster, captured the previous night, was supposed to reach and drop off the *package*, thus saving the lives of his parents, wife and daughter.

John's comrades gave the order to place a time bomb near the bar, but he wanted to keep the number of casualties to a minimum, knowing that there would also be people not associated with the Mexican Mafia on site.

So, he decided to leave the bomb in the men's room, provided he managed to get inside with the deadly package. The young gangster had been to the club many times and knew the layout of the rooms well.

He also knew how many security guards would be on duty to keep customers safe on one of the busiest nights of the week, so there was no way they were going to let him in without checking what was in his backpack first.

Desperate, he had no other choice. In his mind, there were only two scenarios of how this could end. In the first, he saw a bomb explosion and the death of innocent victims, and in the second, the death of his closest family and the loss of all the people who were most important to him in this world. There was only one answer, if someone must die, let it be strangers.

The man stopped across the street from *Casa Mexicana*. Music was pounding from the club, and there was a long queue of colourfully dressed people on the street wanting to get inside. The gangster's gaze moved over the partygoers. Laughing women were joking and drinking alcohol from bottles.

Some of them were already dancing to the rhythm of muffled music coming from inside. Their partners flexed their muscles, trying to look as presentable as possible, with their hair styled with gel and summer clothes suitable for the warm night.   The man also glanced at the security guards, who were meticulously checking everyone's IDs, and the women showed the contents of their bags.

 Mierda! There's no way I'm going in through the front door. He thought.

The only way to do that was to try the back door for staff or look for an open window.

However, both options were incredibly risky in a place teeming with people, and the chance of being seen was almost inevitable. Time was running out, and the gangster, standing in the darkness of a side street, was thinking hard.

Then fate smiled on him. Because he saw that the car of one of the important people in the organization, responsible for the drug business and with whom he worked directly, had just pulled up to the club.

But he couldn't just walk up to him and convince him to help him get into the club without the security guards getting interested in his backpack, without arousing suspicion.

The idea was to use the authority of the gangster everyone knew once he was inside. Because then he could tell the security that he had a package to deliver just for his eyes.

Another 15 minutes passed.

"Oh shit, Pedro." He said when he saw his friend.

Another member of the criminal organization, important in the underworld, is in the company of three friends.

This is my chance. He thought and wasted no time, crouched down with his back to the street so that he wouldn't be seen.

Dressed in a black sweatshirt, he blended into the background and opened his backpack.

He had to act quickly, knowing that Pedro would soon disappear as someone who could enter the club without waiting in line.

The gangster set the timer for 60 minutes, then noticed the black disposable plastic bag and decided it would be a good idea to hide the bomb in it in case he had to open the backpack for the security guards.

A few seconds later, he was ready. He stood up, slung the bag over his shoulder and turned to face the street. Pedro was still there, talking to his friends.

The man breathed a sigh of relief and calmly moved towards his friend.

"Hey, puto!!" he called out when he was close enough.

"Hey, dude! What are you doing here? Did your wife let you off the leash?" Pedro joked.

"Very funny…" replied the gangster while giving high fives to his friend's companions. "…I have a package to deliver to Jose. Do you know where I can find him?" he asked to make it seem like he was there by accident.

"It's your lucky day; he happens to be inside."

"Oh, that's fucking awesome, that'll save me a lot of precious time. I had a good feeling to check it out here." He replied.

"Even the biggest idiot has good ideas sometimes," Pedro replied, which caused an outburst of laughter among his friends.

"Alright maricón, are you coming? Maybe we can have a beer." The gangster began to insist.

"Let's go, let's go, calm down, pendejo, there's no rush! We're waiting for our chicks…" Pedro replied. "…if you're in such a hurry, go in, we'll have a drink next time."

"I`m cool. I'll wait for you."

Ten minutes later, the man looked at his watch; it was already seventeen past nine and only 50 minutes until the explosion, but he was still on the street.

His temporary companions were drinking alcohol and laughing in a party mood while he was getting more and more impatient, knowing that he hadn't yet completed the hardest part of the task, which was to smuggle the device into the club and hide it in a discreet place.

"Here they are!" one of the men suddenly said.

"Hola chicas! What took you so long?! How long do we have to wait for you?!" Pedro shouted to the four scantily clad girls.

"Shut up maricón! Unless you don't want to try them." Replied one of the girls, revealing her ample breasts

"EEEEEE!! CHICA!! BRING IT ON!!" Pedro threw, and everyone started laughing.

"Party!! Here we come!!"

Finally, the bomber thought.

"Why are you so pale?! Are you feeling sick or something?!" Pedro put his arm around him as they reached the entrance.

"I'm fine…" he replied. "…I'm tired."

When they were confronted by the club's four muscular security guards, there were less than forty minutes left until the explosion.

Pedro, at the head of his group, was the first to approach, and the thick rope securing the entrance to the club was immediately raised, indicating that the way was clear.

"They're with me," Pedro emphasized so that there would be no misunderstandings.

"Backpack!" the bomber suddenly heard as he walked past the security guards.

His heart began to beat like crazy. This was the moment when everything would become clear. Either he will be caught, which will mean the inevitable death of his family, or he will outwit the goalkeepers and come out unscathed.

The bodyguard watched him carefully, examining his every move. After what seemed like an eternity, the gangster was opening his mouth to tell the lie he had prepared beforehand when Pedro interjected.

"YO! PUTO! This belongs to Jose, got it?!" he pointed to the backpack. "Now, step aside nicely, you don't want him to know you touched his stuff." He added in a serious voice, proud of himself for having managed to impress the women who were staring at him.

The bodyguard reluctantly gave in and stepped back, allowing the deadly contents of the backpack to get inside.

The first and most difficult part of the task was done. From that moment on, the rest was going to be easy. The gangster checked his watch.

"35 minutes."

"Did you see maricón? That's how it's done!" Pedro shouted excitedly into his friend's ear.

Inside the club, the lights pulsed to the beat of the music and the crowd partied carelessly, unaware of the approaching danger.

The gangster stopped and looked around at the people. There were many people there that he knew personally, and most of them were associated with the Mexican Mafia to one degree or another. But for his own psychological comfort, he had to forget about it then.

If he wanted to save his family, he couldn't think about what would happen 30 minutes later when the package exploded.

Only two thoughts remained in his head: to leave the bomb and get away as quickly as possible.

"JOSE'S THERE...!!" Pedro shouted to him over the music. "...ARE YOU GOING TO TALK TO HIM?!"

The gangster looked in the indicated direction. Jose sat comfortably in a private box, surrounded by beautiful women, luxurious alcohol and a few of his men.

"I NEED TO TAKE A PISST FIRST...!" he replied. "...BE RIGHT BACK!" he added and quickly began to push through the dancing people.

A few seconds later, he entered the men's room. At first, he wanted to put the bomb in the flush of one of the toilets. But when he saw that there was a trash can in the left corner at the end of the room, he thought that would be the most suitable place to hide it.

There was only one problem, there were too many people to do it unnoticed. He checked the time. There were 25 minutes left until the explosion.

Men snorted cocaine, improved the appearance of their hair in the mirror, and others simply relieved themselves of their physiological needs.

The gangster, not wanting to stand out, pretended to stand by the bidet for a moment, then slowly washed his hands and observed the surroundings, but never for a moment did he sense an opportunity to finally get rid of the terrifying package. Time was running out, and he felt increasingly desperate.

Then he decided that he could wait no longer and returned to his original idea. When he was about to enter the toilet cubicle and leave the bomb in the toilet, he noticed the last man leaving the room.

It's either now or never. He thought.

He quickly slipped off his backpack and grabbed it, ran to the trash can, unzipped it, opened the lid, and in one agile move, he threw the black shopping bag with the bomb into the trash can, pushing it hard until it reached the bottom.

He held out his hand, and as he closed the lid of the basket, more people entered. The man, not wanting to make eye contact with anyone, immediately headed for the exit.

He was on the dance floor and quickly heading towards the main entrance when Pedro spotted him.

"YO!! PABLO!!" Pedro called out to him, but the gangster, overwhelmed by adrenaline and his own thoughts, didn't stop. At that point, there was only one priority in his head – *RUN!*

What the fuck? Pedro thought.

15 minutes later, the gunman was in his car and went to the nearest payphone to call the number the brothers had given him.

He wanted to let them know that he had done what he was told and thereby free his family from danger.

When he reached his destination, he picked up the receiver with a still-shaking hand and dialled the number. After a few rings, he heard the person on the other end answering and listening in silence.

"Done…" he said to the silent caller. "…I kept my end of the bargain, now you keep yours."

"…it remains to be seen whether you are telling the truth. If so, you don't have to be afraid anymore." The man's voice answered and ended the call.

The gangster hung up the phone and went out into the street.

"Now it's all in God's hands," he said to himself.

At the same time, the party was in full swing at the Casa Mexicana club, and people were having a great time, including Pedro and Jose in their own circle.

The music was pulsating, the lights were twinkling, and laughter and conversation filled the space.

Pedro, although slightly disturbed by the earlier sight of his friend running out of the club, quickly forgot about him, focusing on dancing and having fun with his friends. In a few seconds, it would be 10:10 p.m., set on the detonator's watch.

...22:09:57, 22:09:58, 22:09:59, 22:10:00...

Just as the watch showed ten minutes past ten, a powerful explosion shook the building's foundations and the neighbourhood.

In a fraction of a second, a shock wave emerged from the room where the charge was hidden, tearing the people closest to it to shreds.

All the lights went out in the club, and the music was replaced by the panicked screams of people inside. Dozens of stunned men and women who survived the explosion rushed blindly and screaming towards the exit.

In almost complete darkness, illuminated only by the flames created by the explosion, they ran in terror, trampling those who had the misfortune of falling.

Heavy black smoke billowed through the front door at the time of the explosion, leaving staff and guests standing outside stunned.

You could hear the screams of the injured, the desperate cries of young women and the coughs of people choking in the quickly spreading stench of smoke. Less than five minutes later, the entire building burst into flames.

Those who managed to escape from the fire sat in the street and trembled with terror. But those who failed to escape that night died inside.

Michael arrived at the scene at 10:20 p.m., after the most dramatic scenes had passed.

Firefighters and paramedics worked quickly to get the situation under control while officers spoke to the victims. The detective got out of the car and couldn't believe the scale of the destruction before his eyes.

"Holy mother of god," he whispered under his breath.

It was a sight he had never seen before or since. He walked closer, feeling the heat of the ruins and the suffocating smell of burning.

All around him were signs of chaos: scattered objects, pieces of furniture, and personal belongings of the victims.

"Preliminary report, detective," one of the officers said, interrupting Michael's thoughts.

The detective took the document, although he couldn't focus on its contents. His gaze wandered around the scene of the tragedy, trying to understand what could have led to this.

"Was it an accident? Or something much more sinister?"

"I need a list of the people present and any witnesses." He ordered, looking through the pages of the report.

Even though his duty was over for the day, the detective's work was just beginning because he knew that every minute and person in this place was worth its weight in gold.

Now, the most important thing was to find out who died, who survived, and what exactly happened on that fateful night.

There would be many conversations, analyses and sleepless nights ahead for Michael, but he was determined to discover the truth, no matter how difficult it might be.

Of the many questions and speculations that arose after this tragedy, only one statement was 100% certain: This night will be remembered in the city's inglorious history forever.

25

Ultimate victory.

"Yesterday doesn't belong to you. Tomorrow is uncertain... Only today is yours."

Five days after the Casa Mexicana massacre, Franco Perez decided to take radical steps to eliminate the Aryan Brotherhood's leadership and influence in the Texas region once and for all, thus putting an end to the bloodshed of his countrymen and associates. To this end, he sent a message to the best sicario in the country, offering high rewards for help, and it wasn't long before willing people began to appear.

In a short time, he had a small army of professional killers who were ready to go to a designated location and eliminate specific individuals one by one. Franco was certain that this move would ultimately bring him victory, so this undertaking became his priority and the apple of his eye.

One of the most important bosses of the Mexican mafia put aside all other matters until the situation in the American backyard was clarified, and there was a mistake which was to cost him his life.

March 1, 1982, 11:58 p.m.

Franco went to bed, thinking about the coming day. Tomorrow, he expected a visit from the hit men who were to come to his villa to discuss the terms of the deal. These were to be the last talks before full readiness, and Perez expected the sicario to leave for El Paso the next day, from where they would begin their *work.*

The gangster's villa was guarded by eight armed guards, five on the walls around the property and three monitoring the area in front of and behind the building, additionally equipped with guard dogs.

The night was warm and calm, and there was no sign of any impending danger. After two o'clock in the morning, Franco Perez was already fast asleep, alone in his luxurious bed.

The light from numerous garden lanterns streamed in through the large bedroom windows, shedding a glow through the white curtains, leaving the part of the room facing the door well-lit. The silence in the room was broken only by the breathing of the sleeping gangster.

Then, the door to the room slowly began to open, and a moment later, the silhouette of a tall man appeared on the threshold. This person stood still for a few seconds, almost completely invisible, and only when he took the first steps into the interior did a pistol with a silencer appear in his right hand. The man's shadow moved quietly across the floor, and his steps were barely audible on the thick carpet.

The garden lanterns cast a faint light on him, which flickered through the curtains, creating ghostly shadows on the walls.

The unexpected guest moved closer to the bed, focusing his eyes on the sleeping Franco Perez, whose calm breathing contrasted with the tense atmosphere in the room.

"Hello, my friend," John said, looking at the defenceless Perez.

He then picked up one of the pillows lying next to his former ally and placed it on his face, which made him wake up.

Franco, woken from a deep sleep, didn't even have a chance to understand what was happening because John put the gun on the pillow separating him from the man's head and fired two shots.

Then he slowly revealed his face: Franco Perez was dead. John stared at his corpse for a moment, then slowly walked away and disappeared out the door, leaving his dead opponent, who didn't even know who killed him, in what he thought was the safest place.

The gangster was found by his maid the next morning when he didn't show up for breakfast at nine in the morning as usual.

Perez's bodyguards and other employees were shocked that someone had managed to get into the guarded compound right under their noses and kill their employer.

This also resulted in the cancellation of all meetings and plans because, without a commander, there was no one to continue further operations.

With this one move, John proved that no one is as untouchable as he thinks, and on that day, the conflict between the Aryan Brotherhood and the Mexican Mafia was finally won.

The day before.

John had arrived in San Antonio, where he was supposed to meet with his brothers, who had been on Mexican soil for some time.

The Aryans had information on how to get to Perez's villa without raising the alarm, and John had to agree on the details of the plan.

In addition, the man had promised himself that he would be the one to pull the trigger when justice was served to Franco, and he was ready to keep his word.

"This is his bedroom," said one of the brothers, pointing to a map of the Mexican gangster's estate.

"The entrance to the tunnel is on this side. It leads to the basement under the kitchen. You go in from here, and here are the stairs. From there, it's downhill."

"And the security? Is there no one in the house?" asked John.

"No. They are forbidden to go inside, but there will be eight of them around generally."

"So, if something goes wrong, you won't have much time before they show up. Are you sure you want to go there alone?" asked another man.

"Yeah, I have a score to settle with him." John replied firmly. "Sure, no problem. The situation is simple: you go in quietly, put bullets in his head and leave. He won't even know what hit him."

"Great job, boys, you really did a good job. Starting tomorrow, our problems with the Mexicans will disappear." John replied.

"Yes, the guy created an emergency exit that will contribute to his death."

"Alright. We'll leave after sunset. Now rest. We have a long night ahead of us." With these words, John ended the meeting.

In this conversation, the brothers referred to the system of tunnels that were built on Franco's orders and were intended to serve as an escape route in the most extreme cases.

As a vigilant and cautious person living outside the law in a world of constant power struggles, Franco Perez had to be prepared for all circumstances, but he was unable to predict that what he considered a security measure would one day fall into the wrong hands and lead to his downfall.

However, this is exactly what happened when members of the brotherhood, after a time-consuming reconnaissance of the area and the internal structures of Perez's employees, captured the son of one of the security guards working on his estate by forcing him to reveal information that would be useful to them in exchange for the promise of releasing his offspring once they no longer needed him.

Through patience and a painstaking strategy of gradually recognizing the enemy's weaknesses, the Aryan Brotherhood had reached the point where they could strike the final blow and defeat their opponent.

The war that had raged for the last few weeks, claiming a record number of lives and ruining many more lives in the process, would now end as quickly as it had begun.

26

Execution.

"Faith and reason are like two wings on which the human spirit soars towards the contemplation of truth."

One Year Later.

Two weeks ago, I was given an execution date and transferred to the Huntsville unit, where I waited for that day.

During my short career in the Aryan Brotherhood, I earned top honours for my participation and was appointed a committee member, replacing Jack as leader of the Polunsky Unit prison.

Even though I didn't kill Luis Ramirez during the biggest riots since the establishment of the institution, everyone knew that it was thanks to me, or rather Gary, that the Latino commander was killed and thanks to which the Brotherhood took power and reigned supreme within the prison walls ever since.

This earned me the respect and recognition of most members of the association and earned me a place in command.

Even if I could not enjoy the position I had gained for too long because the day of my death was approaching, I felt that something had changed in my life and that I had achieved a higher social rank, although it was not as prestigious as a career built in freedom. I had the satisfaction of being appreciated by someone.

Before I found myself in the place where I was counting down the final hours to my execution, Michael would visit me regularly once a week.

The meetings continued to be held in strict secrecy, and I became very used to them, and the detective became my friend.

He would tell me about the situation outside. It was from him that I learned about the bombing at the Latin club Casa Mexicana and that crime had decreased overnight by itself.

I gained information from him without necessarily sharing what I knew myself.

For example, the knowledge that the reason for the lower number of recorded crimes in the city was the death of Franco Perez at the hands of John, which was undoubtedly missed by local law enforcement agencies.

I kept these details to myself in case they might be useful to me in some way.

Sometimes I thought about escaping, but I knew it was impossible.

All I could do was await the inevitable. Michael was the only person who brought me any comfort, even though I knew I couldn't fully trust him.

His visits were like oxygen for me, which I ravenously crave but which does not provide long-lasting relief.

I never thought I would find myself in such a place, but now that the end was near, I tried to accept my fate.

Every hour seemed like an eternity, and every sound was a reminder of the moment ahead. Memories of my past, of my life before prison, were swirling in my head, but now they seemed distant and unreal.

I waited because I had no alternative.

The last few weeks have passed with an expression of regret that I was not able to see Edward as often as I saw Michael, who gradually began to visit me less and less until he finally stopped visiting me.

I had a feeling then that my brother had some serious problems that he hadn't told me about until they finally overwhelmed him to the point that he was unable to go anywhere in person.

However, I still hoped that I would see him one last time during the execution.

The day of the execution, 6:45 p.m.

I had just finished my last meal. I ordered a medium-rare rib-eye steak with fries, gravy and peas and a large glass of cola to drink.

It was my favourite dish, but it didn't taste the way I wanted it to, and I generally didn't feel like eating, which was totally understandable for someone in my situation.

People often say that they are not afraid of death, which is complete nonsense because even the toughest guys feel fear when faced with death and can often shed a tear, and it is completely normal.

The human instinct of self-preservation works at full speed in life-threatening situations, and no one can defend against it.

Therefore, knowing that in less than 15 minutes, I would fall asleep forever effectively made it impossible for me to concentrate on anything else.

I also refused a visit from a priest. I had never been religious, and I had no intention of changing that at the end of my life because I would soon see with my own eyes what it was really like "on the other side."

At 6:50 p.m., the guards came for me.

Only ten minutes left until the scheduled time.

"Are you ready, Mr. Johnson?" one of them asked.

"What if I say no? Will that make any difference?" I replied ironically.

"Give me your hands, please." He replied, ignoring my comment.

"Is my brother in the room?"

"No, Mr. Johnson. But he might show up."

I walked over to the opening in the bars and held out my hands so they could handcuff them.

Once we had that over with, I was led out into the corridor, from where we headed to the site of my last journey.

The corridor was long dark, lit only by the faint light of fluorescent lamps mounted on the ceiling. Each step echoed loudly, sounding like a judgment issued by fate itself.

I didn't feel any fear, just a strange sense of relief that it would all finally be over.

We stopped in front of a heavy metal door behind which destiny awaited. The guards exchanged glances, and one of them opened the door, leading me through the threshold.

The room was small, white and sterile, and in the middle was a specially designed chair with leather straps for the arms and legs. There was silence in the room, broken only by the faint hum of machines.

I closed my eyes, trying to gather my thoughts and recall the memories that mattered most to me. I felt the handcuffs being removed from my wrists, and I was gently led to a chair. I sat up, feeling the cold metal beneath me, and allowed myself to be strapped down.

I opened my eyes and looked ahead. Then I realised that in front of me, there was a window behind which a small group of people were sitting.

I looked around and recognized the family of Thomas Jones and Katy Joys, and my lawyer, who had defended me during the trial, was also there.

To my surprise, neither Edward nor Michael was there, which was a painful shock because even though I expected Ed not to come, I was 100% sure that Michael would be there, but now I realised that his partner, Paul, was there instead, which seemed odd to say the least.

However, this was not the time to think.

If they're not there, then no, it doesn't matter. I thought to myself.

Then, they began to fasten straps to my limbs so that I would not be able to break free. Wanting to occupy my thoughts with something, I looked at the ceiling, focusing for a moment on the pattern of cracks that seemed to create a map of unknown places.

At 6:58 p.m., the guards left me alone in the gas chamber and went outside. Time slowed down, each breath became deeper, and my heart beat slower and slower.

"Mr. Steward Johnson, under Texas law, you were convicted of the charges and sentenced to death by inhalation of lethal gas. Do you have any last words?" I heard a man's voice from outside the room.

"I regret the actions I have committed, as well as those of which I was suspected," I replied.

"At exactly seven o'clock, the gas will be released, which will lead to your death. May God have mercy on your soul."

After these words, I closed my eyes, ready for what was to come. A moment later, I heard the hiss of gas being released into the chamber, and an unpleasant sulphur smell reached my mouth and nose.

…Lub-Dub, Lub-Dub, Lub-Dub, Lub-Dub…

With each new breath, my heartbeat gradually began to slow down.

…Lub-Dub… Lub-Dub… Lub-Dub…

Until finally, I felt blissful sleepiness.

…Lub… Dub… Lub… Dub…

A sleepiness from which I would never wake up.

…Lub… …Dub… …Lub… …Dub…

However, fate had one more surprise in store.

…Lub… …Dub… …Lub…

Epilogue

Two hours later.

Imagine my surprise when I woke up in El Paso Emergency, and Michael was sitting by my bed.

I looked at him with sleepy eyes, hooked up to life support equipment.

"Michael…?" I whispered. "…what`s happening?" I added with difficulty, feeling the remnants of the taste of the deadly gas in my mouth.

"Are you sure you want me to tell you now? Wouldn't you rather rest first?" he asked.

I nodded yes, not wanting to overwork my vocal cords.

"Okay. So, we saved you at the last moment, a few more seconds in that chamber, and it would have been too late…" he began to tell. "…fortunately, Paul was there, and I managed to call the last hope phone in the room in time. To tell you honestly, in my entire career, there has never been a case when he called and saved an innocent person's life, until now," he confessed, looking me straight in the eyes.

I listened carefully, but I had a hard time believing this was happening, and sometimes, I found myself wondering if this wasn't what people call posthumous *purgatory.*

"I found the person who set you up, Steward." He added, and a look of embarrassment began to appear on his face.

I could clearly see that he was hesitating whether to reveal it right away or not.

"Speak." I managed to force it out.

"Okay. Two days ago, we raided the apartment of Stacy Brook, your brother's partner, suspected of drug dealing. I found a pair of shoes that belonged to Edward at the scene."

At that point, I began to realise what the detective was getting at.

"I noticed small red stains on both of them, which we later identified as drops of blood. I sent the shoes to the lab, and it took them a while to get the DNA, which matched the DNA of Thomas Johns's and Katy Joyce's blood. Upon receiving the test results, I immediately contacted the Chief Constable, who authorized a phone call to Judge Logan Smith, and through him, I was able to stop the execution. Bureaucracy is time-consuming, but I managed to make it. They got you out of there at the last minute."

"What about Ed?"

"I questioned him an hour ago, he confessed to everything. He knew that the evidence I had was irrefutable and he told me how he dressed in your clothes, went to the station and did what he did. He gave you some strong sleeping pills, which is why you don't remember anything, after that he faked everything. His car, from your house was driven away by one of the fraternity members, who was very similar in stature to him, that's why I thought it might have been Ed." Michael replied.

"But why?" I couldn't understand my brother's motive.

"As always, for money. He needed to sell the house to have cash to finance the drug trade." He replied.

"Did he confess all this to you?"

"To some extent. I figured most of it out myself, but I still got the impression that he had some serious problems on the outside. Sometimes, it seemed to me that he wanted to go to jail." Michael added, thinking for a moment.

"Thanks for everything."

"You don't have to thank me, it's my duty. When your condition improves, together we will think about how to clear your reputation and organise your life again." The detective replied and then started to head for the exit.

"One more thing, Steward…" he said, suddenly standing in the doorway. "…forgive me for screwing up my job and convicting you before I checked all the clues."

I looked at him and saw real sadness on his face, to which I gave him a thumbs up, and the policeman smiled. After a moment, I was left alone, lying on the hospital bed, processing all the facts in my mind.

"Well, after all, life sometimes gives you a second chance," I stated.

A week later.

After the trial, Edward received the same sentence as his brother Steward and was also charged with participating in a conspiracy to incriminate another individual.

He was sent to the Allan B. Polunsky unit.

The case against Edward was more complicated than it seemed at first. The courtroom was filled with witnesses, and new evidence continued to come to light.

The detective who had previously handled Steward's case now took on Edward's case with even greater determination, wanting to correct his past mistakes.

Eventually, Ed was sent to prison to await his execution date. He was also obliged to hand over all the property he owned to Steward in the form of compensation.

Stacy Brook was also sentenced to 20 years in prison for concealing knowledge of committing a crime and drug trafficking.

Ed was imprisoned, but as a member of the Aryan Brotherhood, he expected the privileges that came with that status.

His business had been struggling since Franco Perez's death, and he knew it was only a matter of time before everything fell apart. But before that could happen, he was arrested, and the cautious Stacy managed to keep the $75,000 that was now supposed to be Steward's, which was a decent amount to start a new life.

News of Steward's fate spread quickly among the brotherhood behind the prison walls, and when Ed got there, everyone already knew what he did and how he tried to frame his own brother, who, for them, was a respected person in their environment.

Therefore, on the very first day, when Ed went out into the yard and was called by Jack to talk, the unaware man confidently walked towards the group of brothers among whom Jack was waiting for him, thinking then that in a moment, he would be welcomed into their group with open arms.

"You are Ed?" Jack asked.

"That's right, I've been in the fraternity for a few years," Ed replied.

At the same time, showing the *AB* tattoo on his hand as proof of his words.

"I worked with John outside." He added.

"Excellent, you'll be useful here too," Jack replied with a mocking smile.

"It's good to know, all for the good of the brotherhood!" Edward replied enthusiastically.

"Welcome." Jack stepped aside in a hospitable gesture, revealing the way to the depths of the group.

"Thanks."

Ed took a few steps and saw that he was among men who were looking at him strangely.

At first, he didn't feel any threat from them, but a few seconds later, he realised that he was surrounded. A few of them approached him, and he felt the painful blades of knives piercing his skin from all sides.

"You fucking rat." He heard.

When he tried to scream, one of the brothers covered his mouth with his hand, so the only sounds he could make were the indistinct moans of someone suffering from a persistent toothache.

After a minute, the brothers separated, leaving Ed bleeding out. The man lay on the ground and took his last breaths, watching the clouds pass by in the sky, and then everything went silent. He closed his eyes, and nothingness enveloped him.